POSTCARD HISTORY SERIES

Lynn MASSACHUSETTS

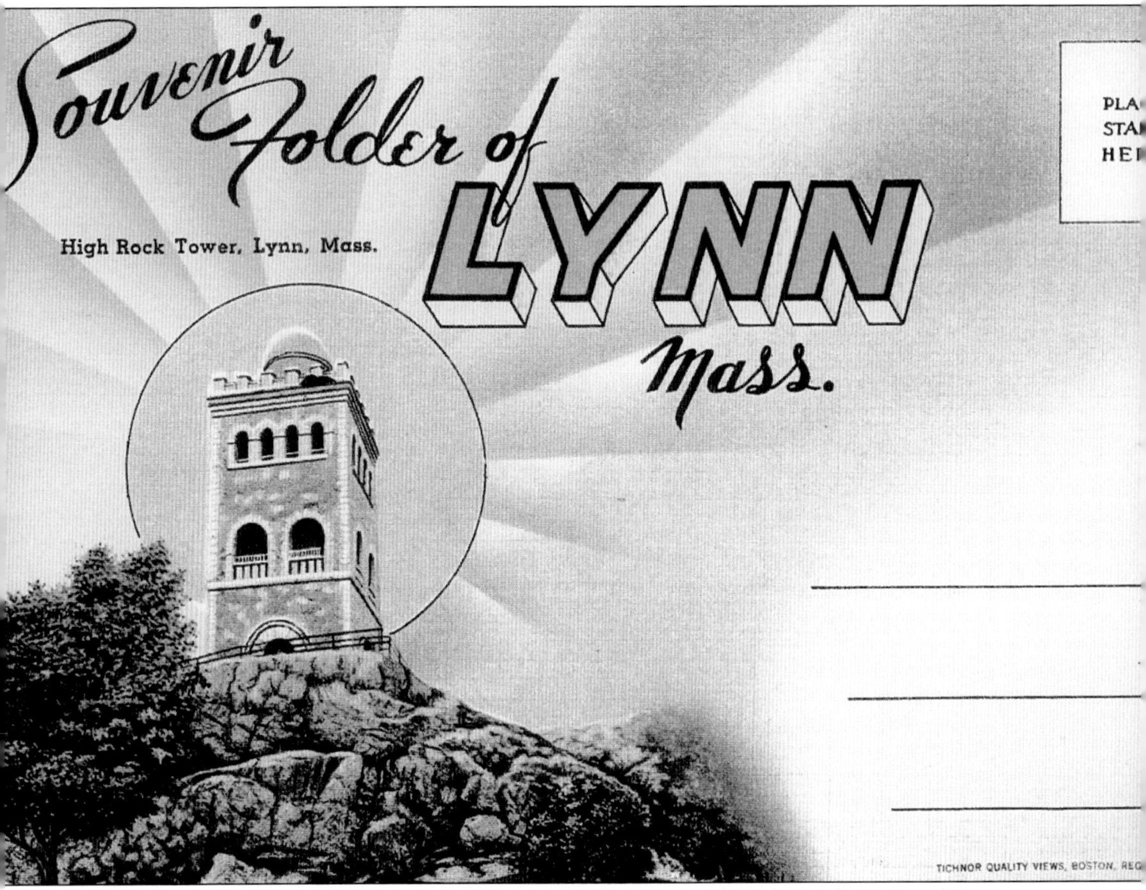

No image is more popular on Lynn postcards than that of High Rock Tower. This souvenir folder from the 1940s folds out to show 18 additional views of Lynn.

POSTCARD HISTORY SERIES

Lynn
MASSACHUSETTS

Diane Shephard for the Lynn Historical Society

ARCADIA
PUBLISHING

ISBN 978-0-7385-8986-2

Published by Arcadia Publishing
Charleston, South Carolina

Printed in the United States of America

Library of Congress Catalog Card Number: 98-87445

For all general information contact Arcadia Publishing at:
Telephone 843-853-2070
Fax 843-853-0044
E-mail sales@arcadiapublishing.com
For customer service and orders:
Toll-Free 1-888-313-2665

Visit us on the Internet at www.arcadiapublishing.com

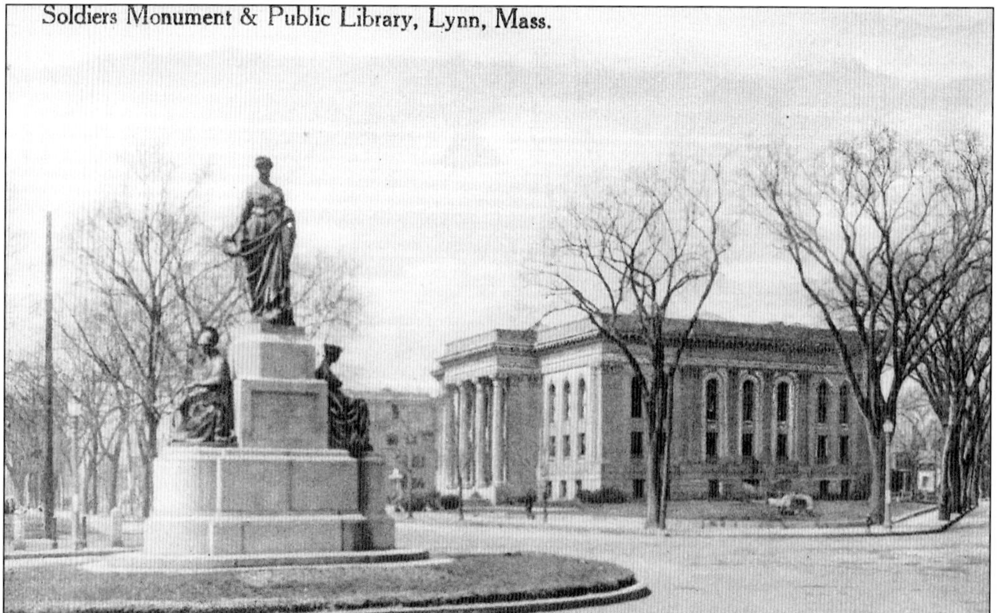

The Soldier's Monument was erected in 1873 as a memorial to the Lynn men who fought for the Union during the Civil War.

Contents

Acknowledgments

The author would like to extend her thanks to Lynn Historical Society President Bill Conway for access to his fine postcard collection and for his generous permission to reproduce many of these cards. Thanks also to Stephen Schier for lending family photographs, to Fay Greanleaf for her early work on the project, and to Society Director Ken Turino for assistance in planning and layout. All images are from the collection of the Lynn Historical Society unless otherwise noted.

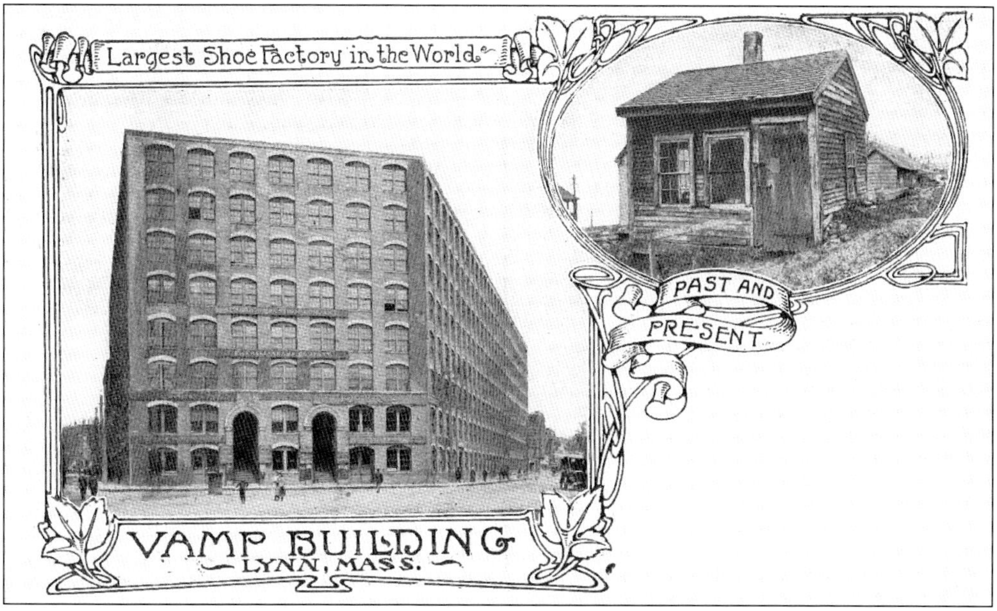

Lynn's Old Home Week celebration in 1907 was the source of numerous commemorative and souvenir cards. This one celebrates the rise and progress of the shoe industry from the humble 10-footers of the early days to the giant factories of the 20th century. (Conway collection.)

INTRODUCTION

Most collectors agree that the picture postcard in America had its beginning at the World's Columbian Exposition of 1893. While these were not the first postcards as such—the federal government and private advertisers had been utilizing the medium since the 1860s—the cards issued at the Chicago Exposition were the first to be designed specifically as souvenirs. The colorful and inexpensive mementos struck a responsive chord with the public and in seemingly no time, postcard collecting had become a full-fledged craze.

The golden age of the picture postcard, from about 1898 to World War I, was also a period of both prosperity and optimism throughout much of the country as the United States began to take its place among the world's leaders. Nowhere was this spirit more evident than in Lynn, Massachusetts. Having survived a devastating fire in 1889 that had destroyed the better part of its industrial center, Lynn had rebounded in fine fashion. By the turn of the century it was the nation's leading manufacturer of women's shoes and the newly formed General Electric Company was on its way to becoming an economic giant.

Lynn's fortunes would peak during this period, as would souvenir postcards of the city. As many as five different companies printed and published postcards in Lynn at the beginning of the century, and many more views were printed out of town. The postcards reproduced here are largely, though not exclusively, from this era.

The Lynn that appears in these pages is reflective of the times, not only in its images but in its spirit as well. It is a city proud of its present, hopeful for its future, and occasionally nostalgic for its past. There are very few clouds present in the sunny aspect it has turned to the world. Labor unrest, overcrowded living conditions, and the myriad other real-life problems with which the city was then grappling have no place in this picture-perfect world of sunny beaches, bustling businesses, and solid institutions.

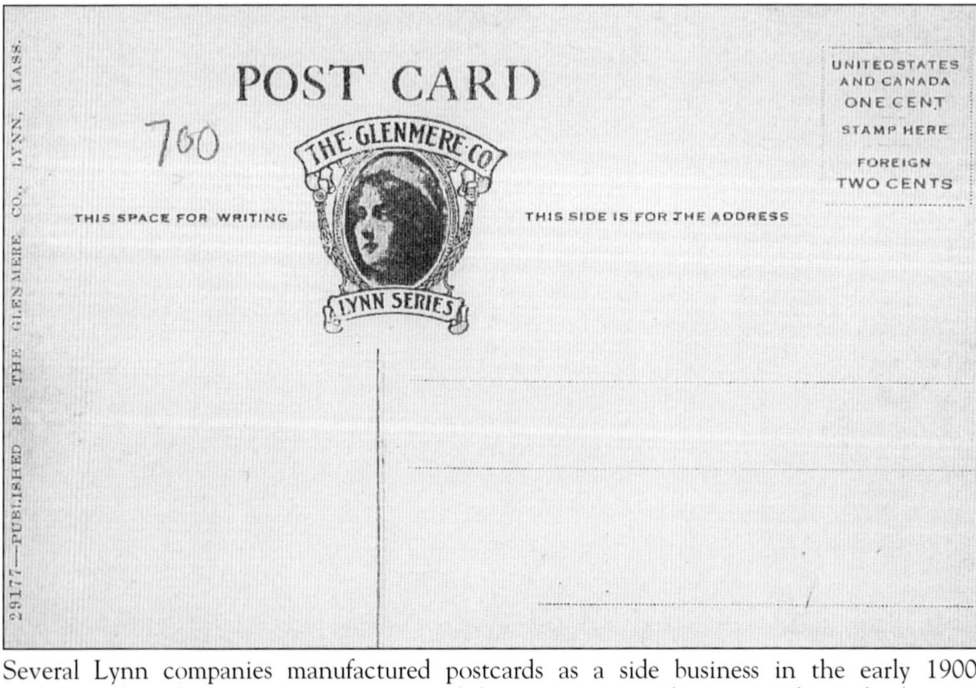

Several Lynn companies manufactured postcards as a side business in the early 1900s, including the Glenmere Company on Euclid Avenue, primarily a toy and novelty business. (Conway collection.)

One

ALONG THE SHORES

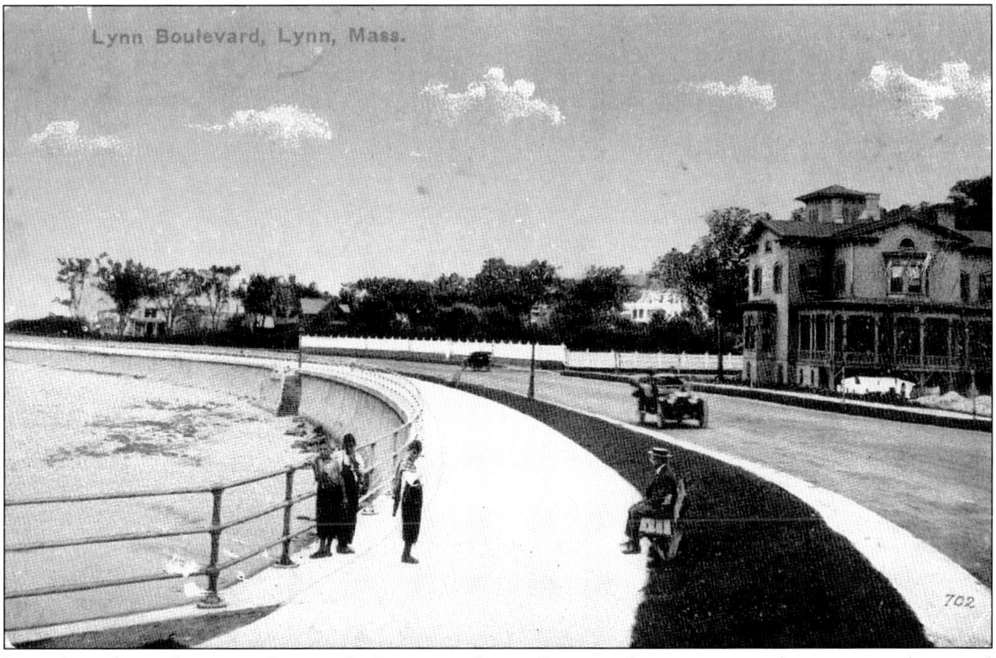

Lynn has always been justly proud of its waterfront. Scenes of recreation, relaxation, and natural beauty along the shore are the most common subjects for Lynn postcards.

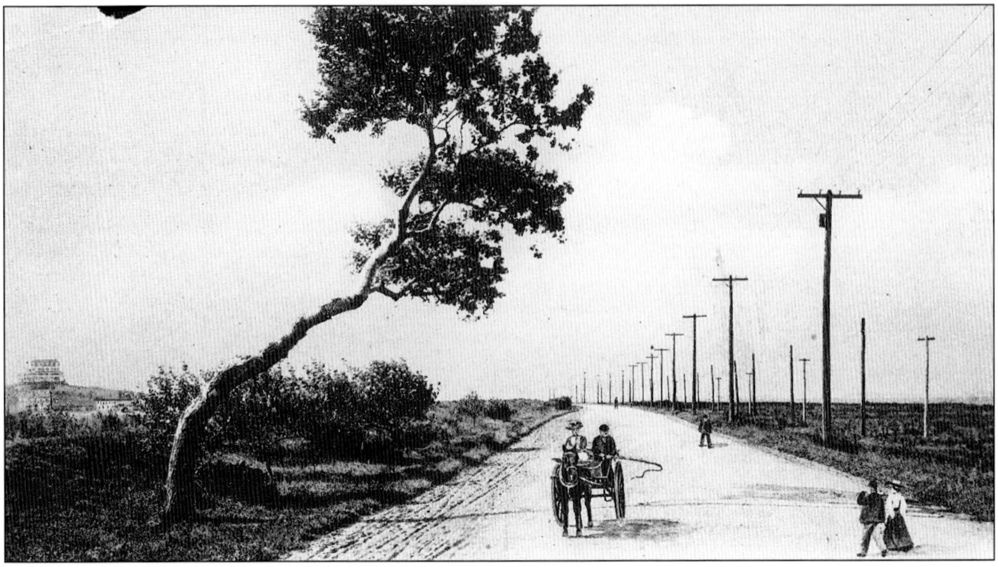

At one time, two weather-beaten, halfway trees, both poplars, were well-known landmarks on the Lynn-Nahant roadway. Only one was left standing in this 1910 view; it fell to a heavy storm in 1916.

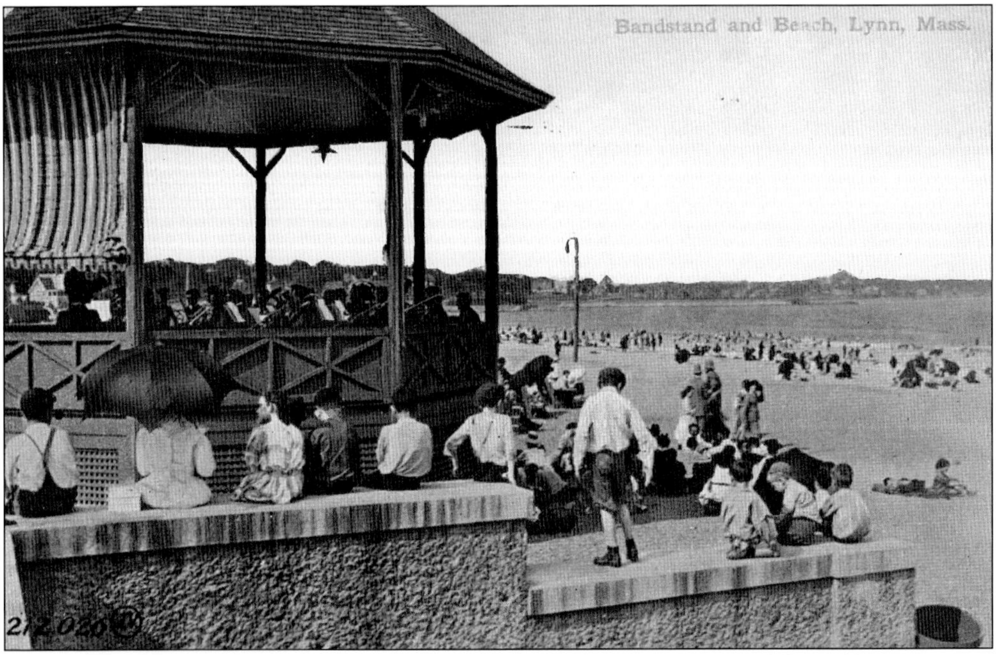

After many years in private hands, much of Lynn's beachfront was opened for public recreation in the early 20th century. Sunday afternoon band concerts were a popular respite for the largely working-class population.

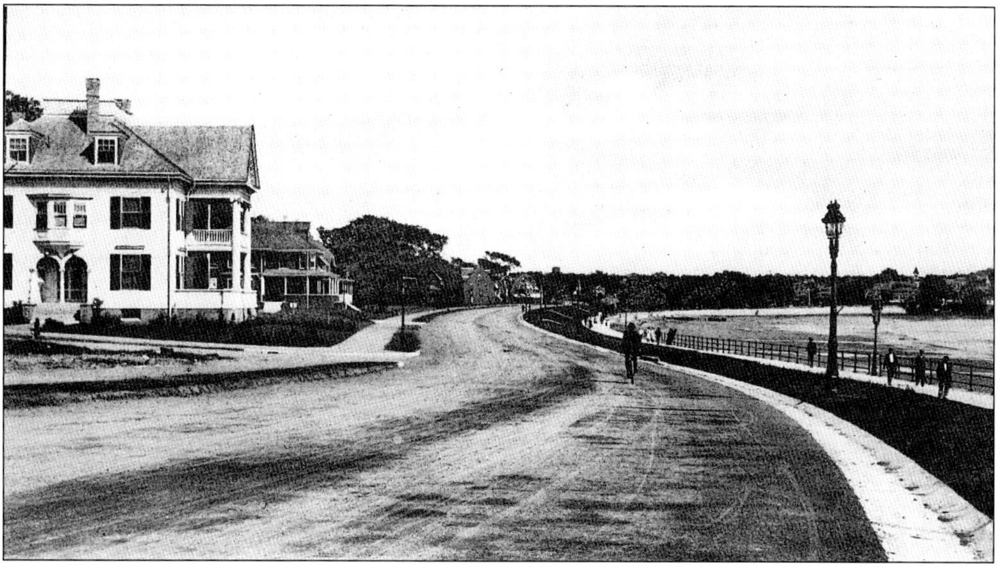

Under the auspices of the Metropolitan District Commission (MDC), a shore boulevard (now known as Lynn Shore Drive) was begun in 1904 and opened in 1907.

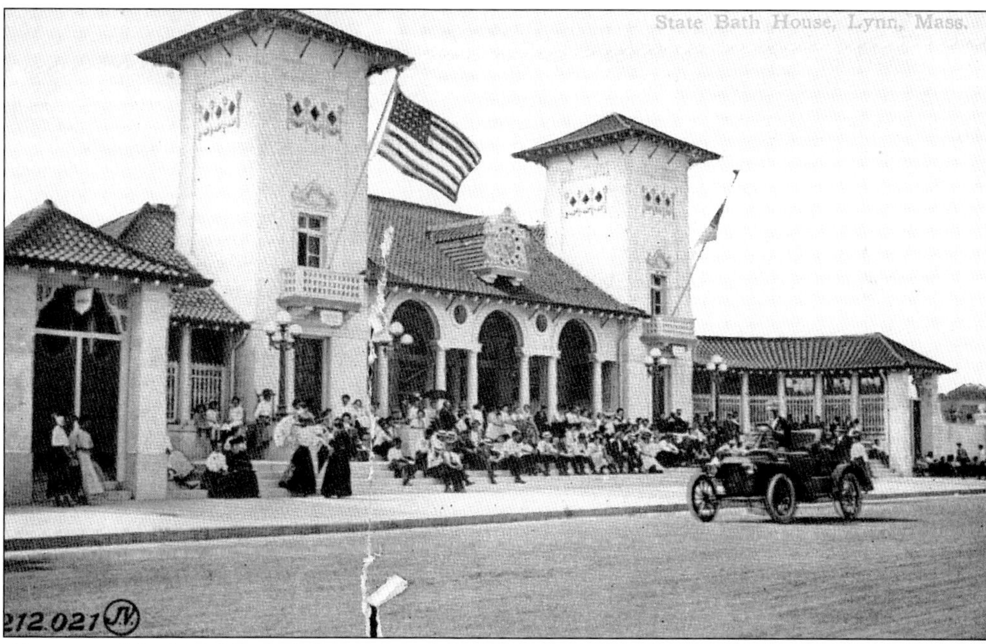

Also part of the MDC Lynn/Nahant Beach Reservation, a handsome bathhouse was constructed in 1907 and was well patronized, as seen here in 1910.

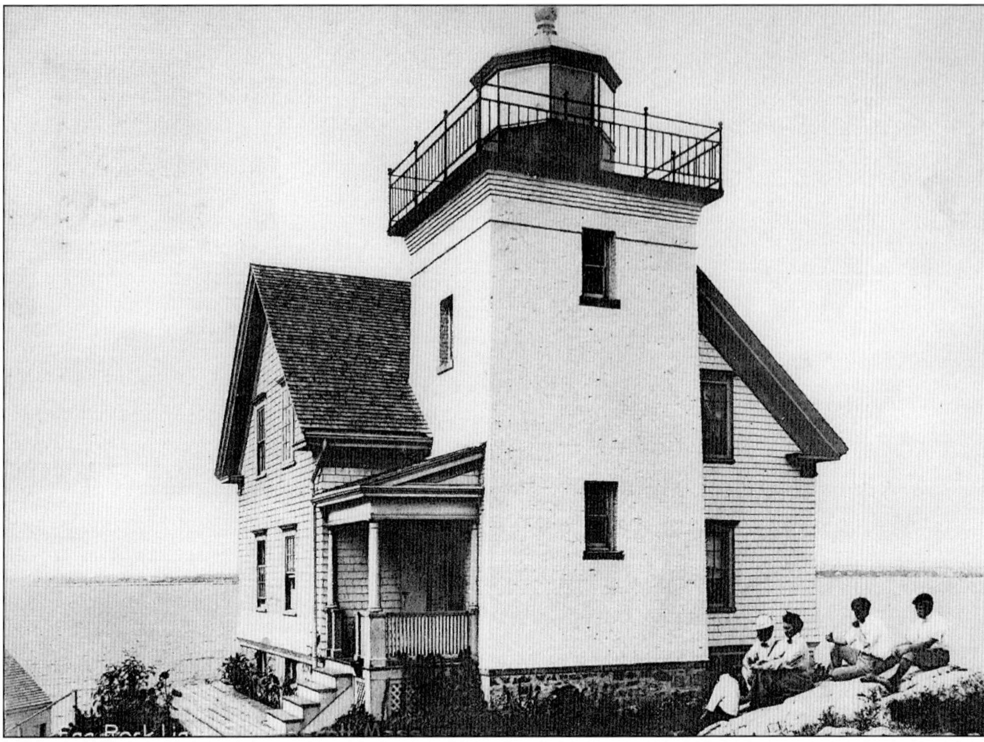

In response to frequent requests by Swampscott fishermen, the federal government built a lighthouse on Egg Rock in 1856. This view shows the second light, constructed in 1898. The light was abandoned in 1922 and the island is now home to a bird sanctuary.

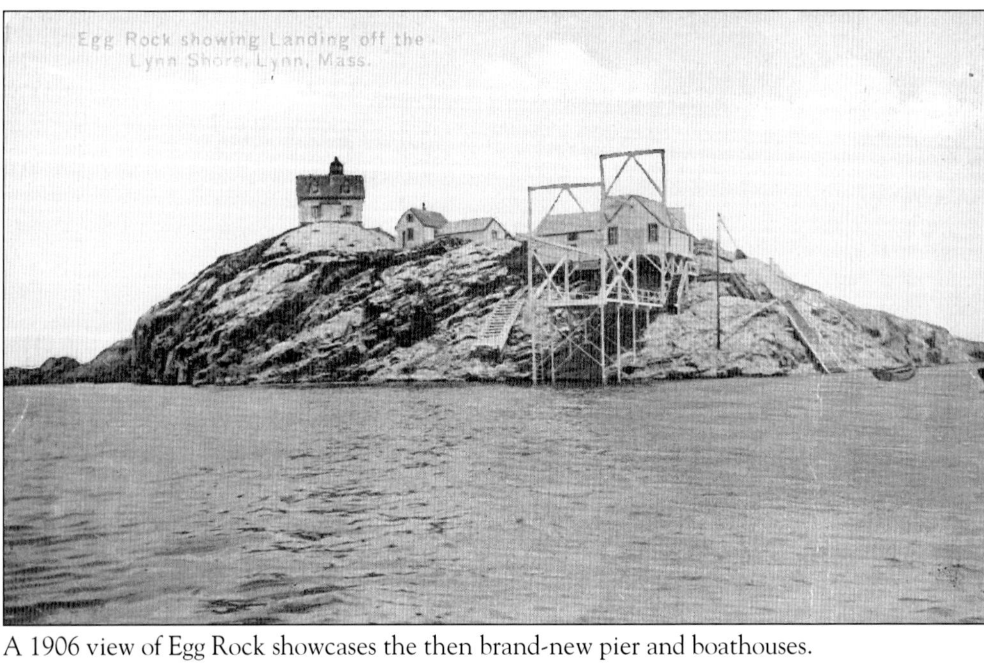

A 1906 view of Egg Rock showcases the then brand-new pier and boathouses.

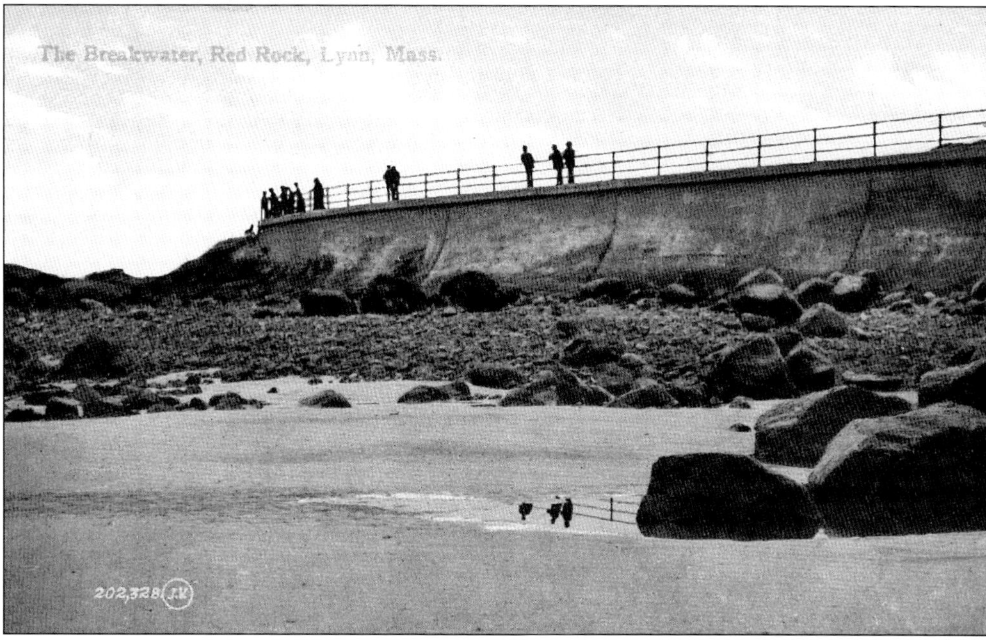

Here we experience low tide at the Red Rock breakwater c. 1905.

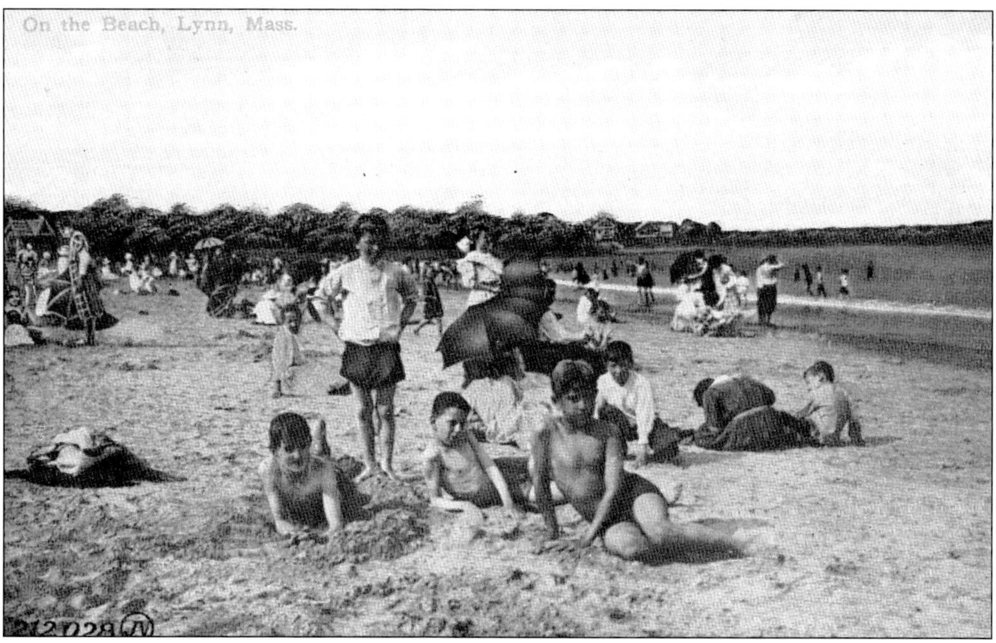

Although the girls in the background have had to stay fully clothed, there's not much in the attire of these boys in 1910 that would distinguish them from their modern counterparts.

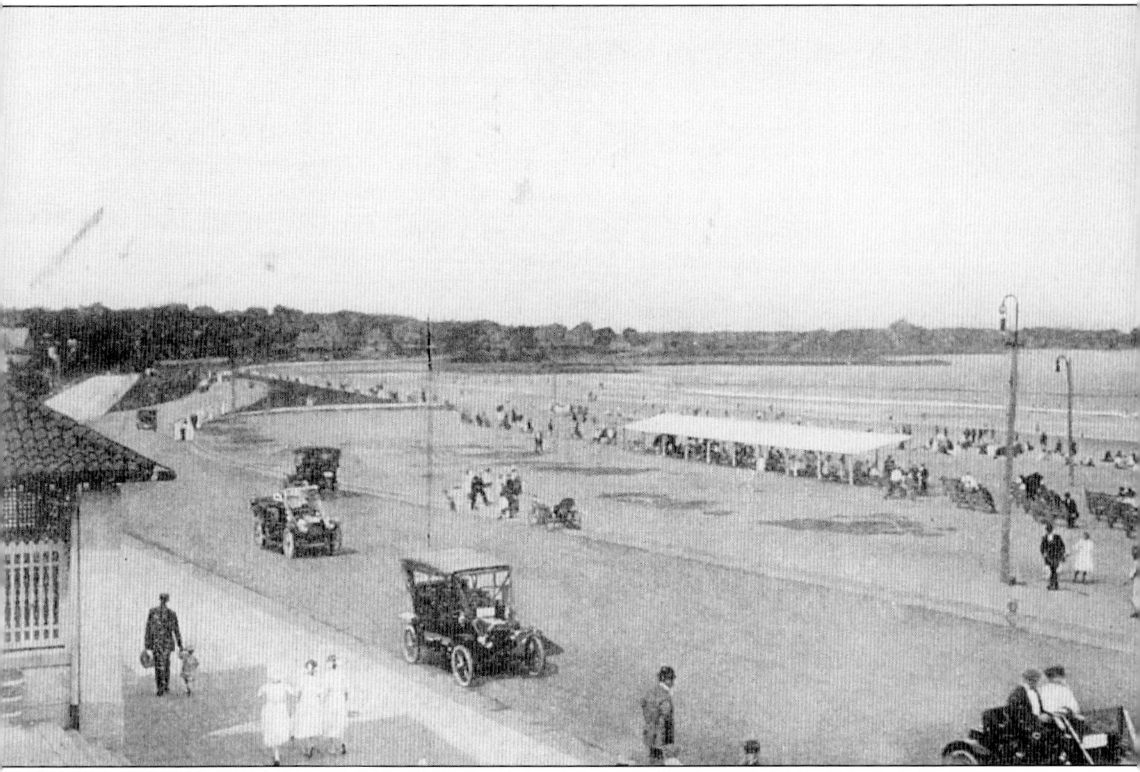

This oversize c. 1915 postcard, which features views of Lynn Shore Drive from both directions, is large enough so that it had to be folded in half to be mailed. At first glance the message

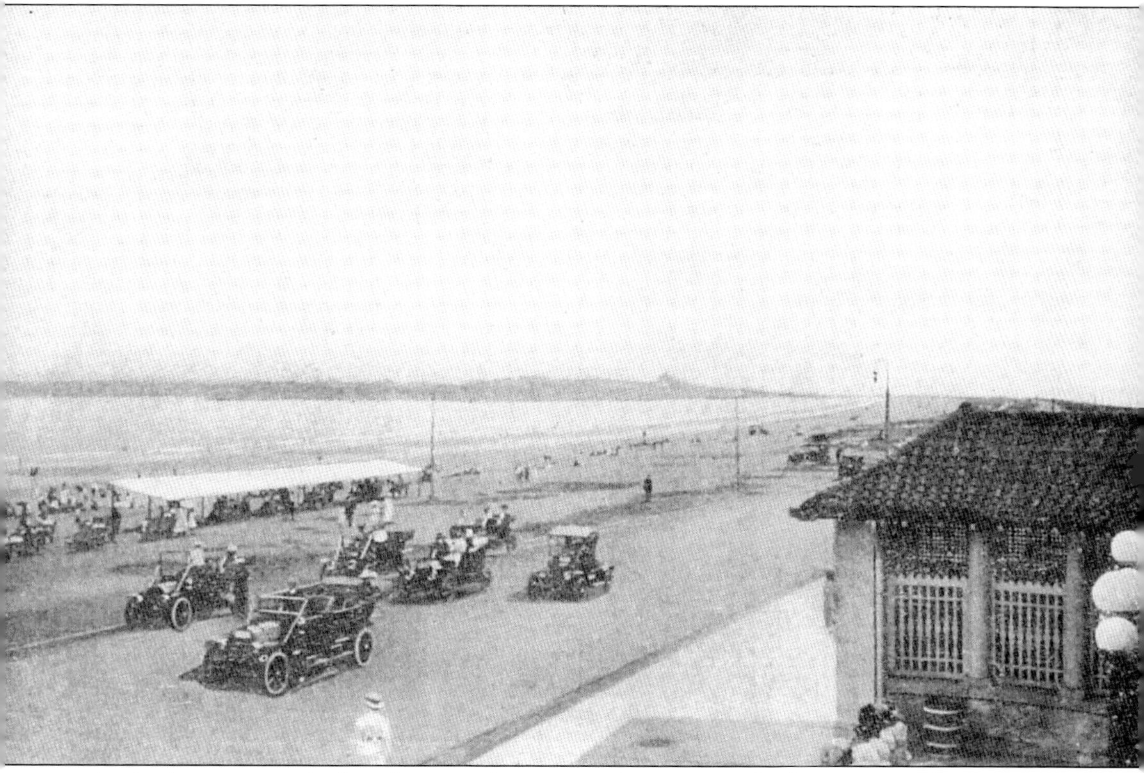

on the back appears to be handwritten, but it is in fact a printed advertisement for Sorosis brand shoes.

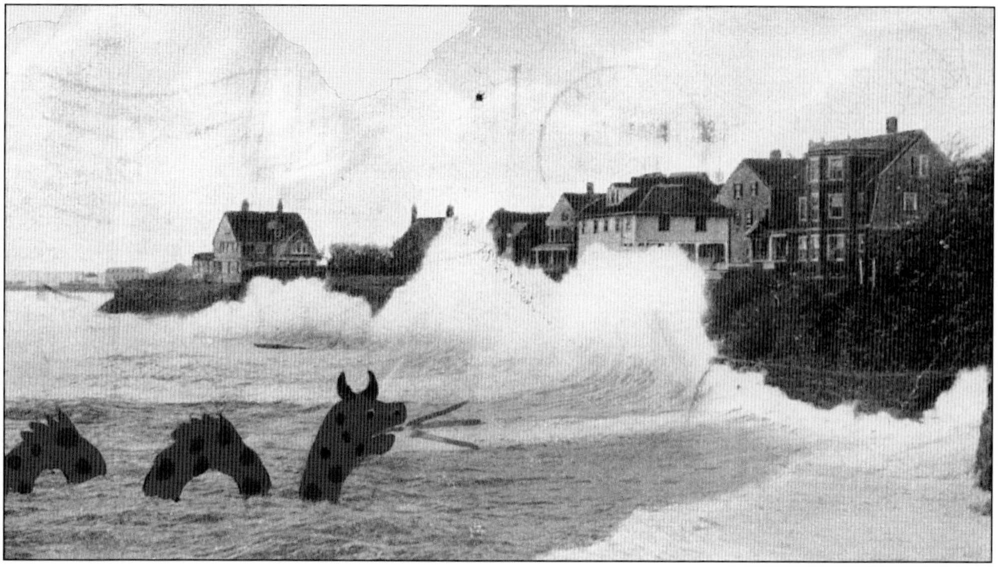

An unusual visitor has been added to this 1905 view of the breakwater.

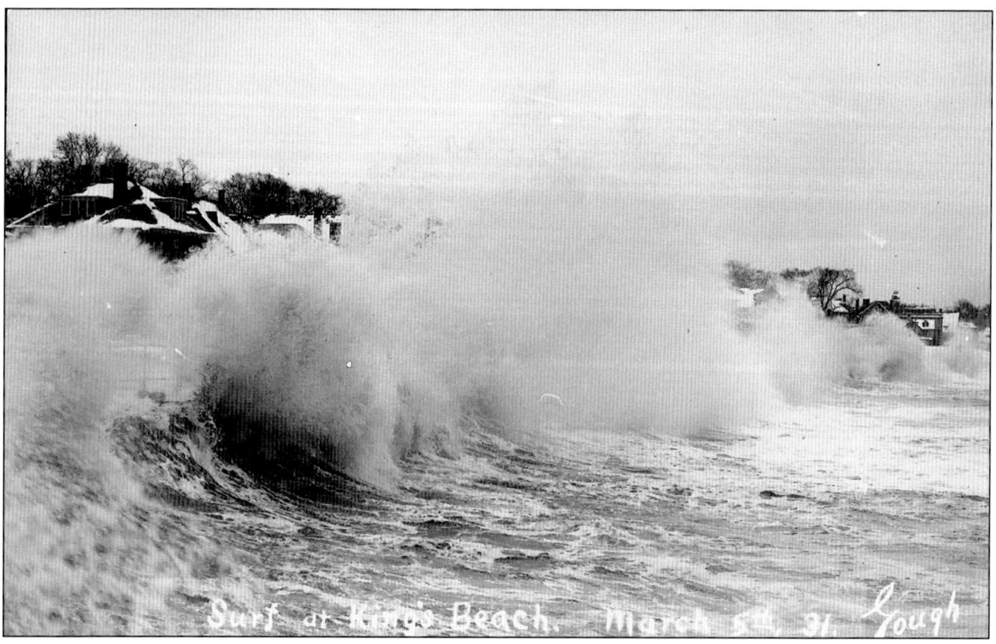

The storm of March 5, 1931, produced these spectacular breakers.

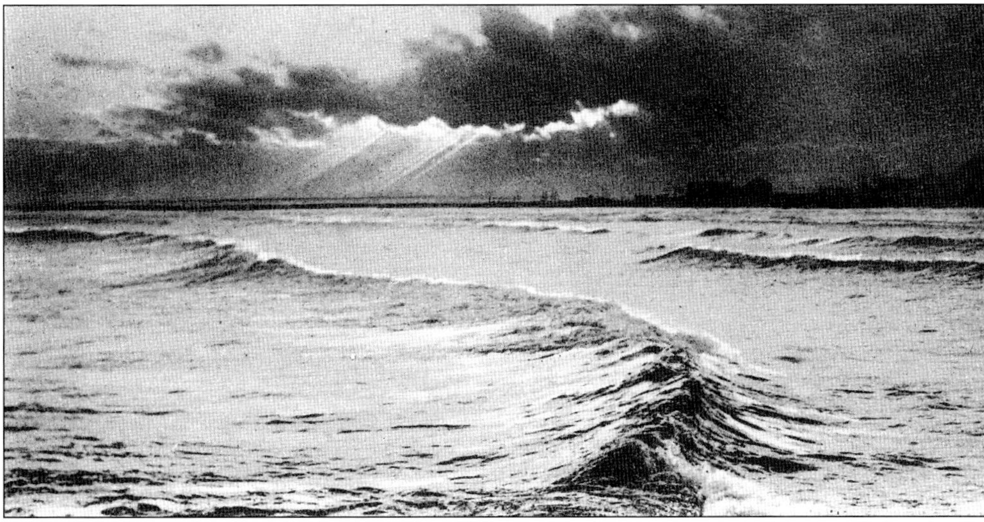

The sun is breaking through the clouds after what appears to have been a severe storm in this c. 1910 postcard published by the Puritan Art Company of Lynn but printed in Germany.

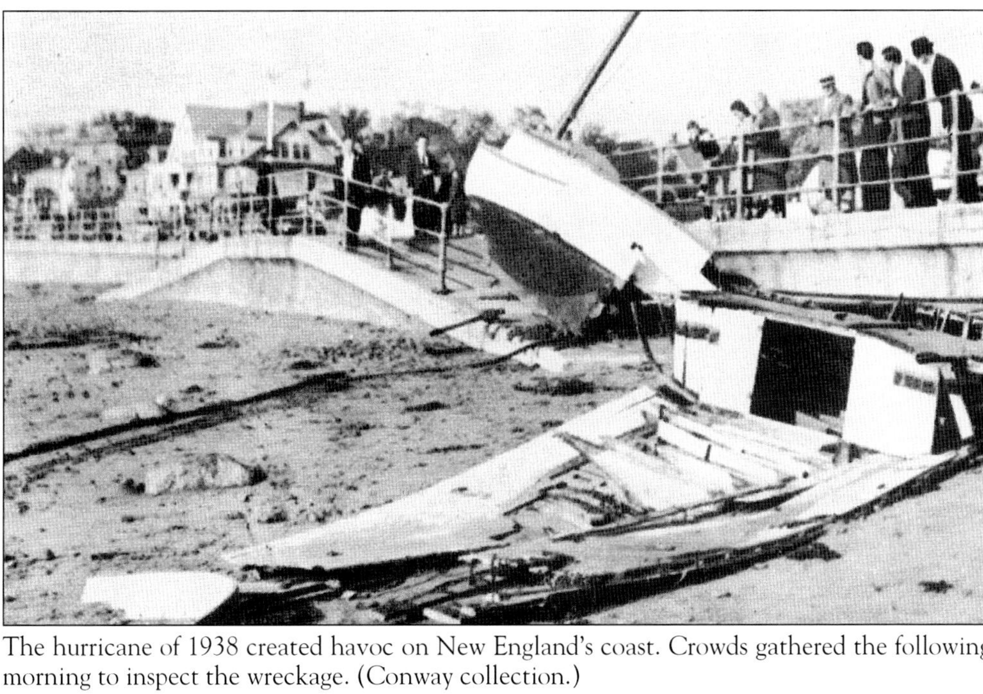

The hurricane of 1938 created havoc on New England's coast. Crowds gathered the following morning to inspect the wreckage. (Conway collection.)

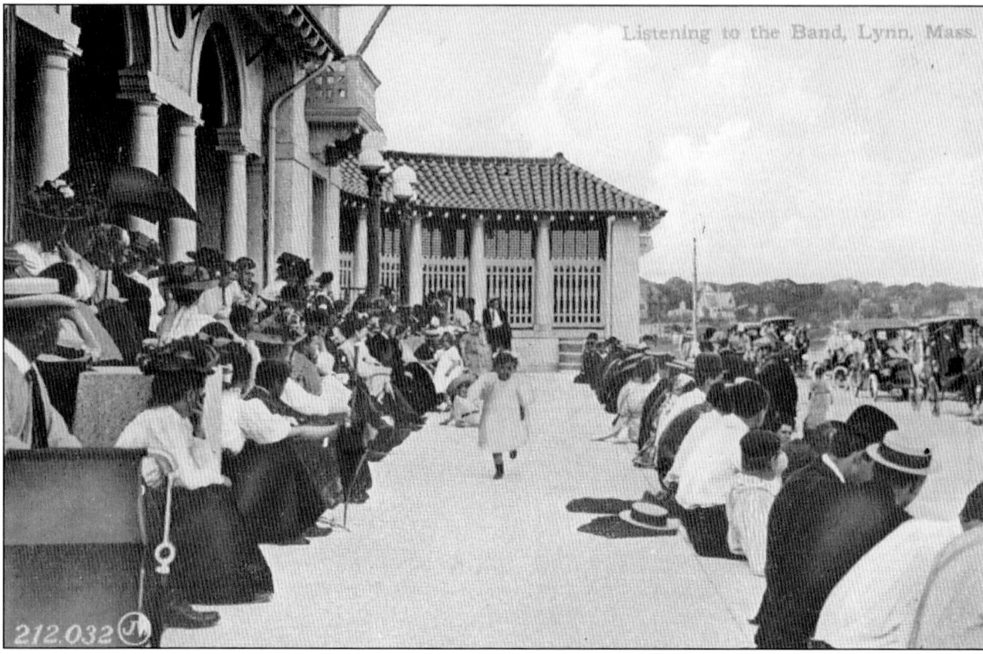

Not everyone was riveted by the band concert heard from the steps of the state bathhouse in 1910.

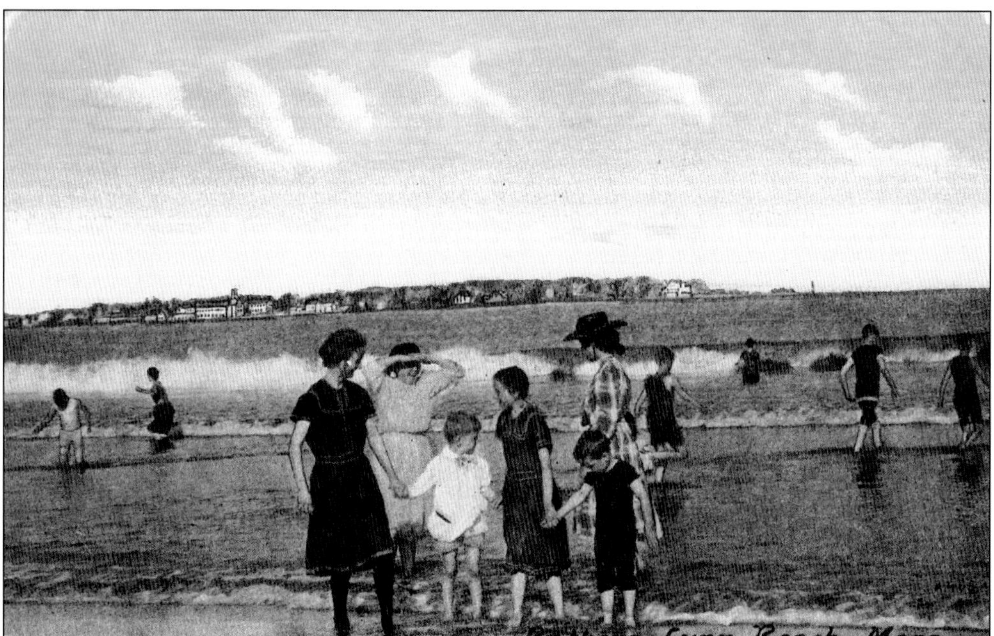

A family group enjoys Lynn Beach c. 1910.

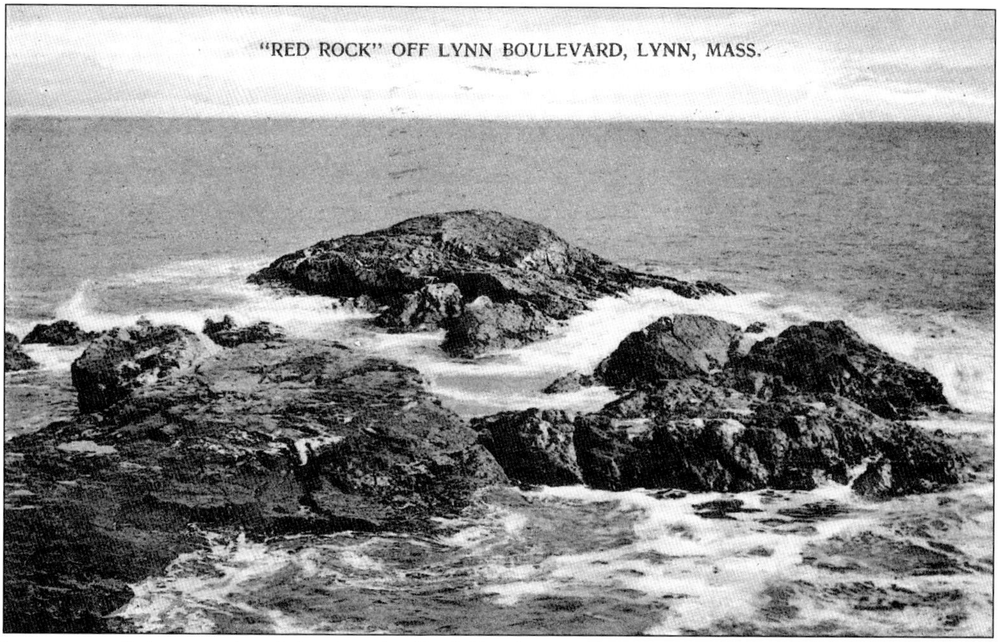

Long a well-known local landmark, Red Rock was incorporated into the MDC's shore reservation and was the site of a rest stop along the boulevard.

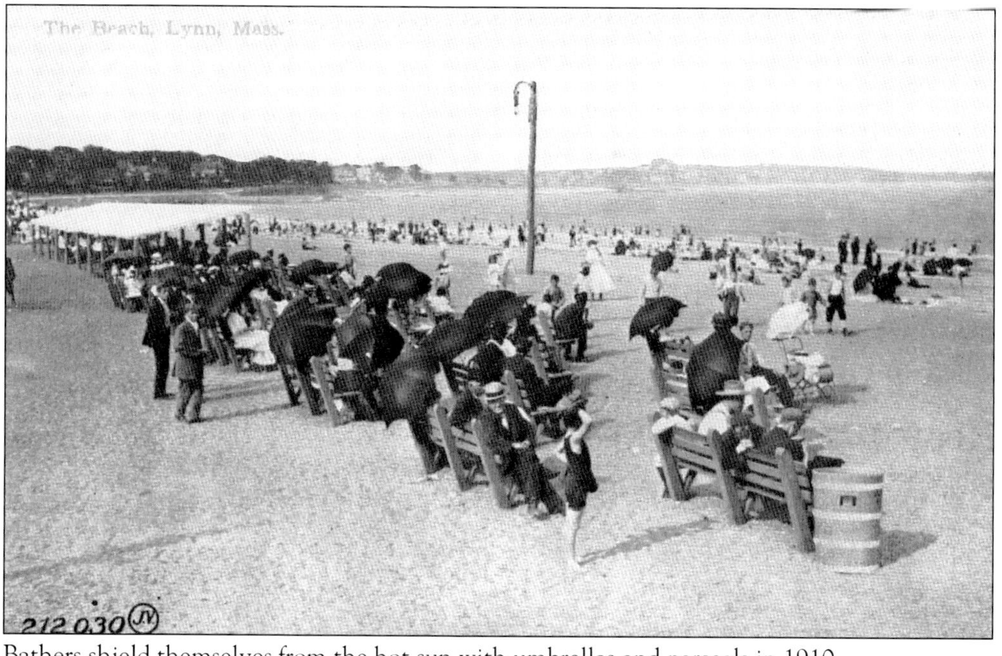

Bathers shield themselves from the hot sun with umbrellas and parasols in 1910.

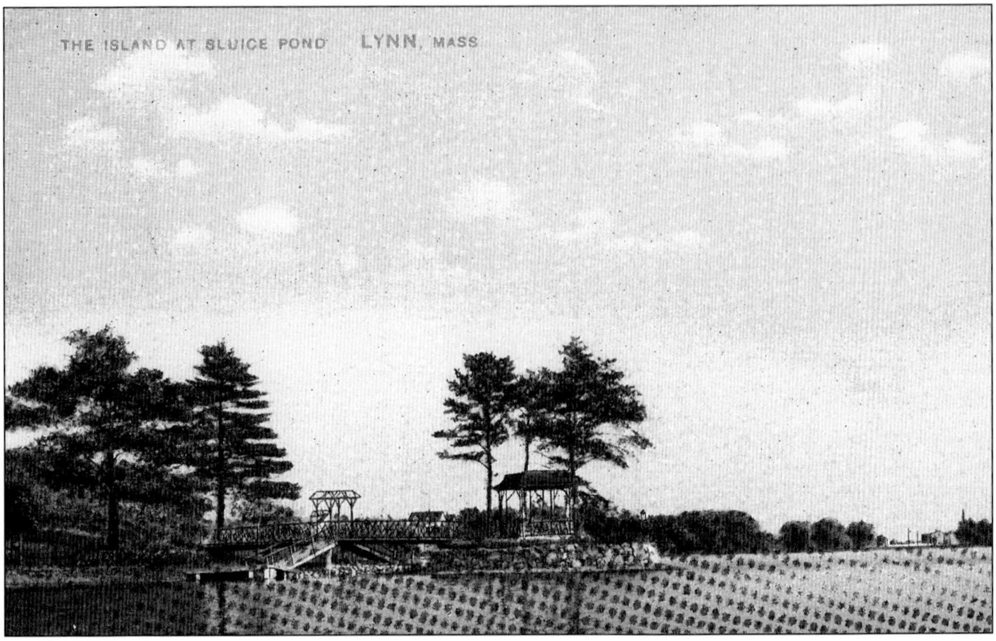

Lynn is blessed not only with ocean beaches but several good-sized ponds as well. Sluice Pond, off Lynnfield Street, is a man-made pond that takes its name from a 17th-century mill and sluice that once operated on its banks.

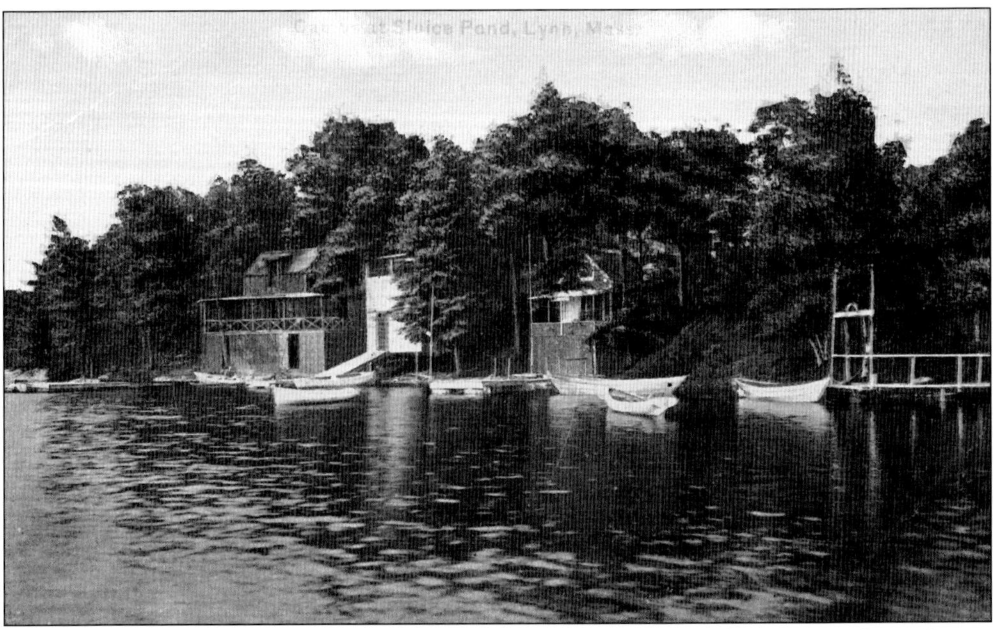

In the early 20th century, Sluice Pond was a popular vacation spot for Lynn residents. Rustic cabins dotted its banks.

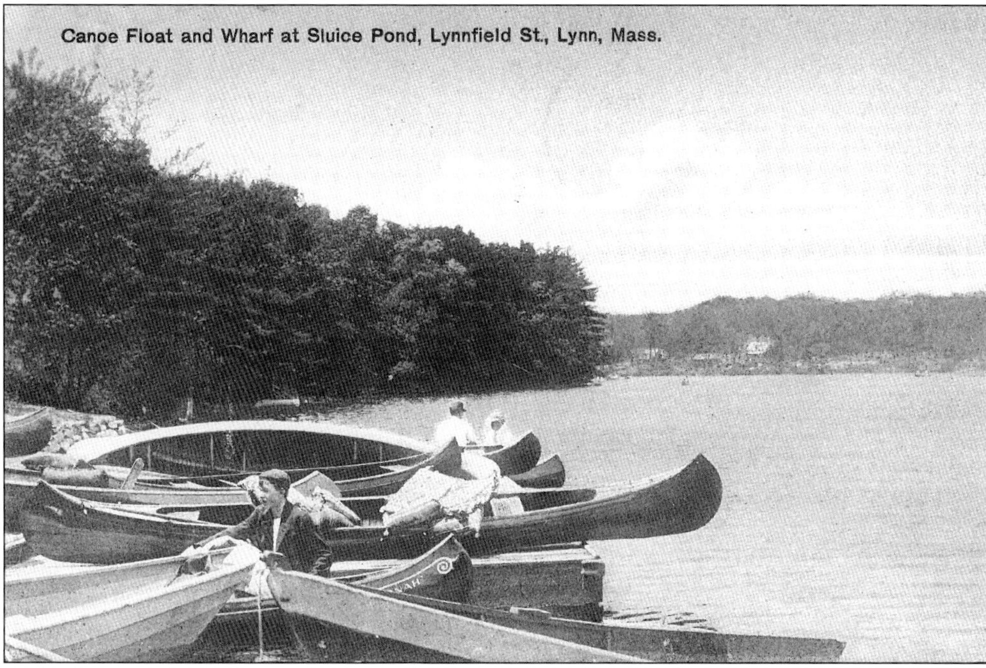

The *Lynn Item* of July 25, 1916, urged Lynners, "If you cannot get away on a vacation until the very last day of summer and are therefore obliged to stay in Lynn, turn your sorrow into rejoicing and your footsteps Peabody-ward, hire a canoe and spend the day at Sluice." These two views, from 1909 (above) and 1916 (below), show that many heeded the advice.

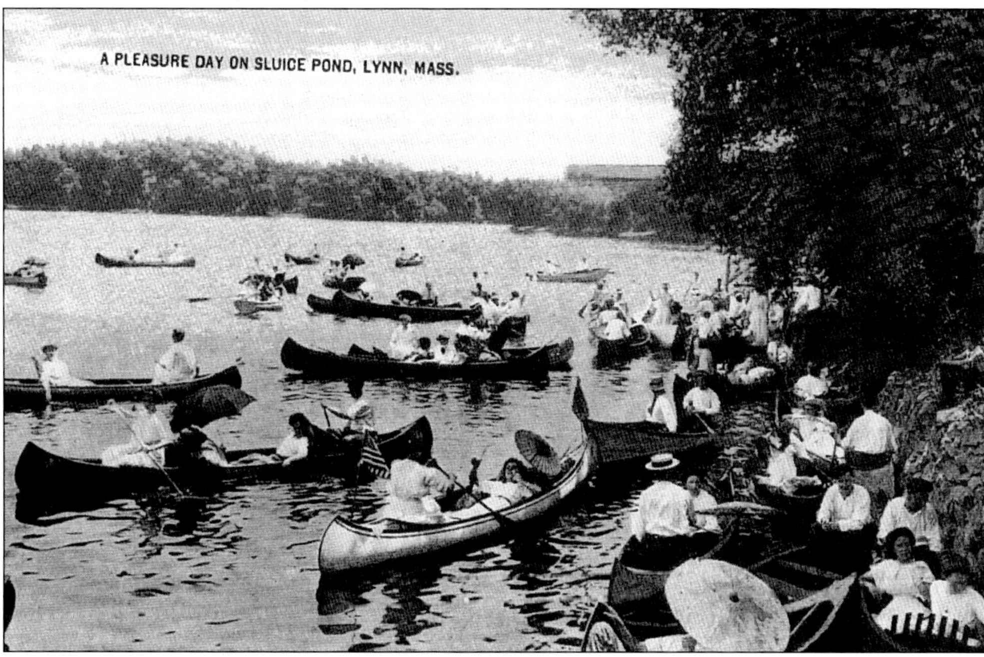

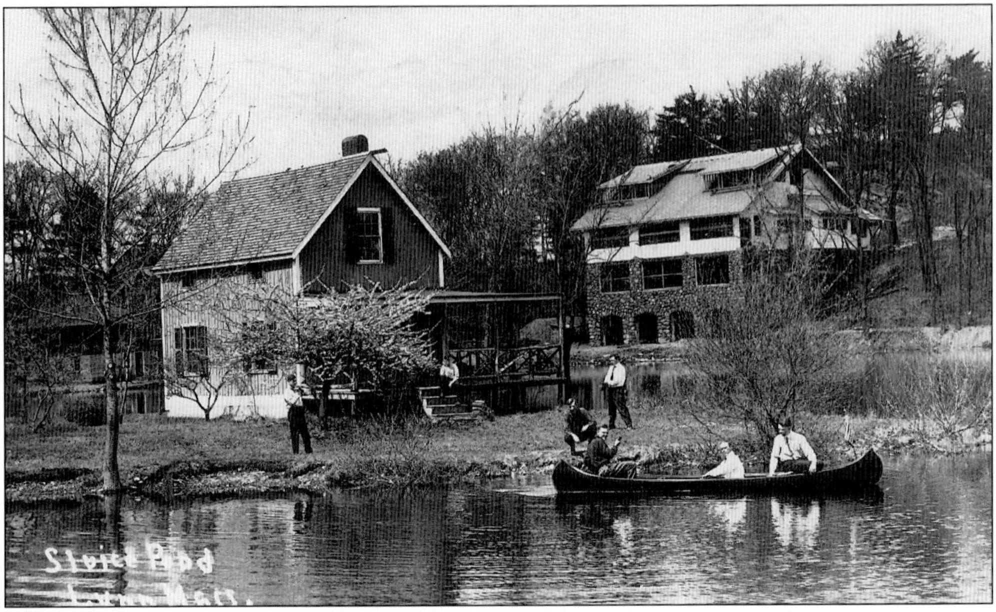

Briarcliff Lodge, originally referred to as "the Lynn Woods Chateau" or "the Dancing Bungalow at Wyoma," opened in June of 1916. It has belonged to the City of Lynn since 1937. (Conway collection.)

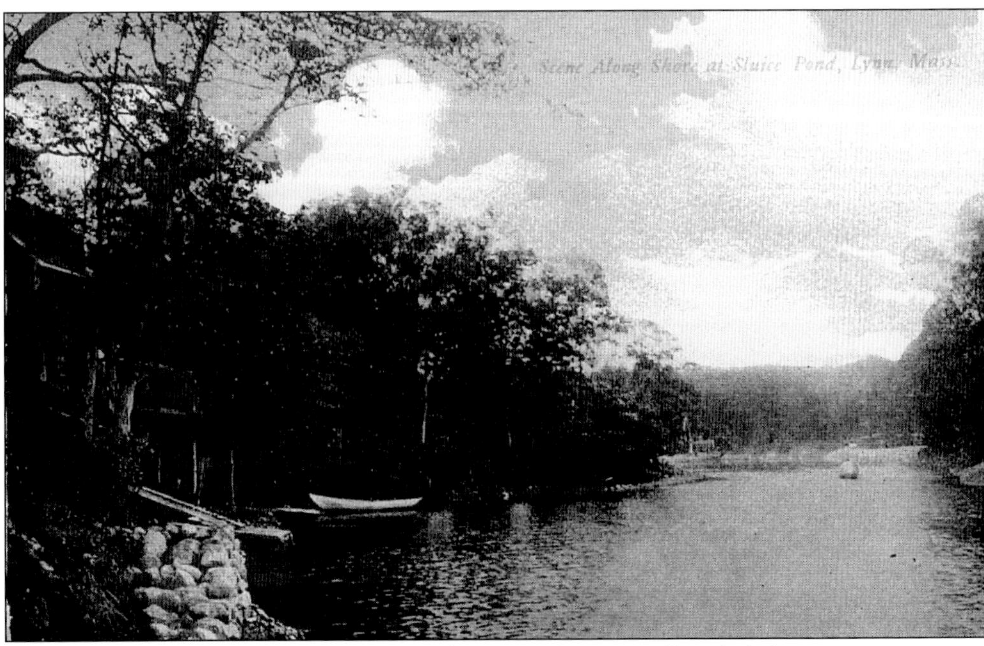

Despite Sluice's popularity as a recreational spot, its 50 acres still included quiet corners.

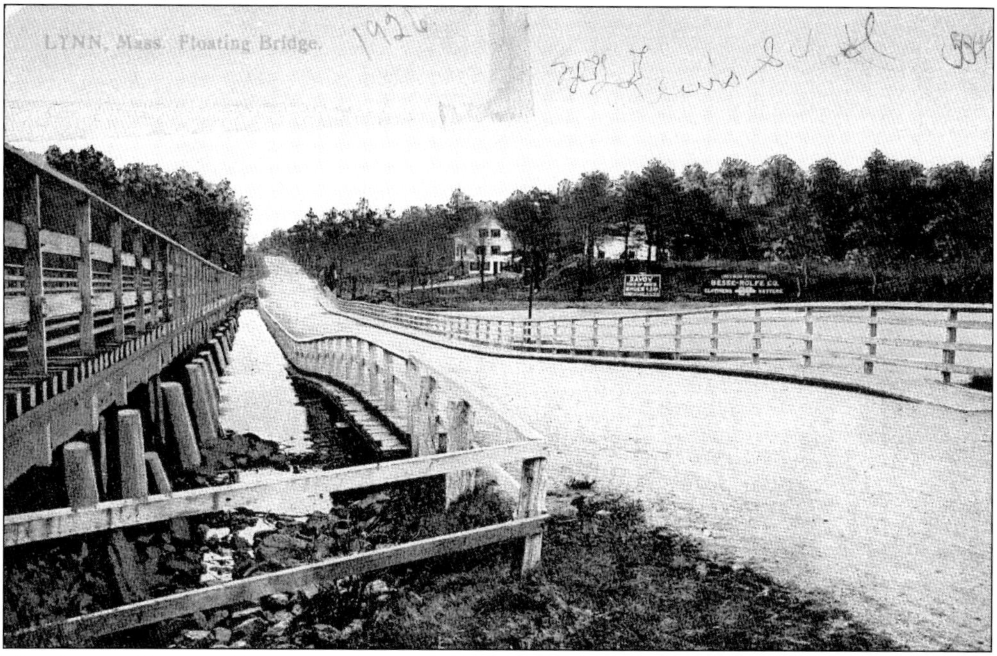

The famous Floating Bridge was built in 1804 as part of the Boston-Salem Turnpike. It was constructed as a pontoon because the pond's bottom was too soft and peaty to support a conventional bridge. This fact gave rise to the popular myth that Collins Pond, as it was then known, was bottomless.

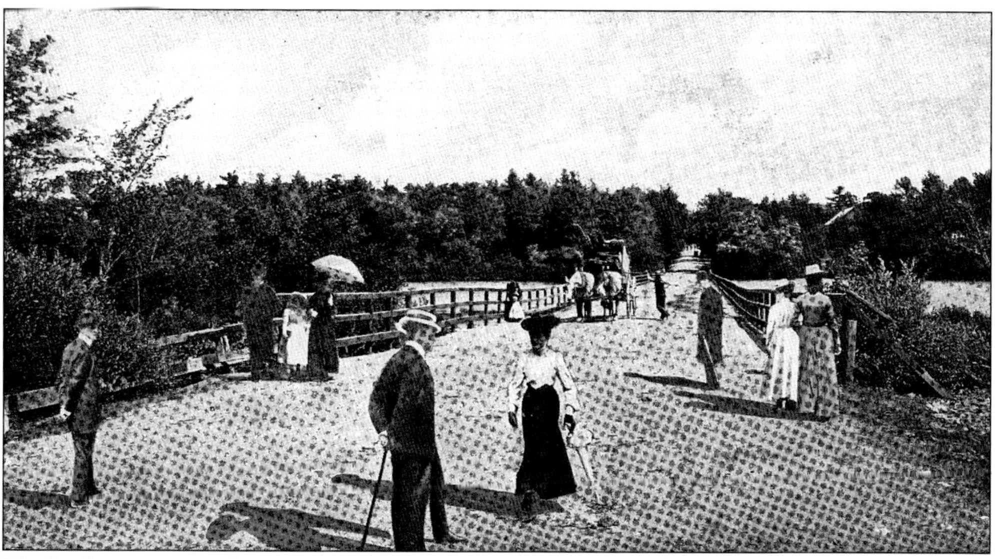

The bridge was a popular site for curiosity seekers and made a pleasant destination for a summer walk. It was replaced in 1921 and named after Matthew L. Buchanan, Lynn's first World War I casualty.

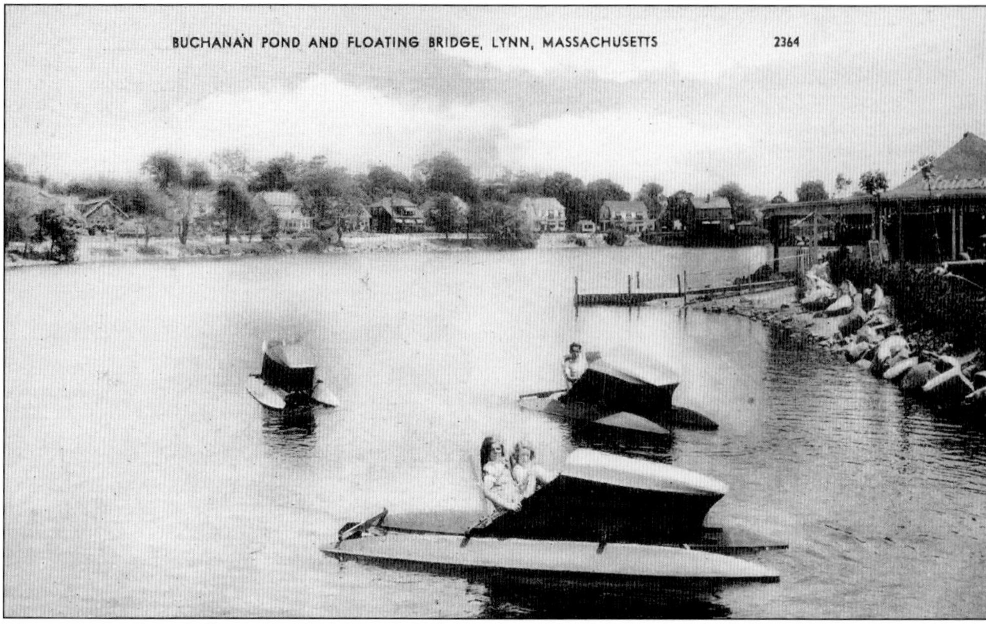

The relatively small size of Buchanan Pond was no deterrent to these boating enthusiasts c. 1920.

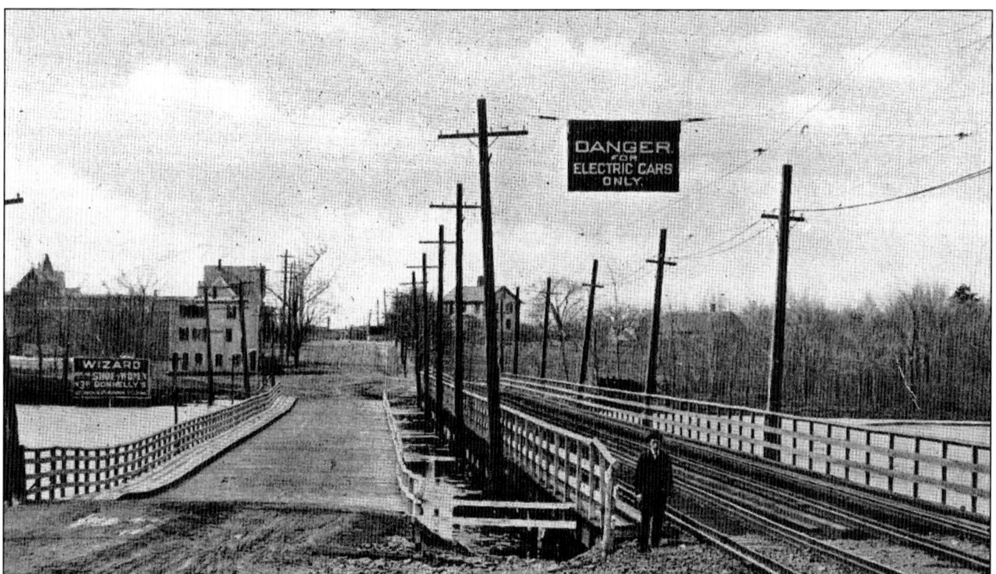

The construction of the Boston and Northern Street Railway bridge must have gone a good way toward dispelling the notion of Buchanan Pond's infinite depth. (Conway collection.)

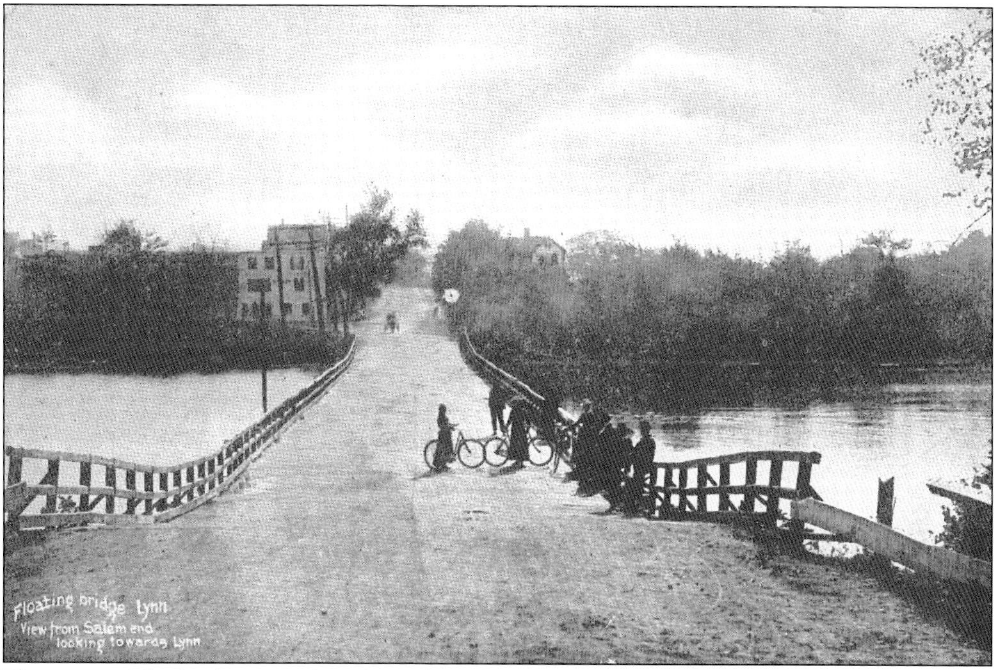

This view of the bridge was taken from the Salem side. (Conway collection.)

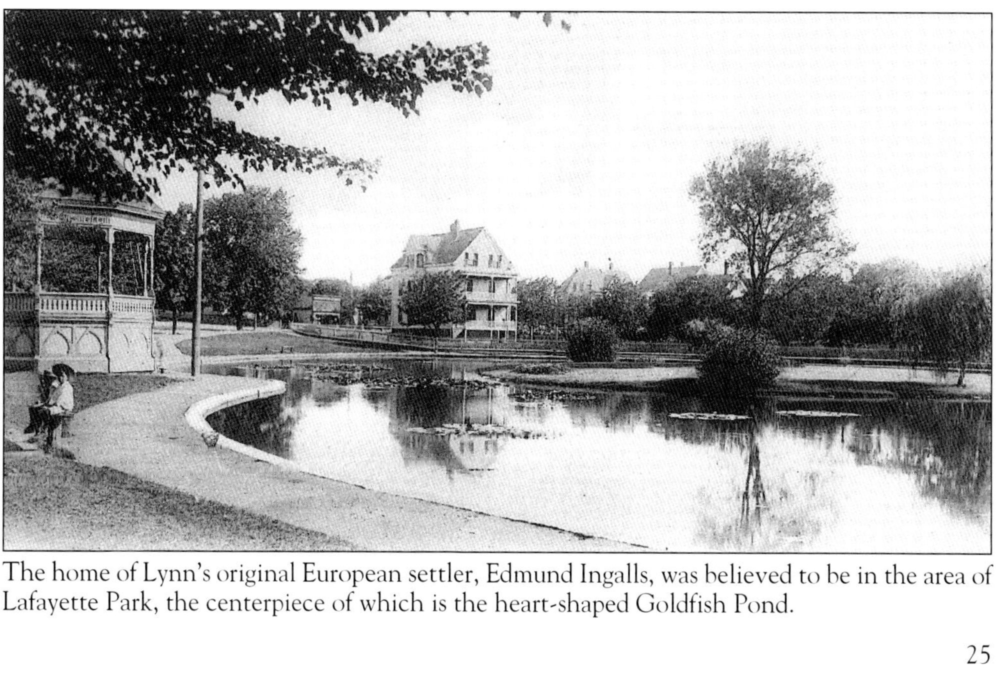
The home of Lynn's original European settler, Edmund Ingalls, was believed to be in the area of Lafayette Park, the centerpiece of which is the heart-shaped Goldfish Pond.

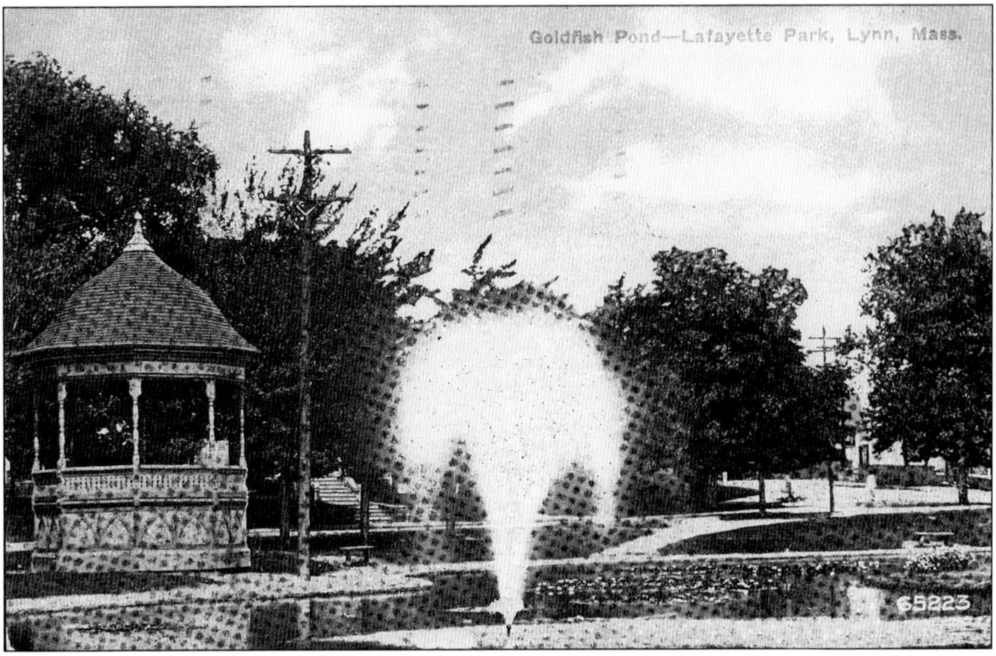

According to tradition, Goldfish Pond derives its name from the goldfish "borrowed" from the Stetson Estate in Swampscott by neighborhood boys as early as the 1840s. Successive generations replenished the stock over the years until Goldfish Pond became the preferred term over "the Swamp" or "Ingalls Pond."

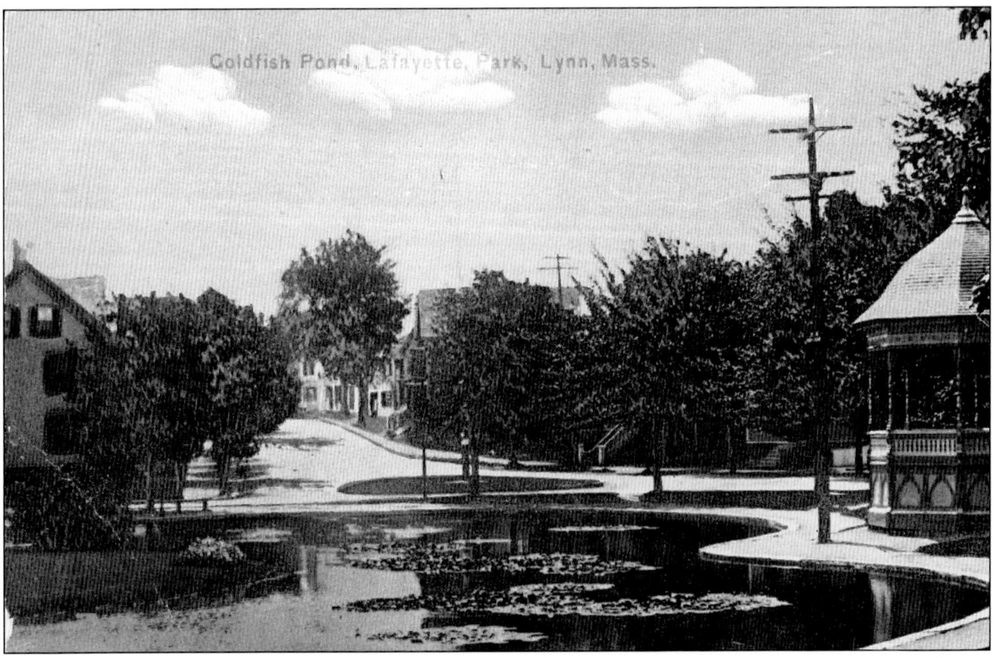

A 1910 view of Goldfish Pond looking down Lafayette Park shows the 1890 bandstand. An earlier bandstand had been located on the island in the center of the pond.

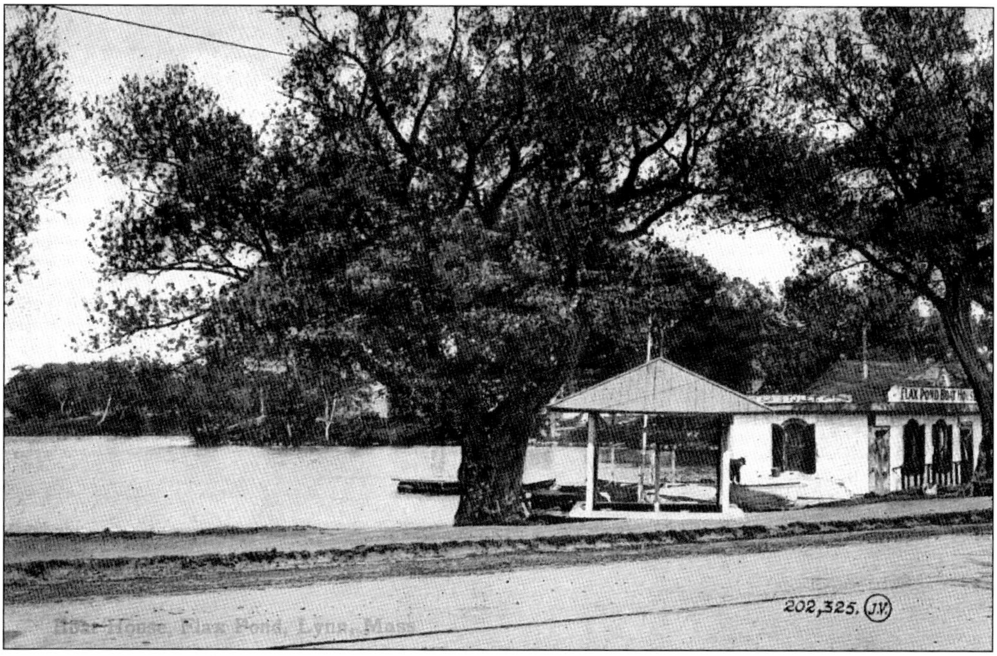

Seventy-one-acre Flax Pond is another of the important "Lakes of Lynn." Burcks boathouse stood on the Chestnut Street side until it was shown to be occupying city property.

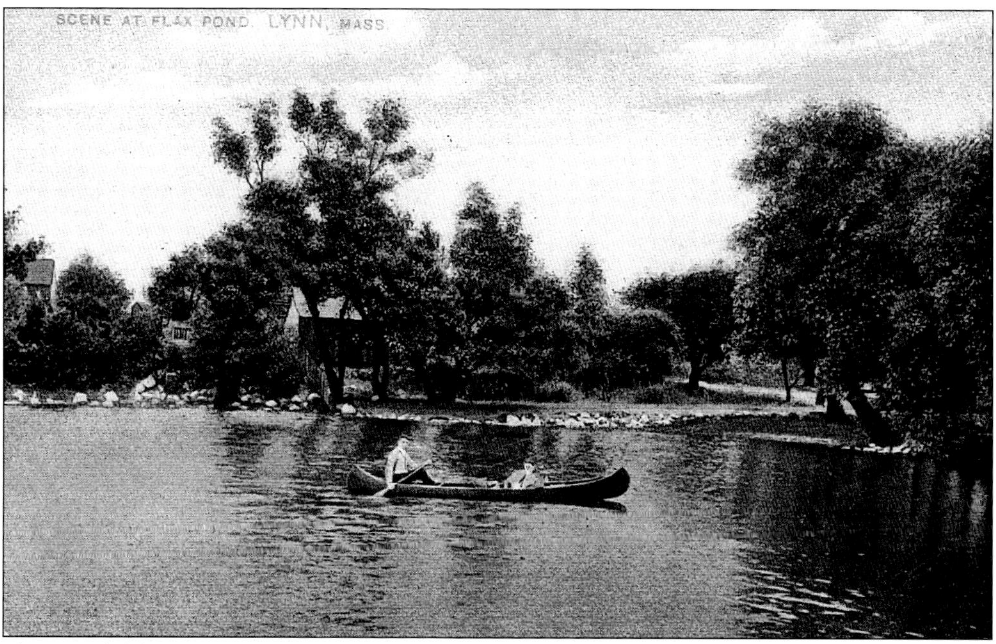

Flax Pond, like its sister, Sluice Pond, was a popular spot for canoeing, swimming, and, in the winter, skating.

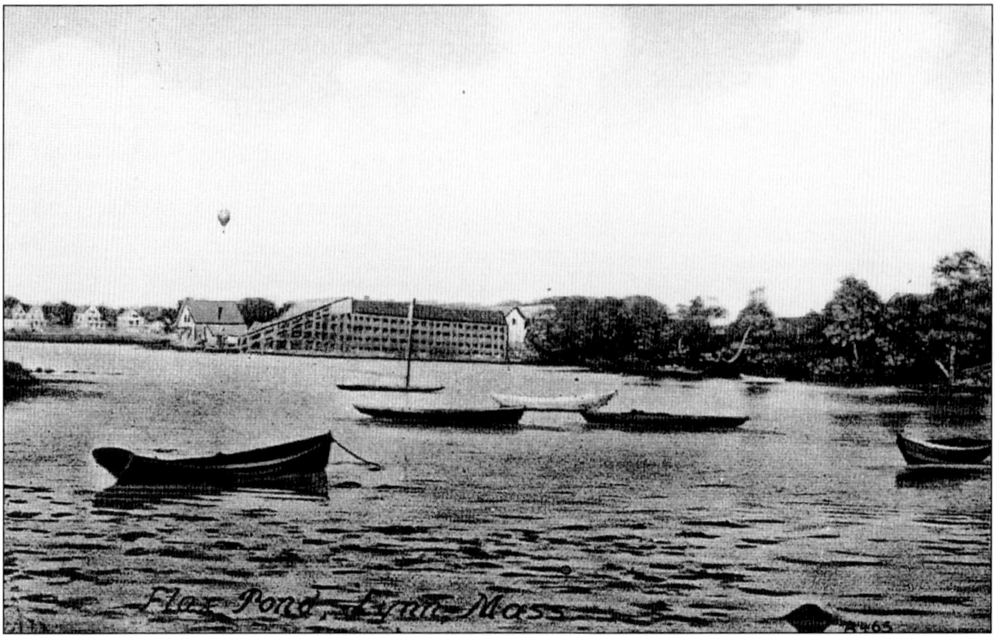

Aside from its recreational uses, Flax Pond was an important center for the ice industry. Some of the icehouses can be seen on the far side of the pond in this 1910 card.

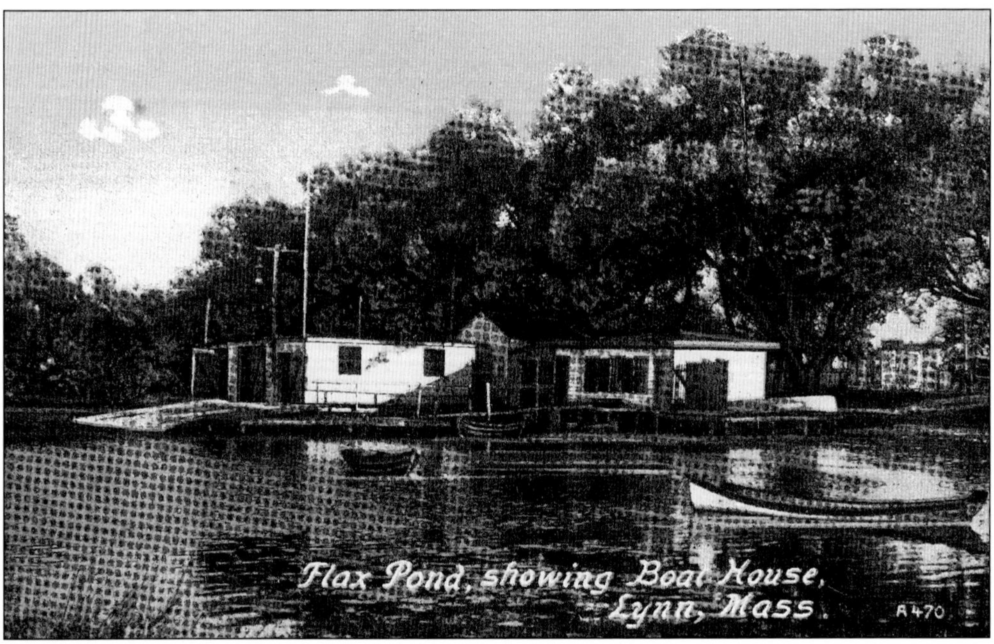

This is another view of the popular boathouse on Flax Pond.

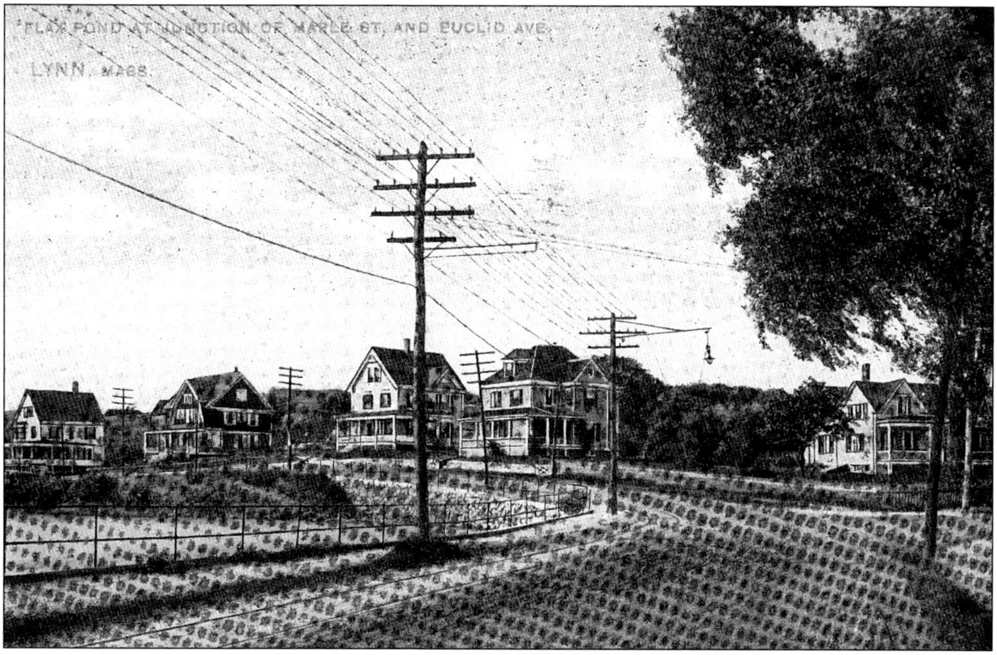

At the time of this picture in 1910, the so-called Lakeside area of the city was still rather sparsely settled.

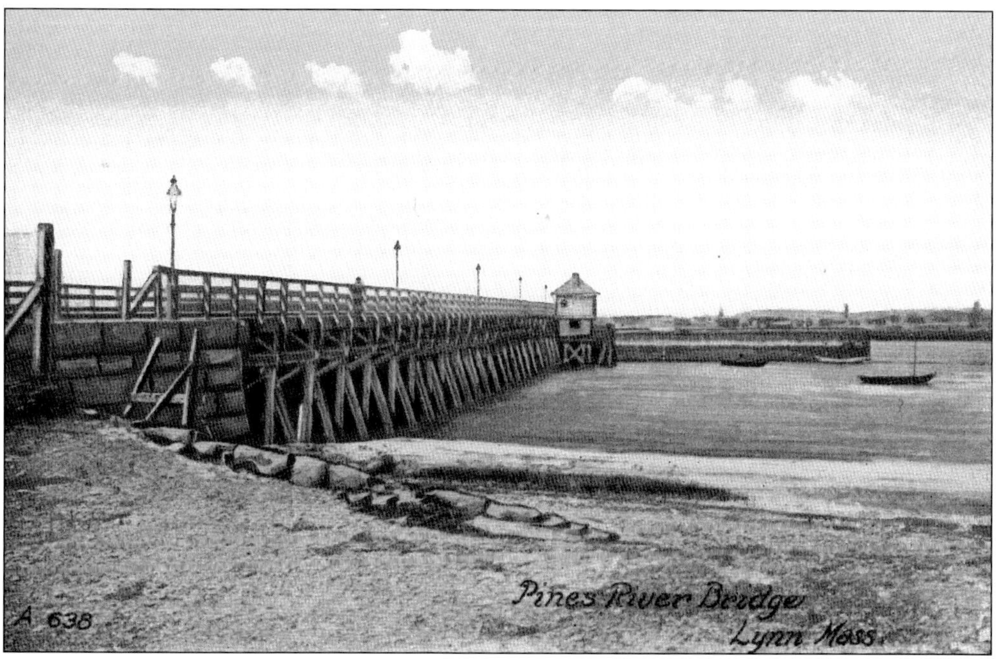

The Pines River Bridge was constructed in 1875 at the point where the Pines River meets the Saugus. It was destroyed by fire in 1921.

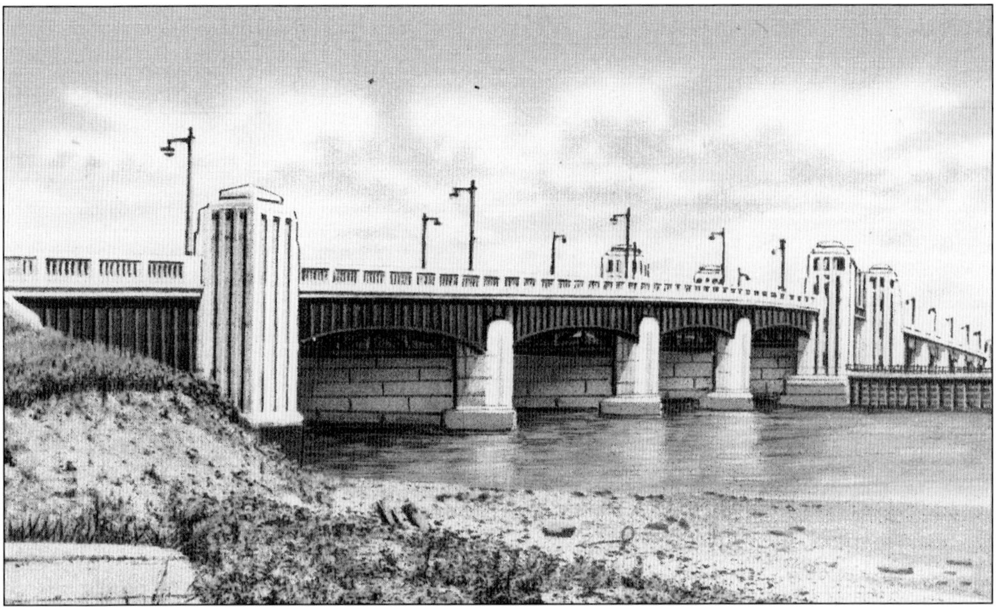

In 1935 the General Edwards Bridge over the Saugus River opened to accommodate the increase in automobile traffic. Clarence Edwards was the commander of the World War I 26th Infantry (the Yankee division), which was made up of National Guard units from New England.

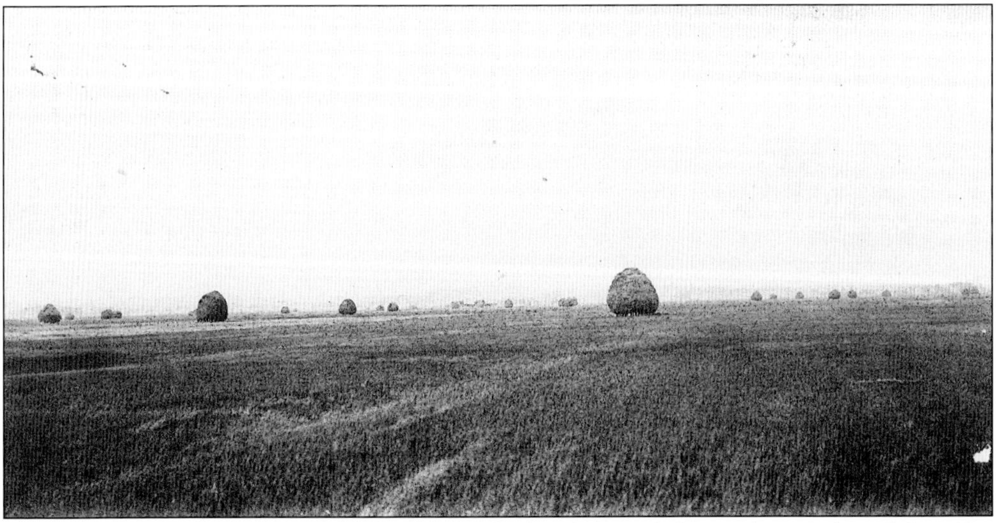

This 1900 view of the Lynn marshes evidences little substantial change from Colonial days. For centuries the salt marshes provided local farmers with a bountiful hay crop.

Two

STREETS AND SQUARES

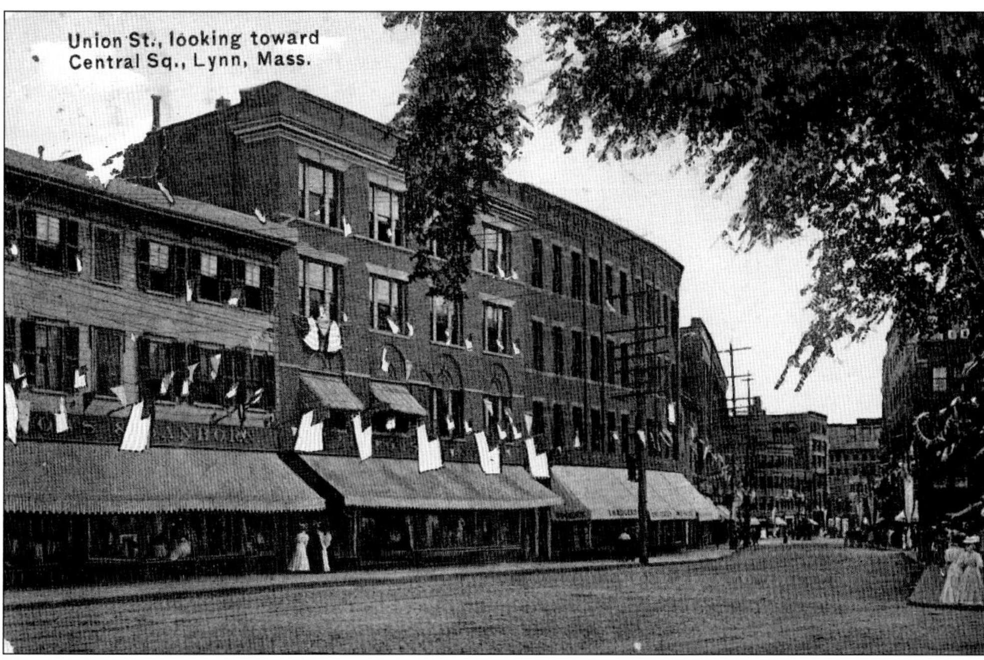

This card depicts Union Street looking toward Central Square and shows two popular department stores, Burrows and Sanborn and T.W. Rogers. The stores are decked out in flags and buntings, most probably for the 1907 Old Home Week Celebration.

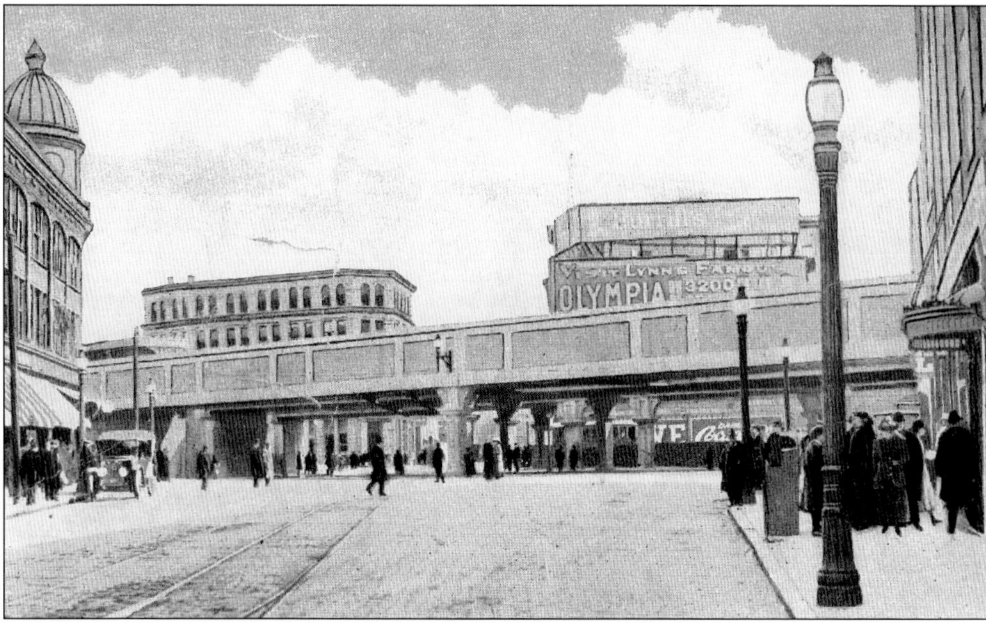

Railroad grade crossings have been the cause of numerous accidents over the years. In 1913, the Boston & Maine eliminated the grade crossing at Central Square and elevated its tracks as shown here.

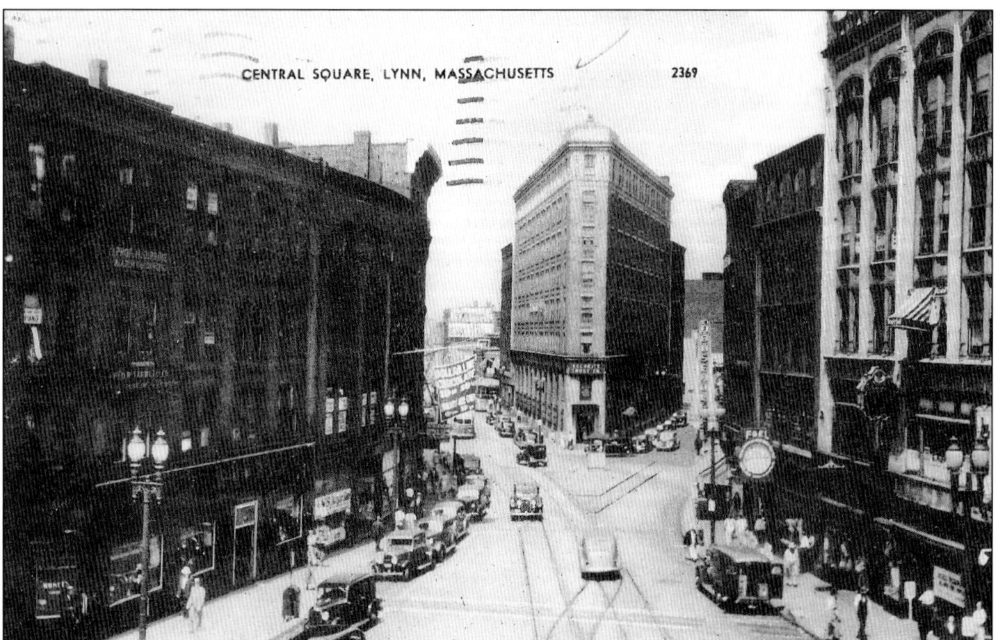

Central Square owes its existence to the construction of Lynn's first railroad depot on Union Street in 1835. At that time, the business center of the town shifted from its traditional focus at the Common. This 1947 card shows a thriving downtown scene. (Conway collection.)

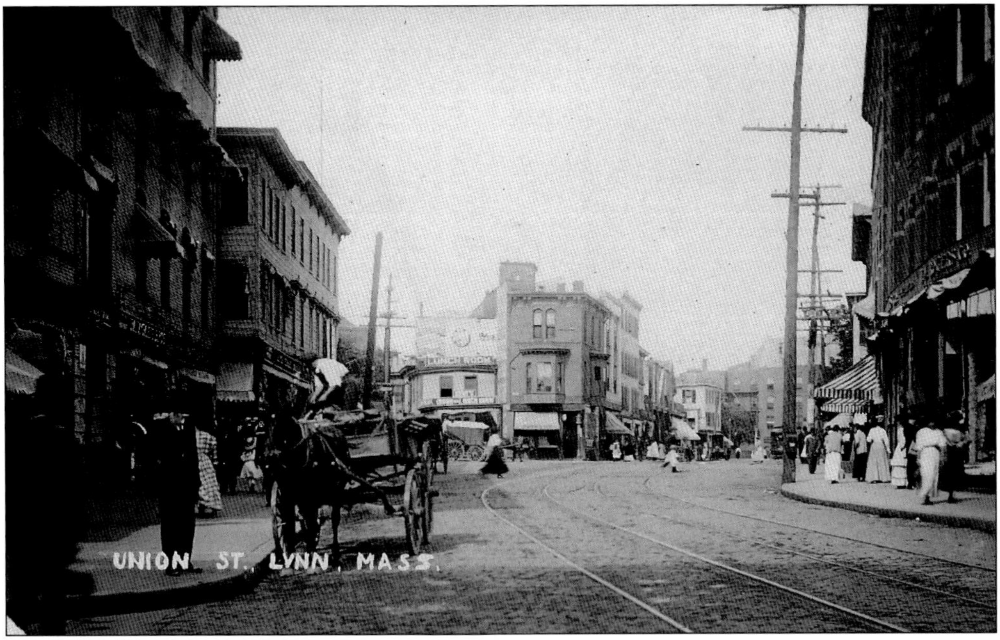

This 1910 view of Union Street looks toward Union Square, later called Freeman Square. The building at the center of the picture is Warren Toppan's pharmacy at Toppan's Corner; next door is Kent's Union Square Lunch Room. (Conway collection.)

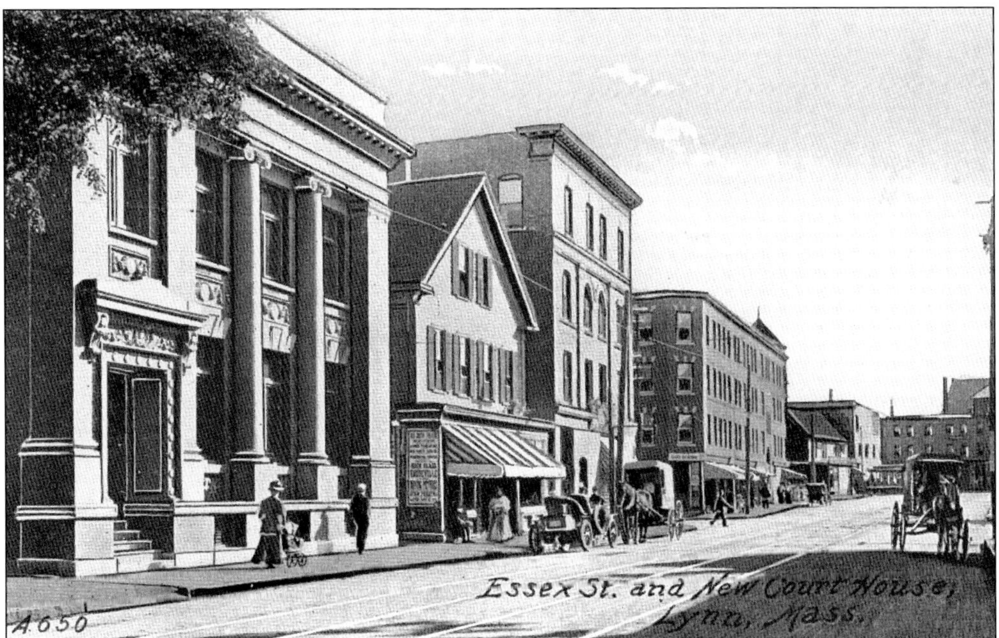

The new courthouse illustrated here was built in 1909. Although this card gives the impression the building was made of granite, it was constructed predominantly of red brick. It was razed in 1971.

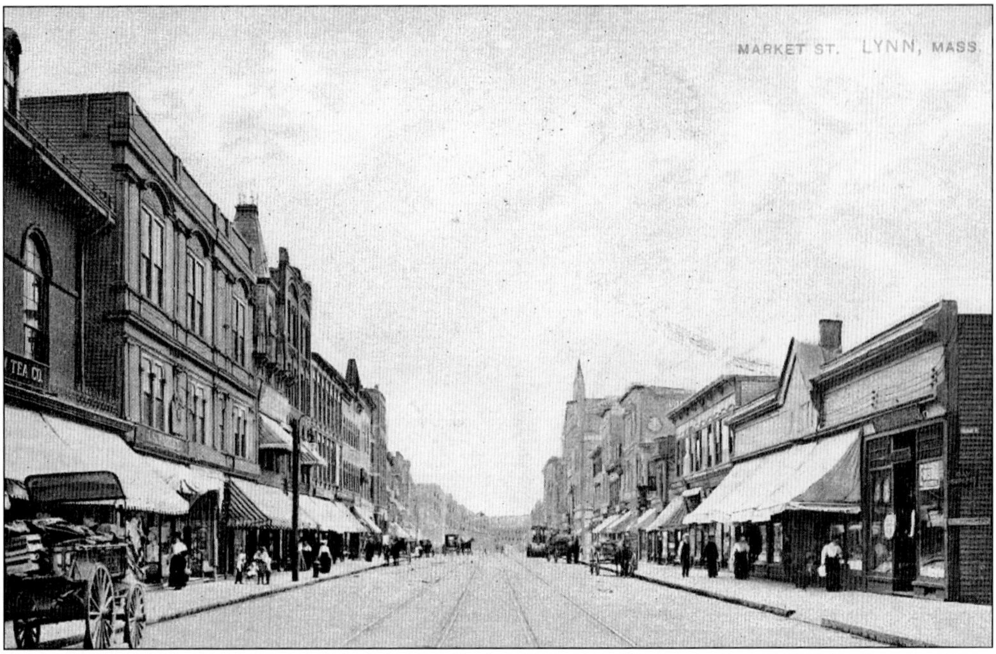

This view shows Market Street looking north from City Hall Square *c.* 1910. The first building on the right is Charles Stackpole's phonograph store with a window advertisement for Edison products. Across the street are J.S. Farley's Dry Goods and the Grand Union Tea Company.

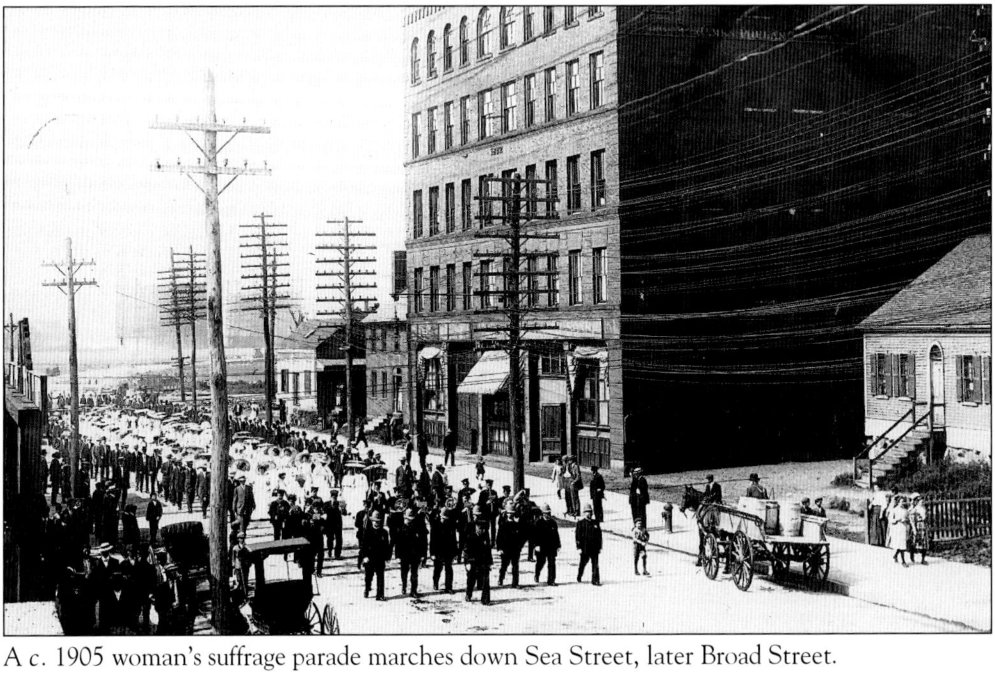

A *c.* 1905 woman's suffrage parade marches down Sea Street, later Broad Street.

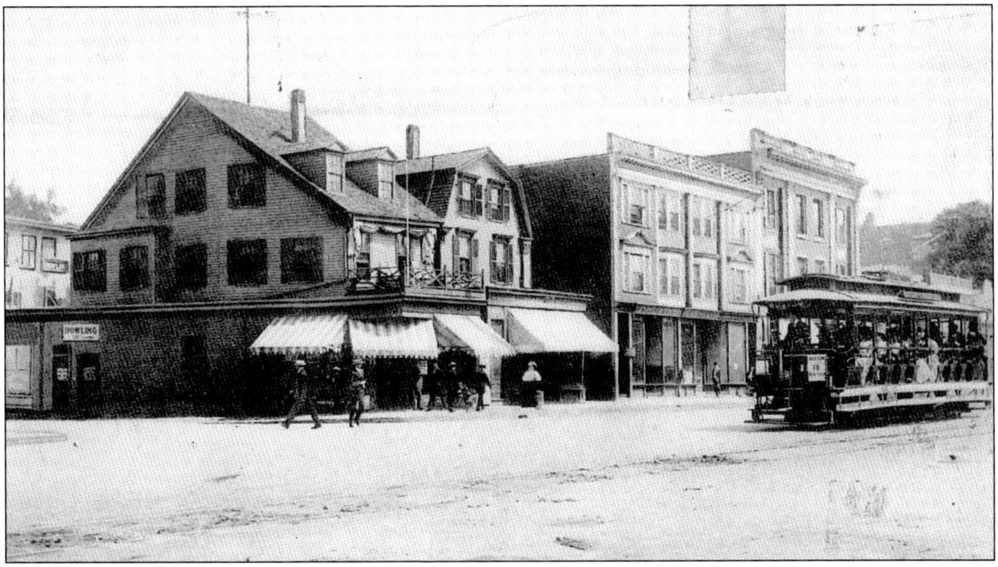

Market Street is shown here at the corner of Centre Street in 1910. The bowling alley on the corner charged 10¢ a string. The open trolley is a Boston and Northern car.

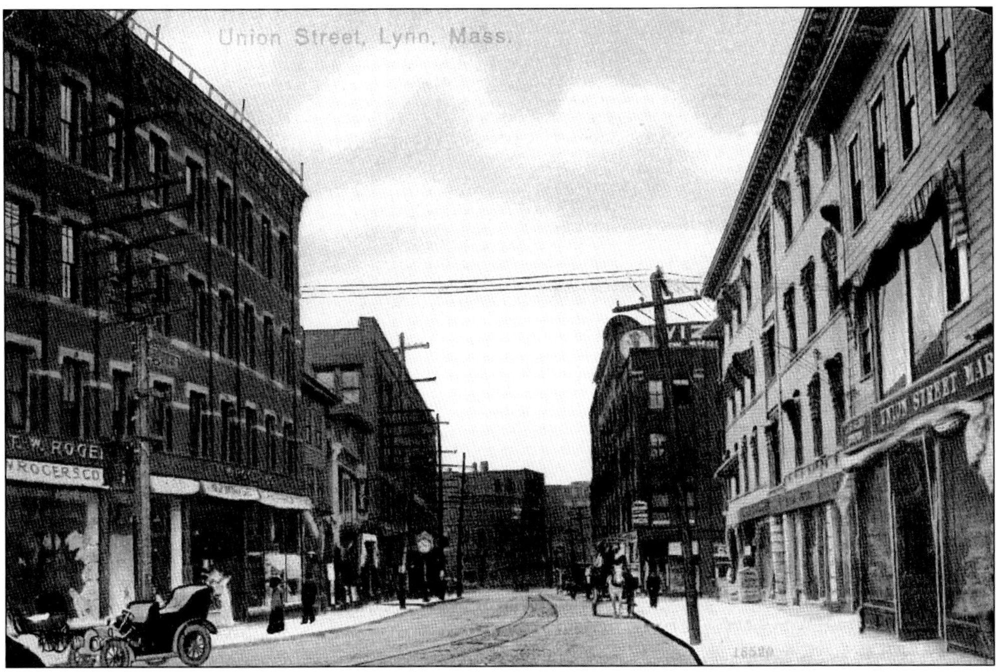

This 1910 view of Union Street, published by the T.W. Rogers Company but printed in Germany, shows several modes of transportation—a horse-drawn wagon, streetcars (evidenced by the tracks), an automobile, and even, on the extreme left, a baby carriage. The Union Street Market on the right was part of J.B. Blood and Company.

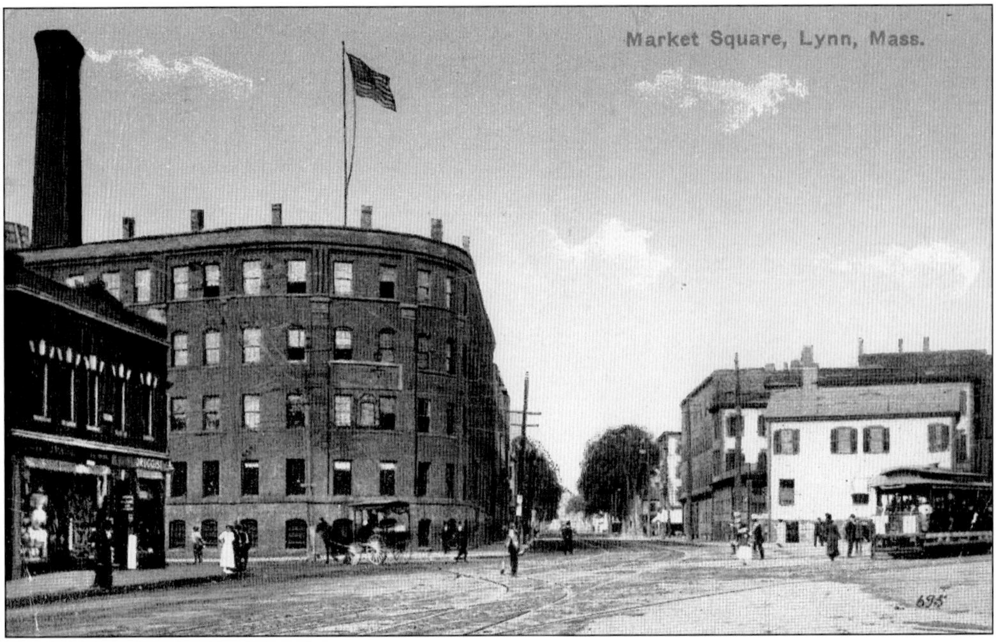

This view features Market Square and Western Avenue. The small, white building on the right was the much-altered Lynn Hotel, built in 1803. At the time of this picture, 1913, it was known as the Market Square Hotel and was winding down its long career as a hostelry. It was demolished in 1923. The large brick factory on the left belonged to Lucius Beebe; behind it are the West Lynn Works of General Electric. (Conway collection.)

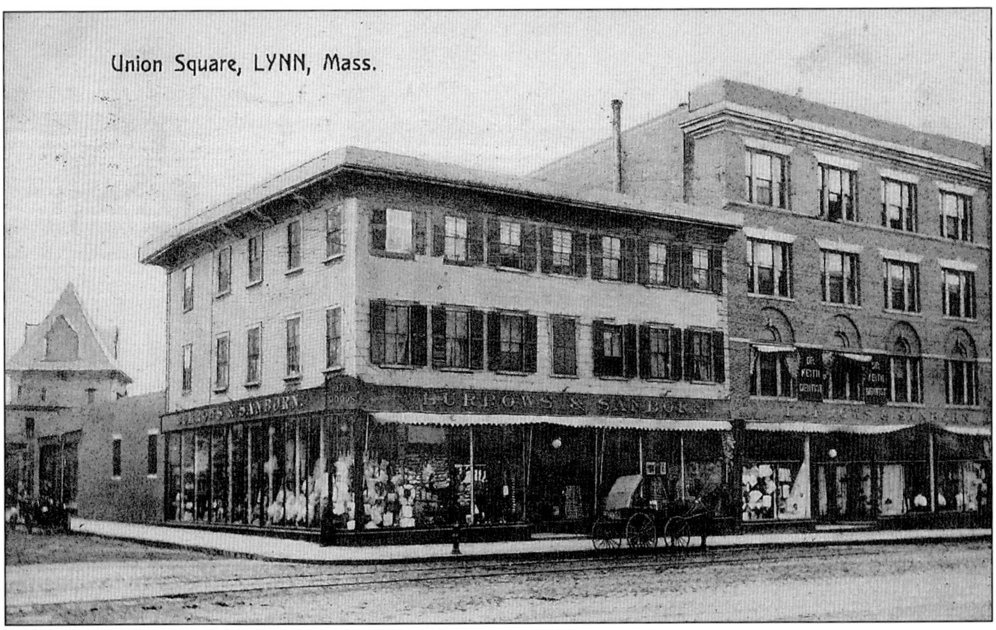

Burrows and Sanborn was at Union Square in 1913. Established in 1872, the department store was a downtown fixture until the 1960s. The roof of the Boston & Maine depot is visible on the left.

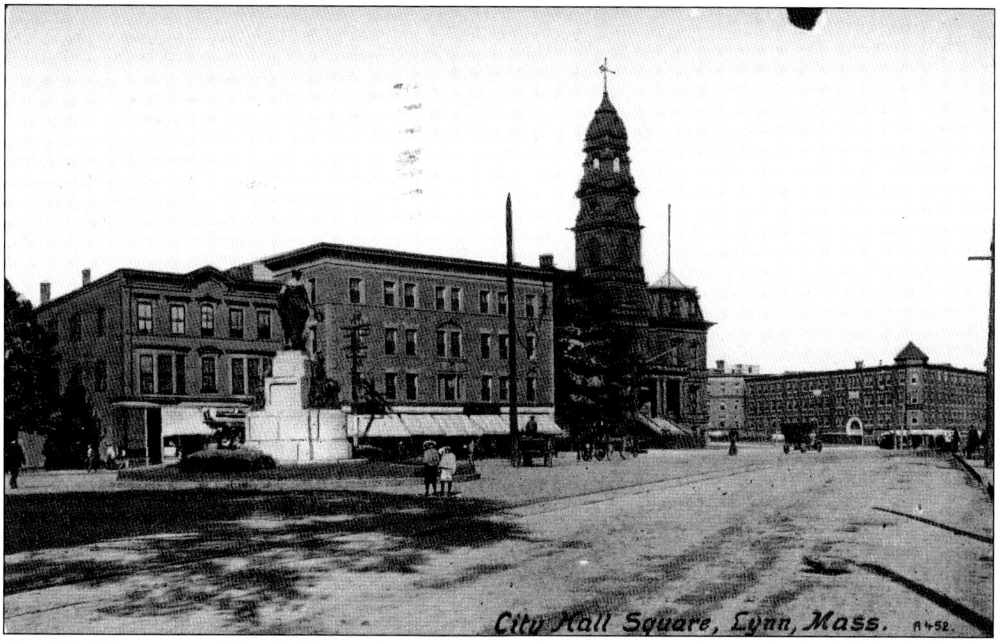

City Hall Square and the Soldier's Monument are shown here in 1910. The large brick building to the left of the old city hall is the Rhodes Building, built in 1898. It housed a number of small businesses, as did the Littlefield Block to the right at the corner of Essex Street.

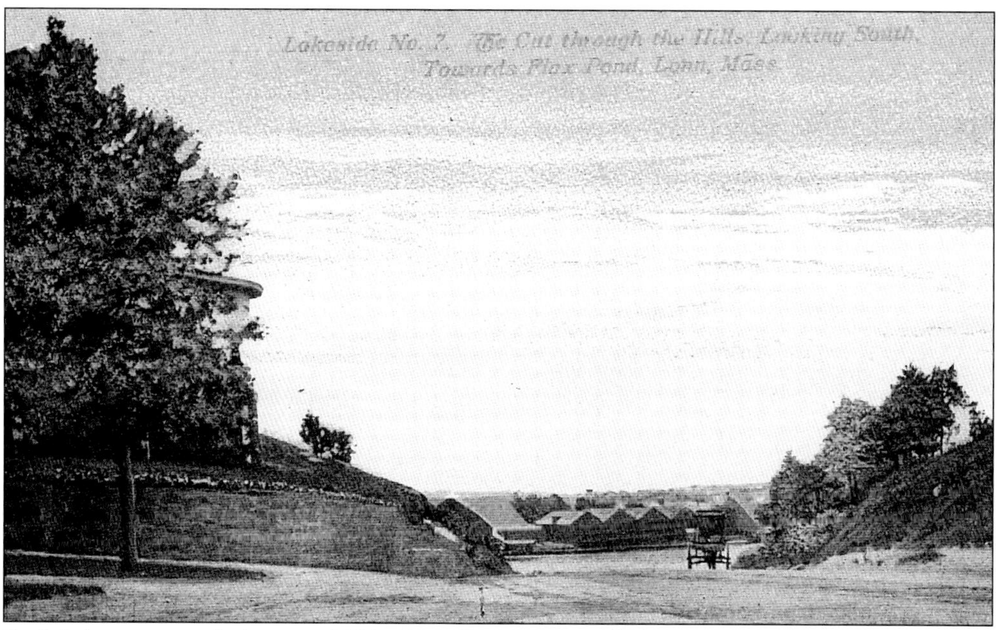

Euclid Avenue was laid out in 1892 when the area around Flax Pond became developed. This view was taken near the intersection with Lakeview Avenue.

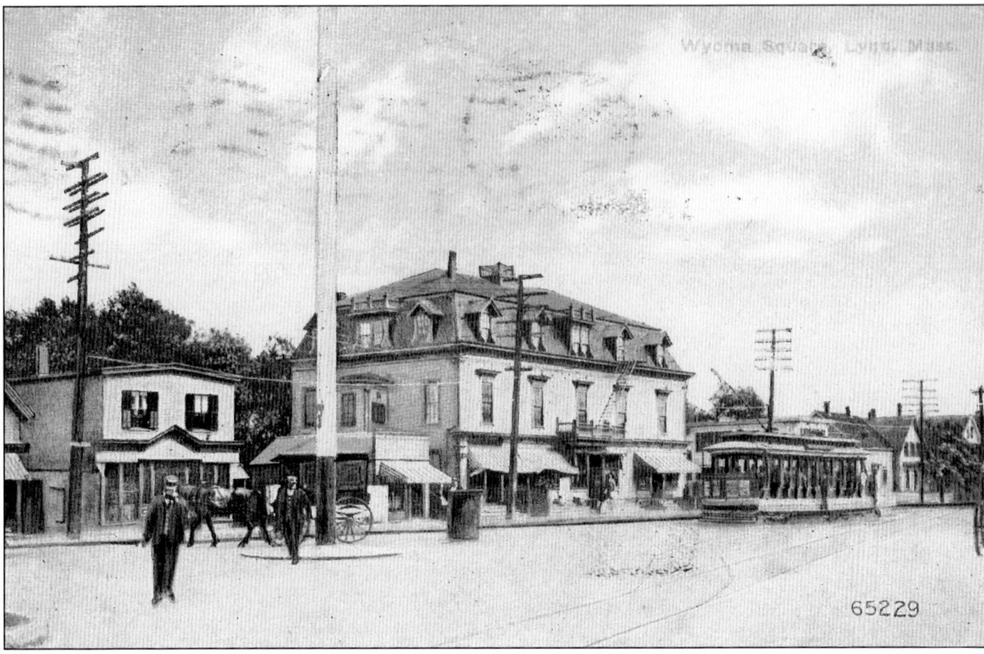

Originally known as "Bachellor's Plain" or "Dyehouse Village," the area of Lynn now centered on Broadway and Lynnfield Street was given the name "Wyoma" by Lynn poet and historian Alonzo Lewis, who considered the latter more poetic. The large building in the center is Wyoma Hall, which housed the Wyoma Grocery company and the Broadway Pool Room in 1909.

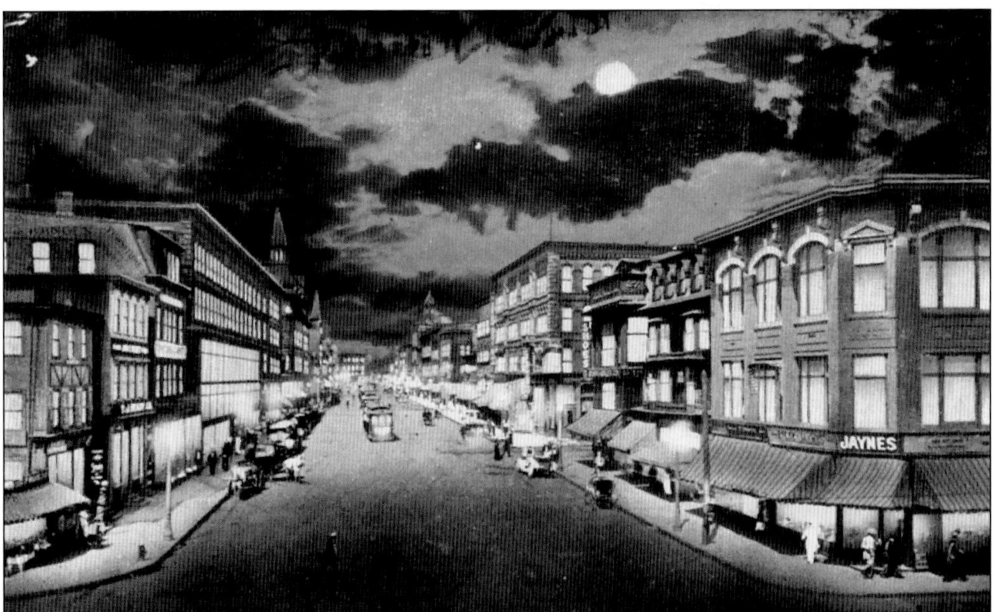

This *c.* 1915 view has been colored to give the appearance that every window on Market Street is illuminated. Given the size of the crowd that is visible, this may have been exaggerating the busyness of the scene somewhat.

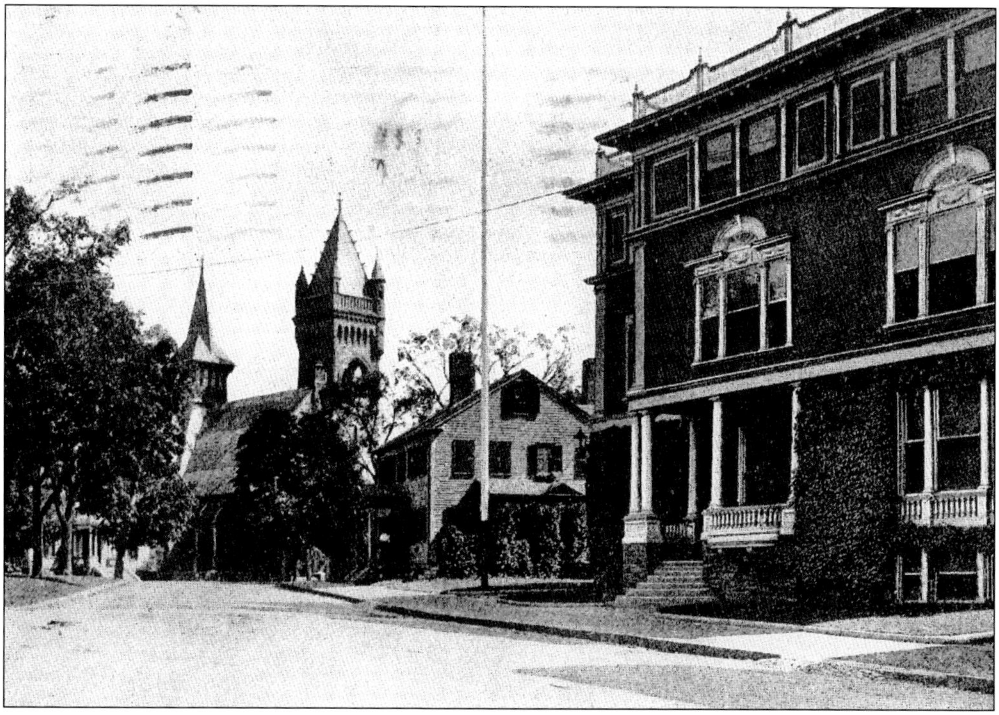

Washington Square was home to the Oxford Club and the Universalist church. This card was published by the P.B. Magranes Department Store in 1910.

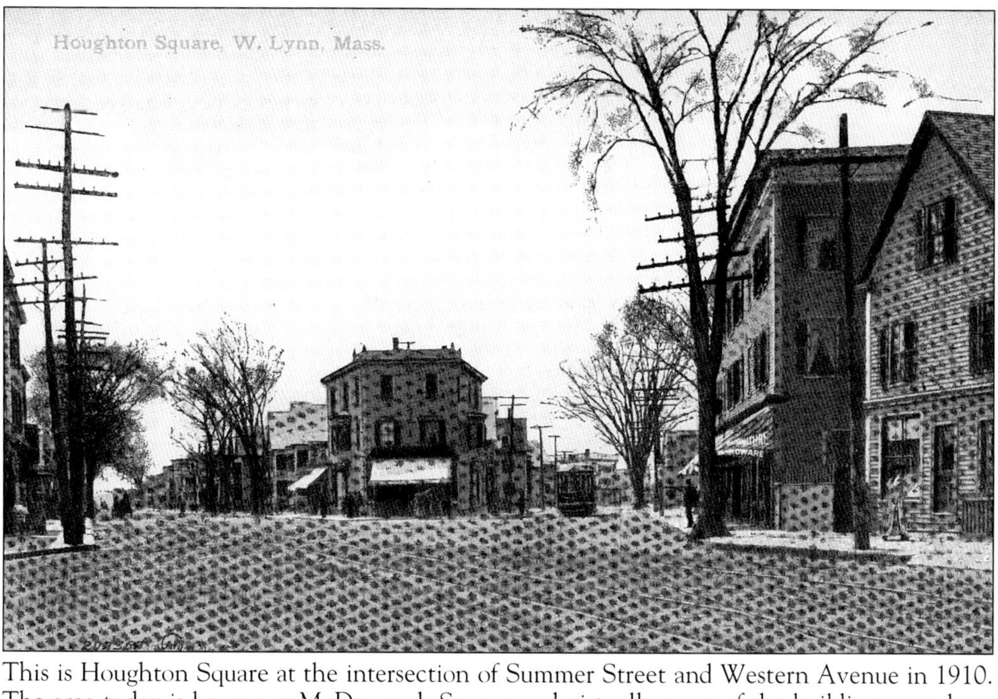

This is Houghton Square at the intersection of Summer Street and Western Avenue in 1910. The area today is known as McDonough Square and virtually none of the buildings seen here are still standing.

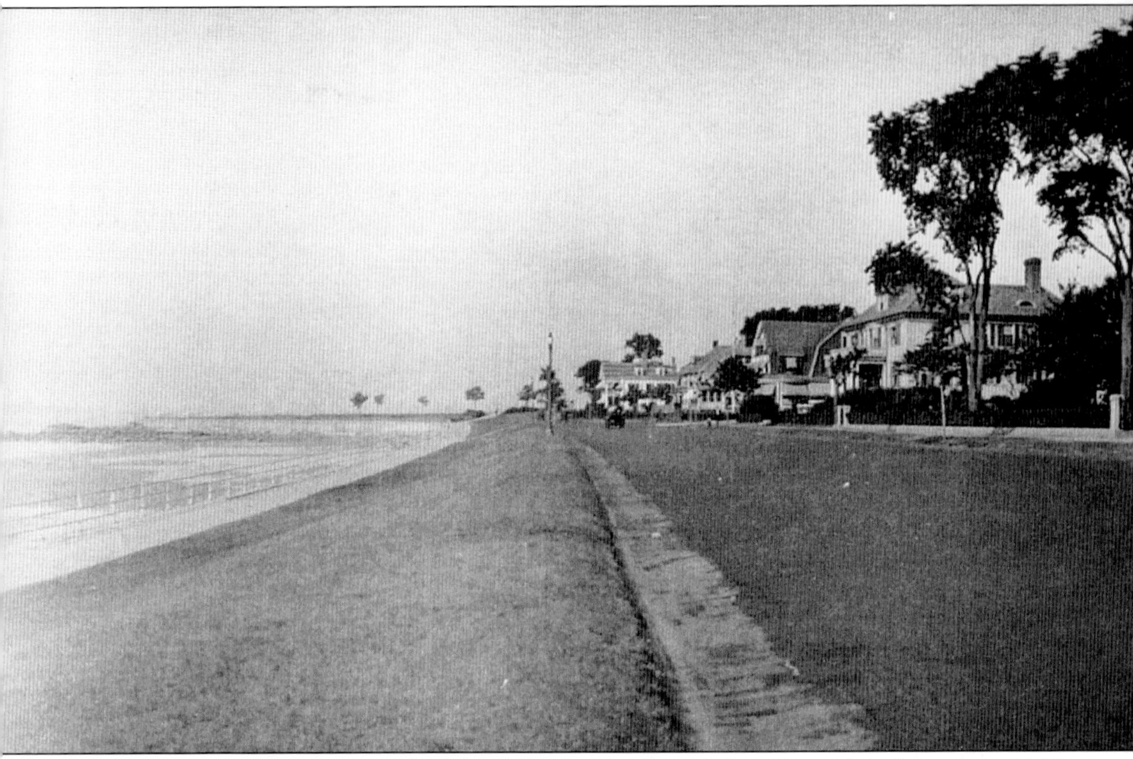

These two panoramic views of the fine homes along Lynn Shore Drive date from about 1910.

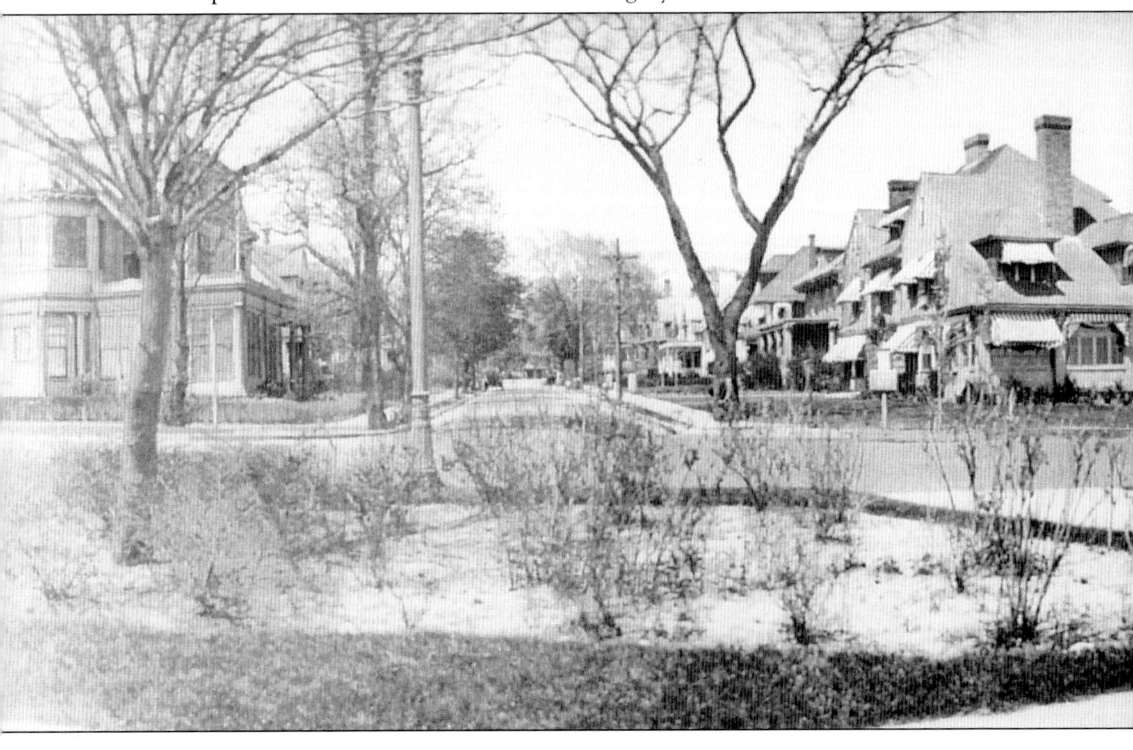

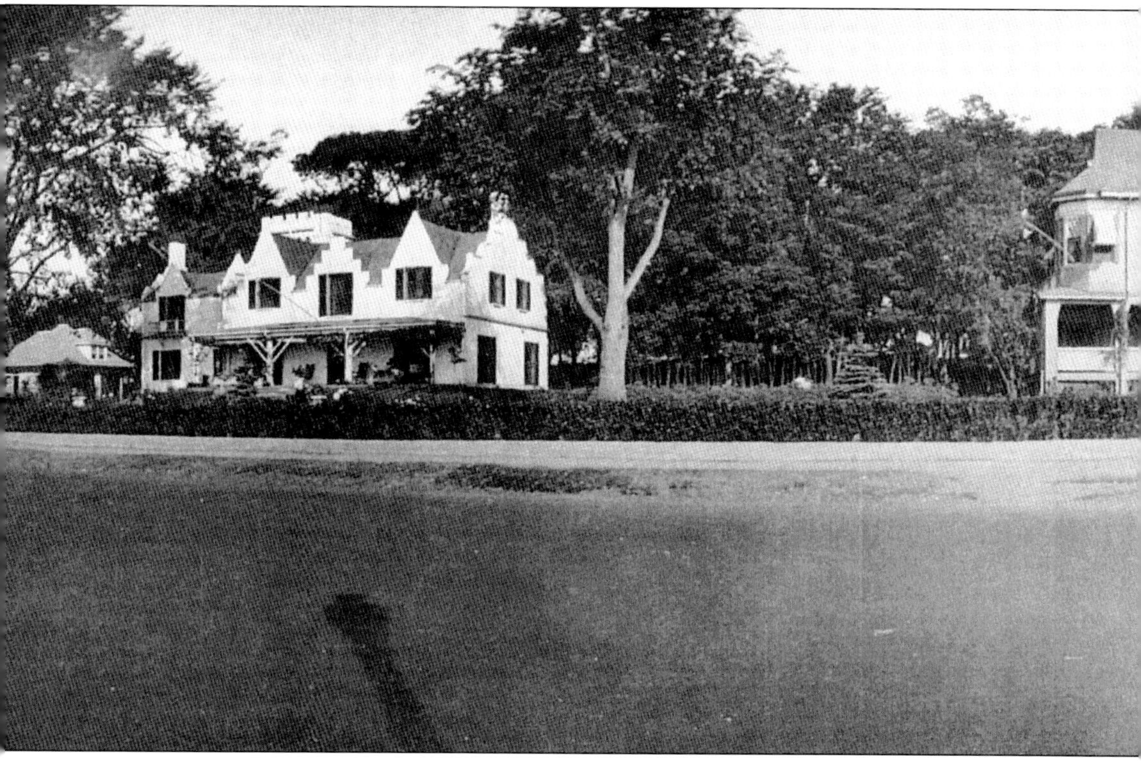

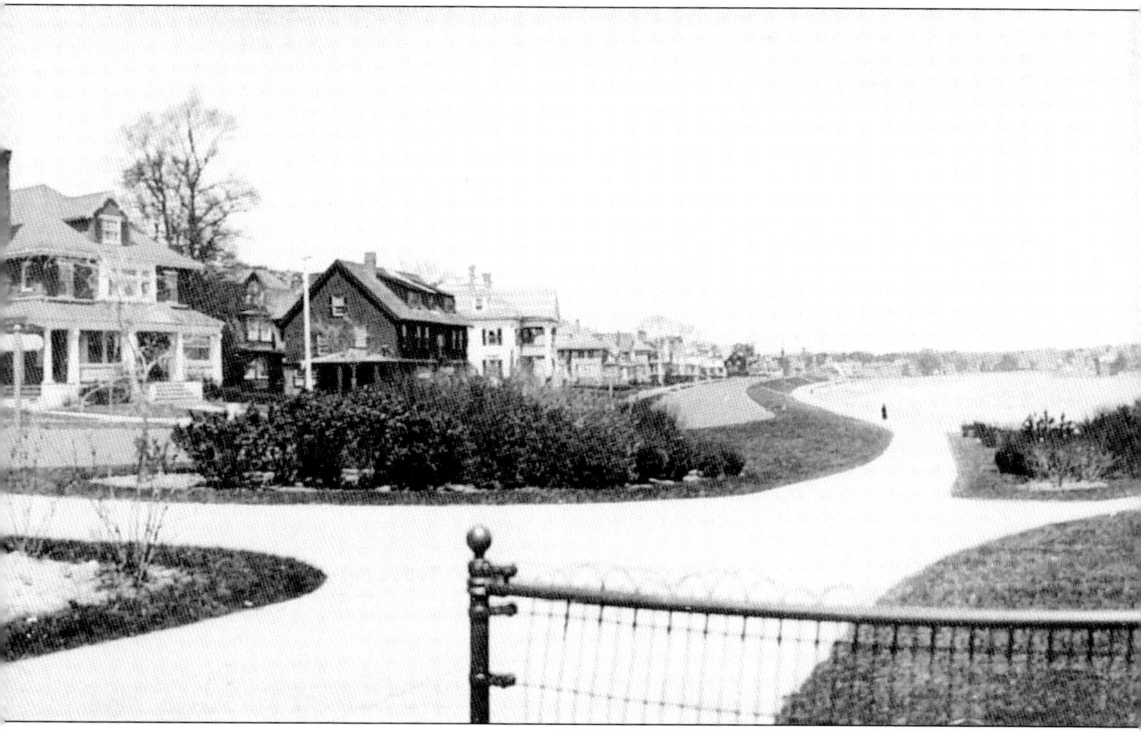

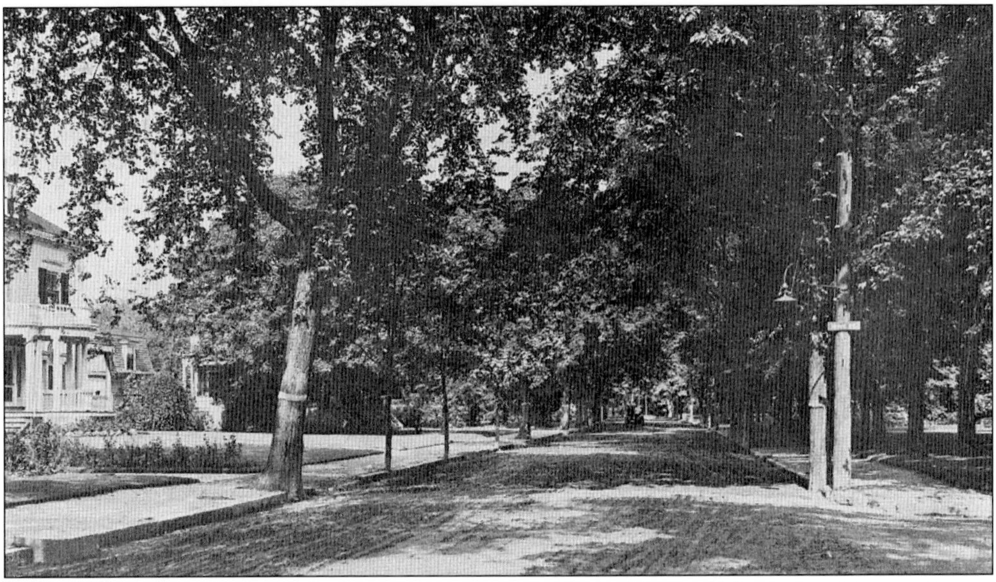

The home of Edward LaCroix, a leather manufacturer, is visible on the left side of Ocean Street, seen here from the foot of Wave Street in 1903. Built in 1895 by architect James T. Kelley, it is a fine example of the Colonial Revival style and is still standing today. Many of Lynn's wealthy businessmen built homes in what became known as the Diamond District during the late 19th and early 20th centuries.

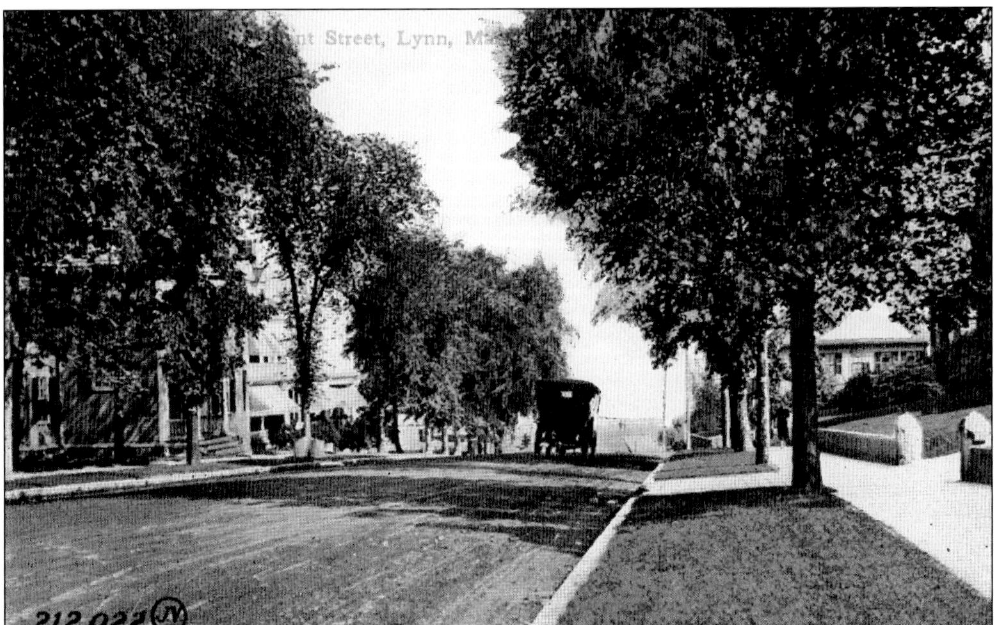

Nahant Street is shown looking toward the sea from about Ocean Street. At the time this picture was taken in 1906, Nahant Street contained a mixture of 18th-, 19th-, and 20th-century homes in a pleasant suburban setting.

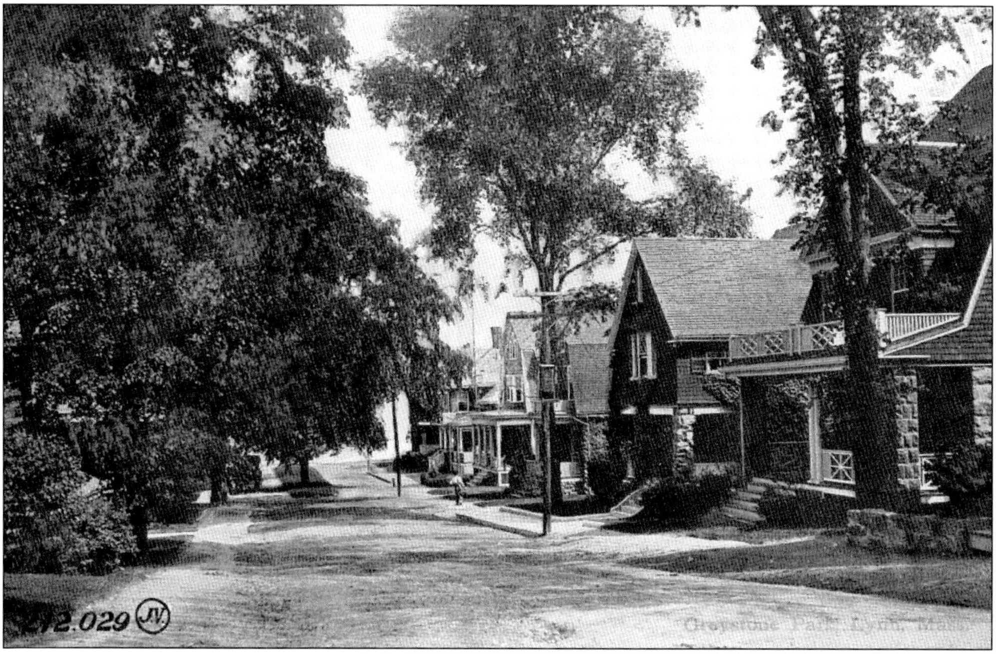

Once a part of the estate of famed 19th-century-actress Jean Davenport, Greystone Park was laid out in 1895. The handsome suburban homes shown in this 1906 view are nearly all still standing today.

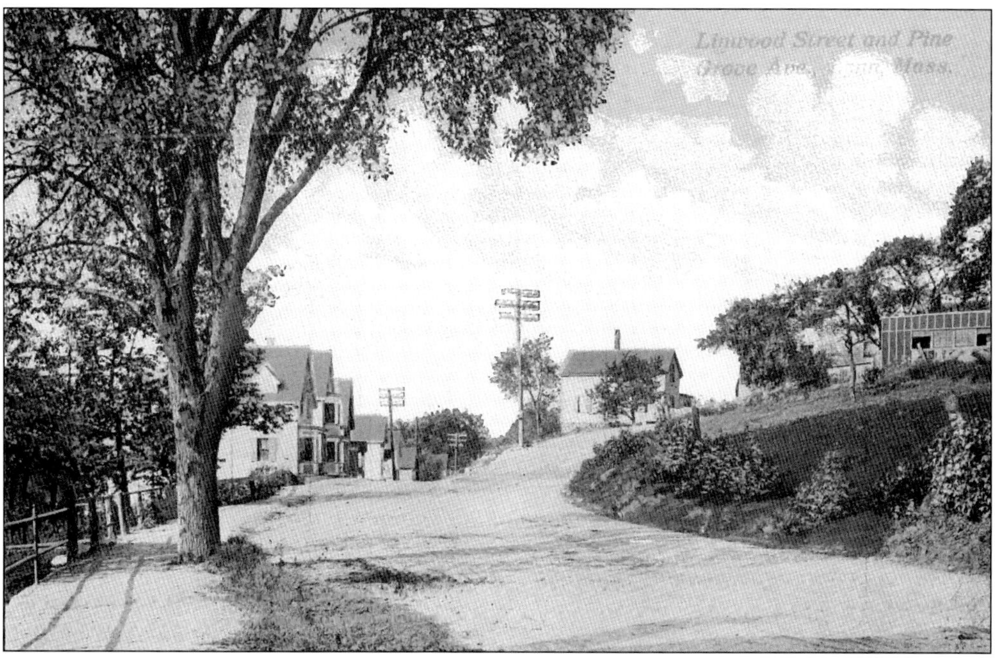

Pine Hill was relatively sparsely settled throughout much of Lynn's first three centuries. By the mid-19th century, however, the area's reputation for healthfulness and beautiful scenery led to its gradual development as a suburban neighborhood. Many of the single-family cottages (such as those shown here) housed workers. (Conway collection.)

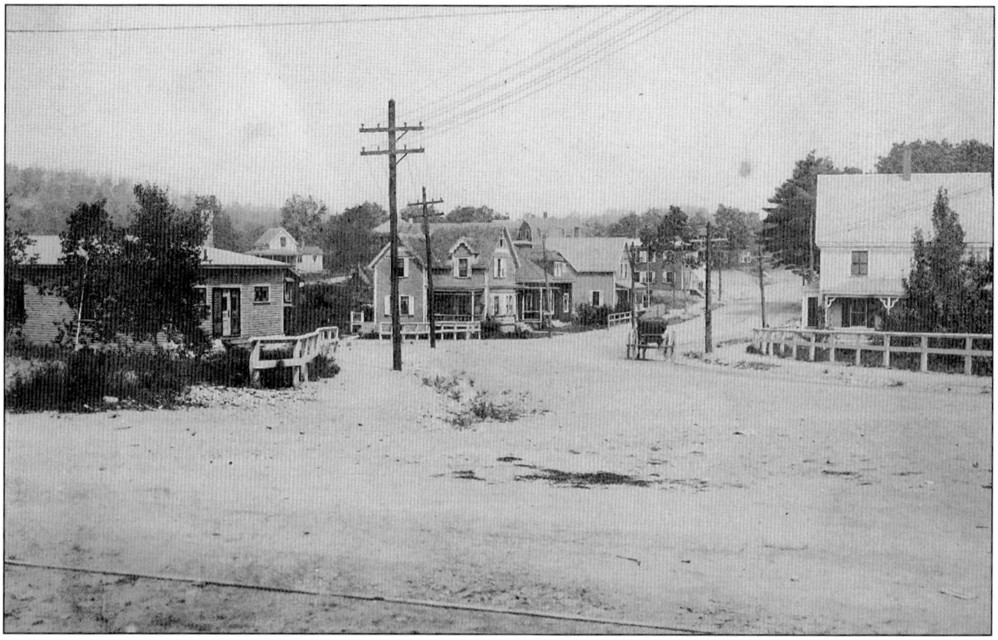

Lynnfield Street is seen here from Great Woods Road. The street railway, as evidenced by the tracks in the foreground, went a little further up Great Woods Road and then turned around. This view cannot be dated with certainty but it is clearly from the early 20th century.

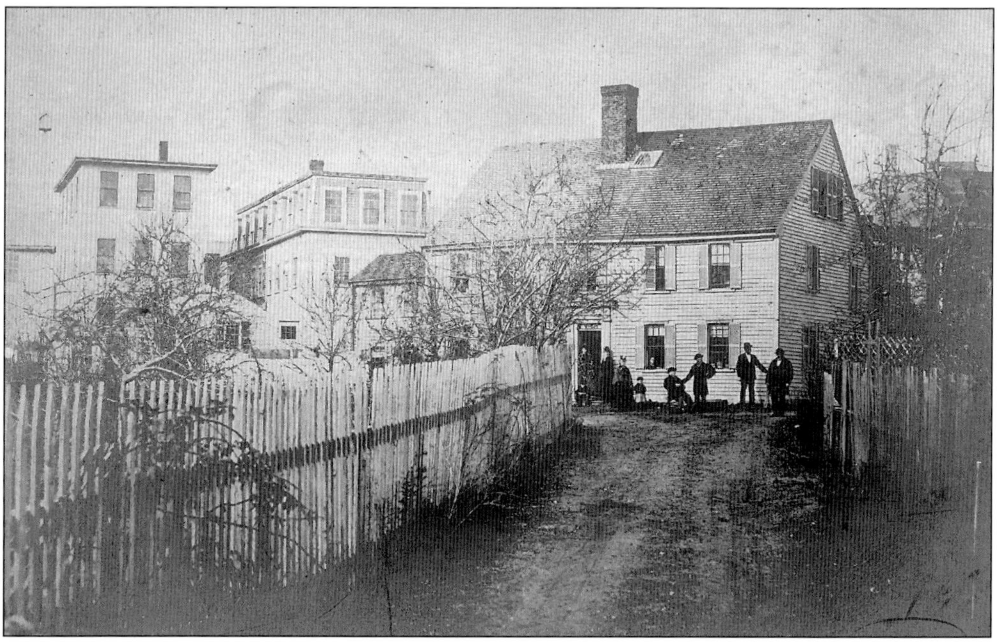

The Breed-Thompson house was built in 1740 and stood at the bottom of an unnamed lane off Broad Street. The buildings in the back faced Union Street and all of them, as well as the old house, were destroyed in the great fire of 1889. The image was chosen as the subject for a much later postcard, probably because of its charming and quaint qualities.

Three

Woods, Parks, and Open Spaces

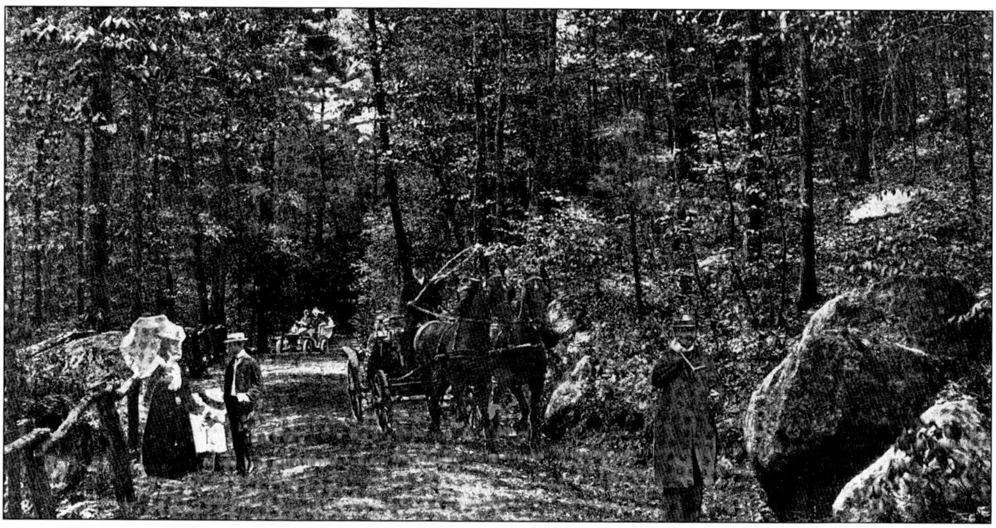

Lynn Woods was acquired by the City of Lynn during the 1880s and 1890s. The sender of this 1907 card chose this image to illustrate the religious maxim that states, "It is a long and crooked path that leads to the Heavenly Gate."

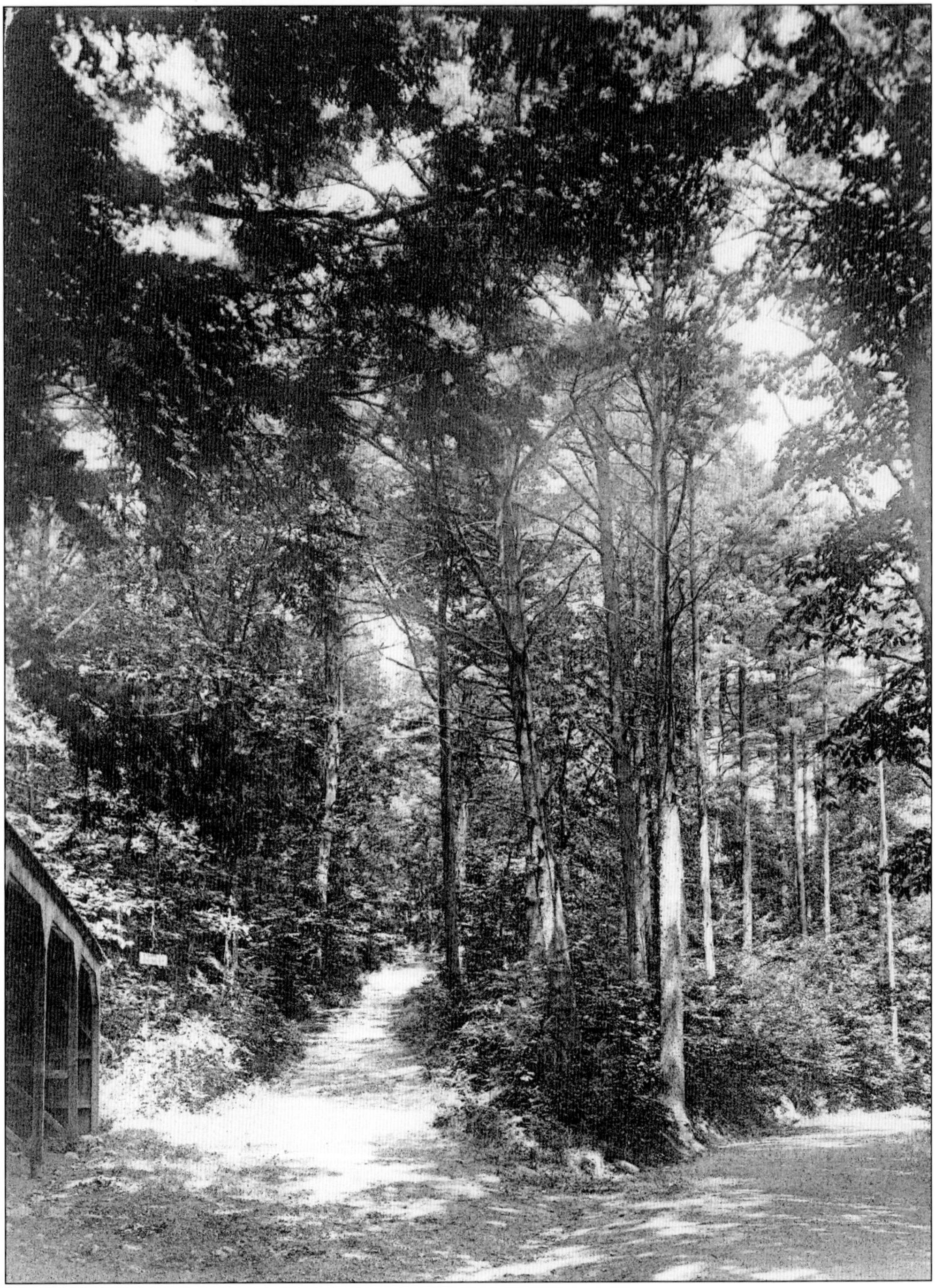

City parks during the late 19th century usually contained many formal design elements. Against that trend, and according to advice of renowned landscape architect Frederick Law Olmstead, Lynn Woods was allowed to remain in its natural state. Said Olmstead, "Nor can you ever hope to introduce decorative features of the sort commonly expected to be seen in parks in such manner that they will not be discordant with the general character and offensive to good taste." Here is a 1915 view of which Olmstead would no doubt approve.

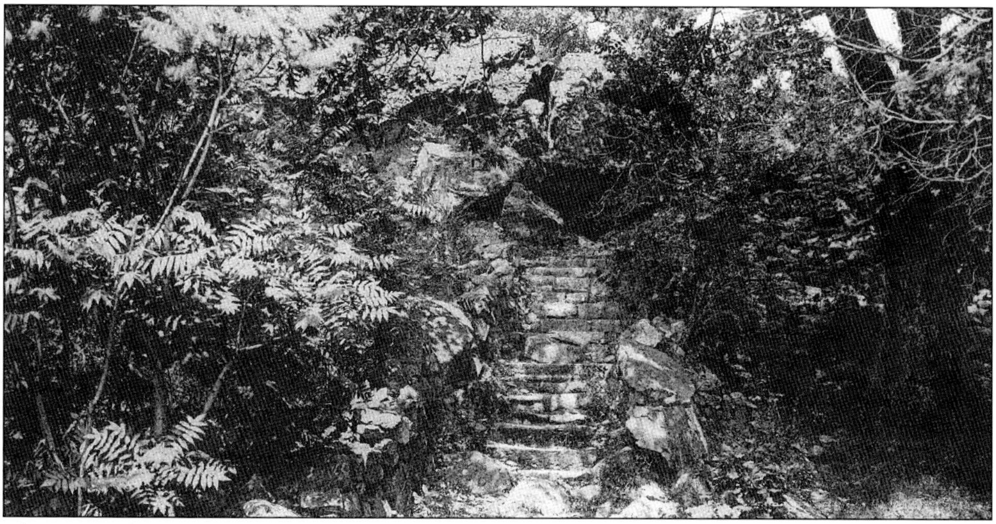

There is perhaps no better known or more romantic legend associated with Lynn than that of Dungeon Rock and the pirate gold supposedly buried there. Here we see the rough-hewn steps leading up to the rock.

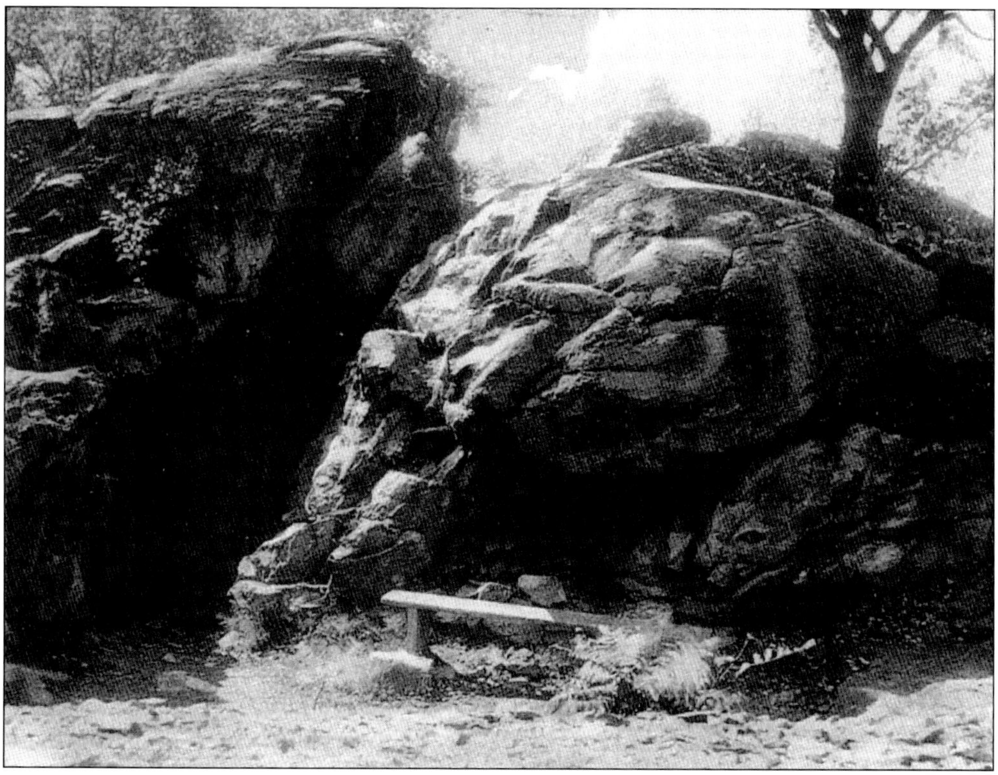

This is the entrance to Dungeon Rock Cave, where, according to legend, pirate Thomas Veal was buried alive along with his ill-gotten treasure when an earthquake shook Lynn Woods. As early as 1834, historian and poet Alonzo Lewis complained about the destruction being wrought by treasure-hunters and souvenir-seekers.

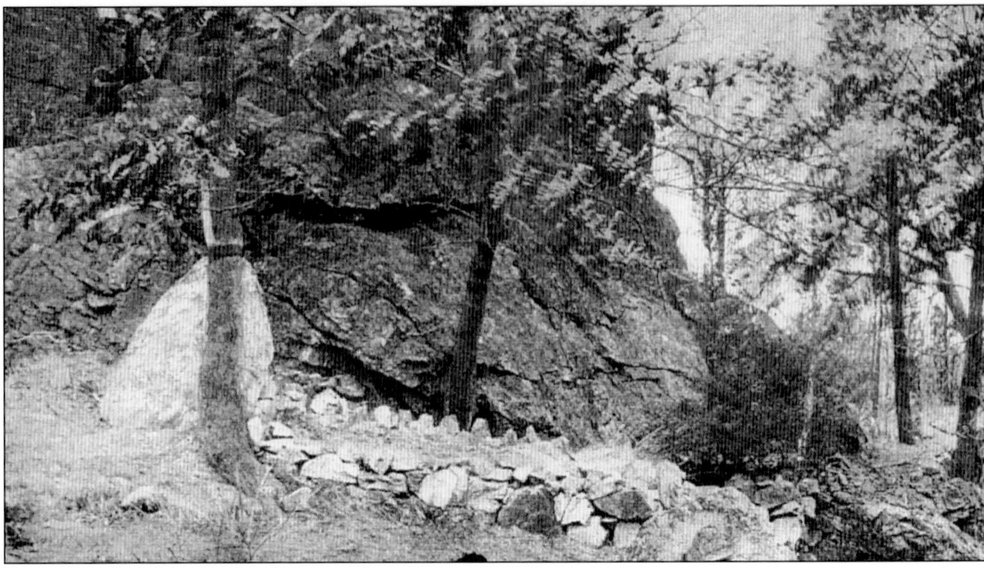

In 1852, when the area now comprising Lynn Woods was entirely in private hands, Hiram Marble purchased Dungeon Rock with the hopes that spirit guides would lead him to the treasure; he was unable to find it. Upon Hiram's death, his son Edwin continued the work with no more success. After having dug 137 feet through solid rock, Edwin Marble died and was buried in the grave shown here, near his lifelong obsession.

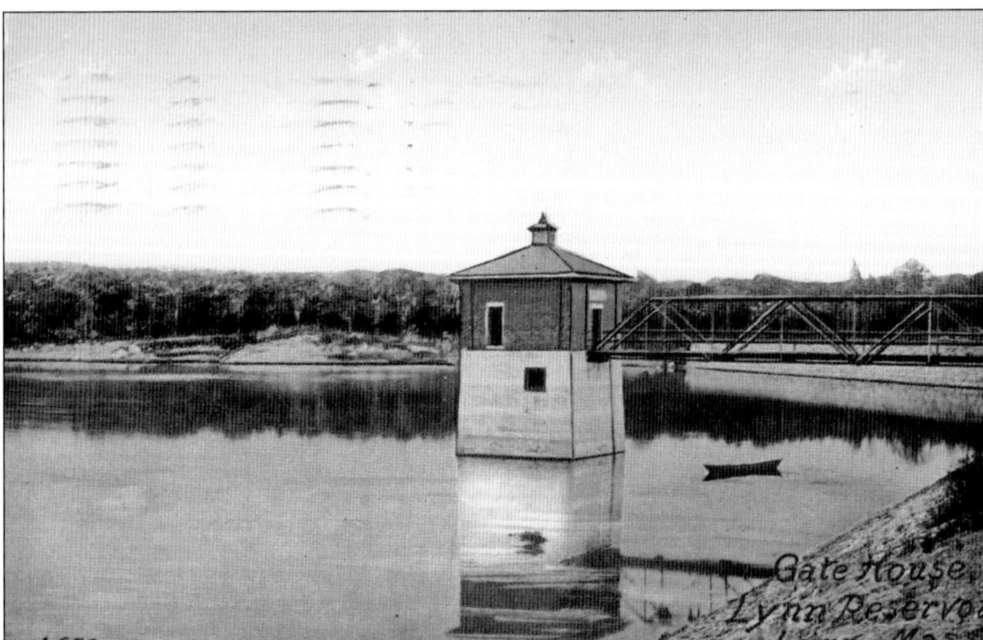

Breed's Pond in Lynn Woods is a man-made pond built by Theophilus N. Breed in 1843. The city purchased it in 1870 for a water supply and built the gatehouse the same year. This card dates from 1910.

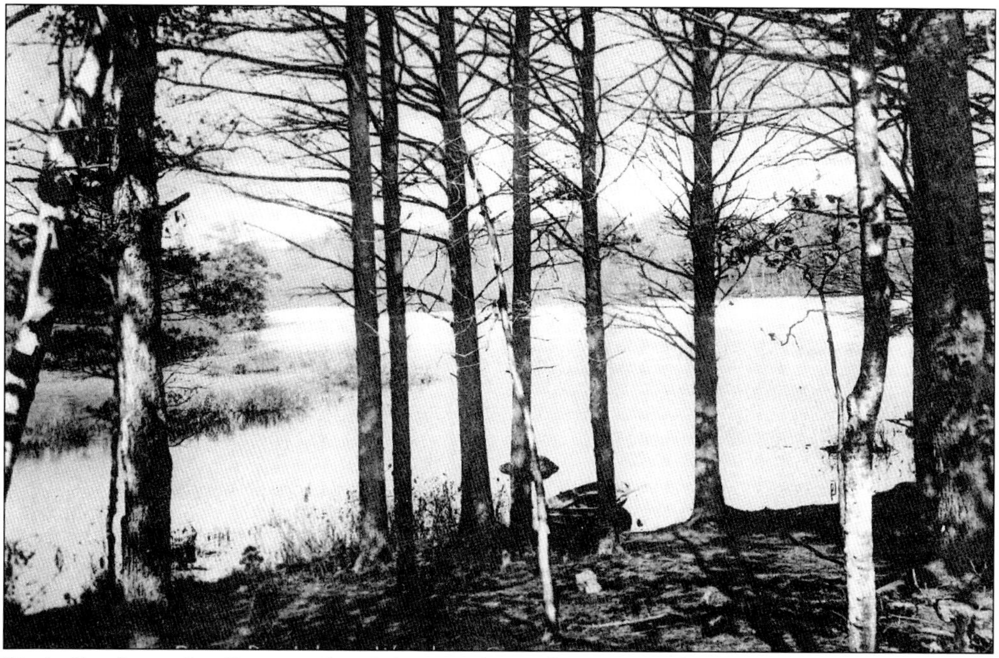

Birch Pond, on the Saugus side of the woods, is also man-made. It was created in 1878 by damming Beaver and Birch Brooks and serves as a storage basin for the city's water supply.

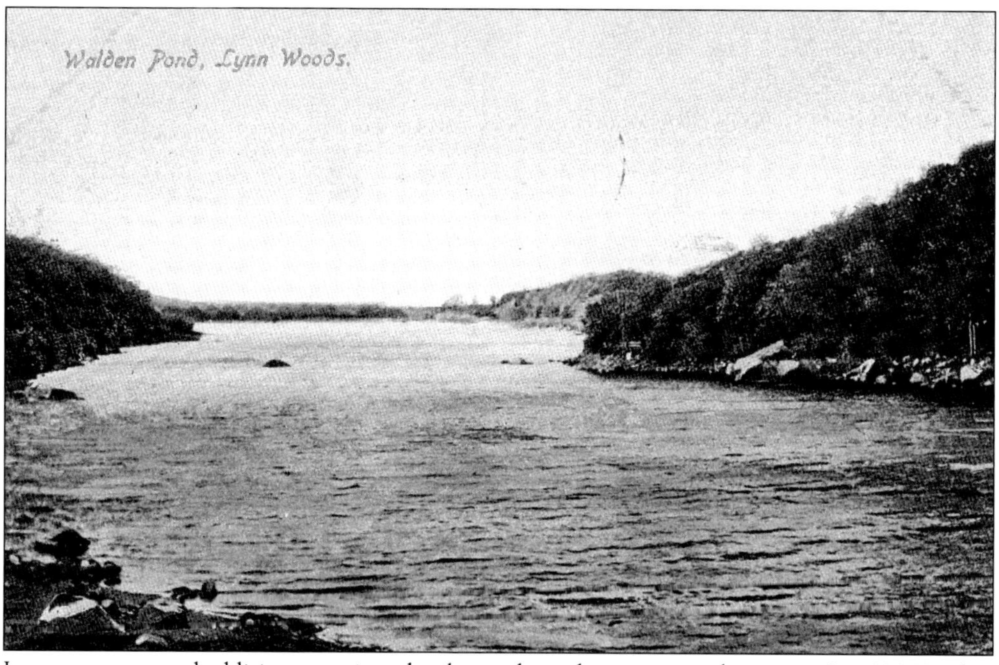

Improvements and additions continued to be made to the water supply system. In 1889 Hawkes and Penny Brooks were dammed to form Walden and Glen Lewis Ponds, the latter of which was eventually joined to the former. Lynn's Walden Pond, not to be confused with Thoreau's, was named after former-mayor Edwin Walden, the city's first water commissioner.

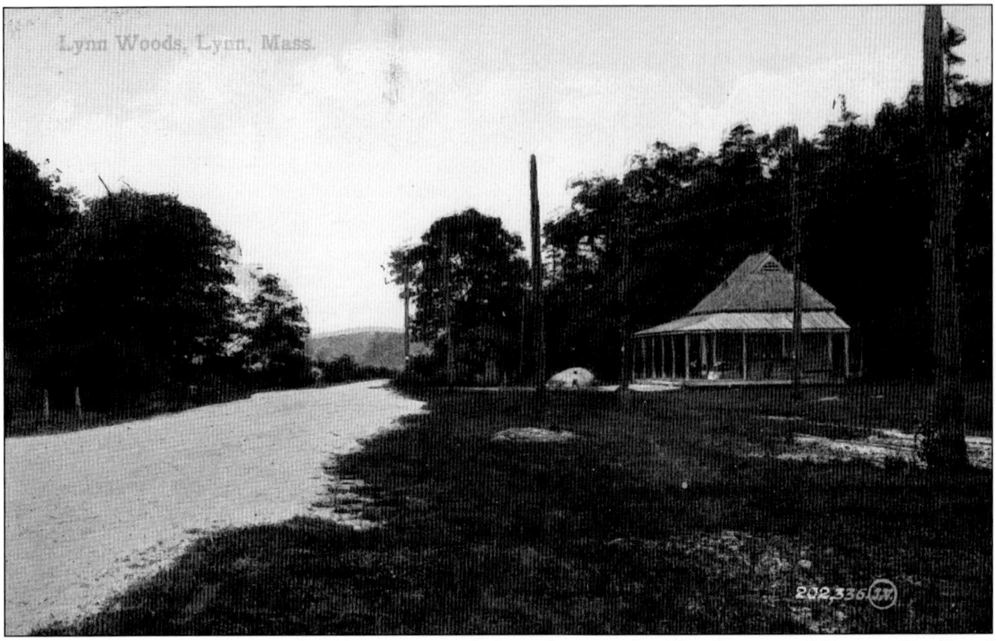

By 1891, trolley-car service had been extended to the woods. The Lynn and Boston Railroad Company operated the station and refreshment stand at the Great Woods Road entrance. This is a 1905 view.

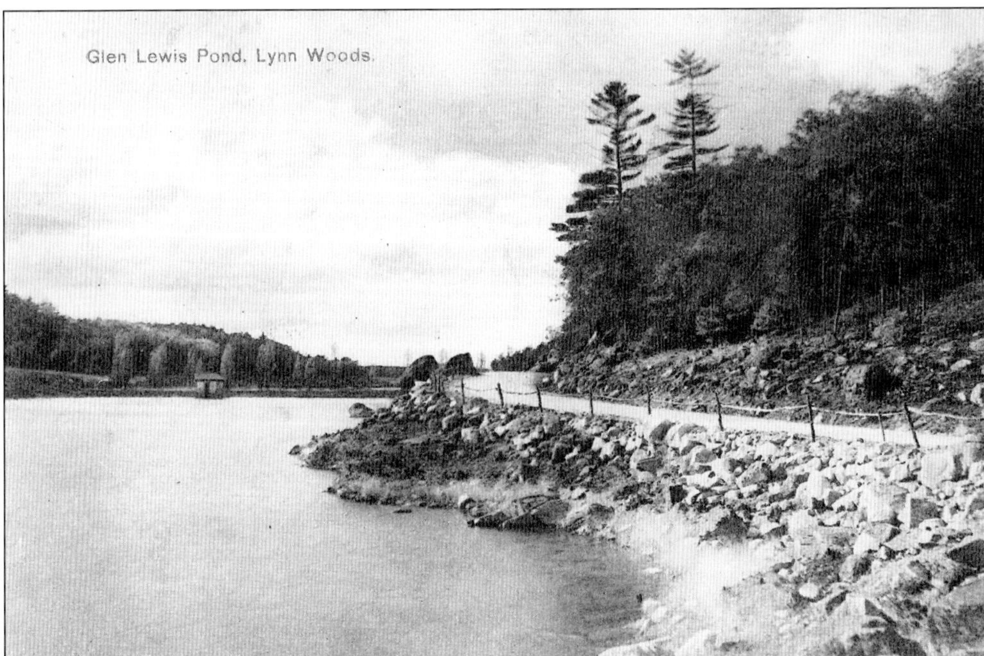

The road along Glen Lewis Pond is shown here as it appeared in 1918. The gatehouse is visible on the opposite shore.

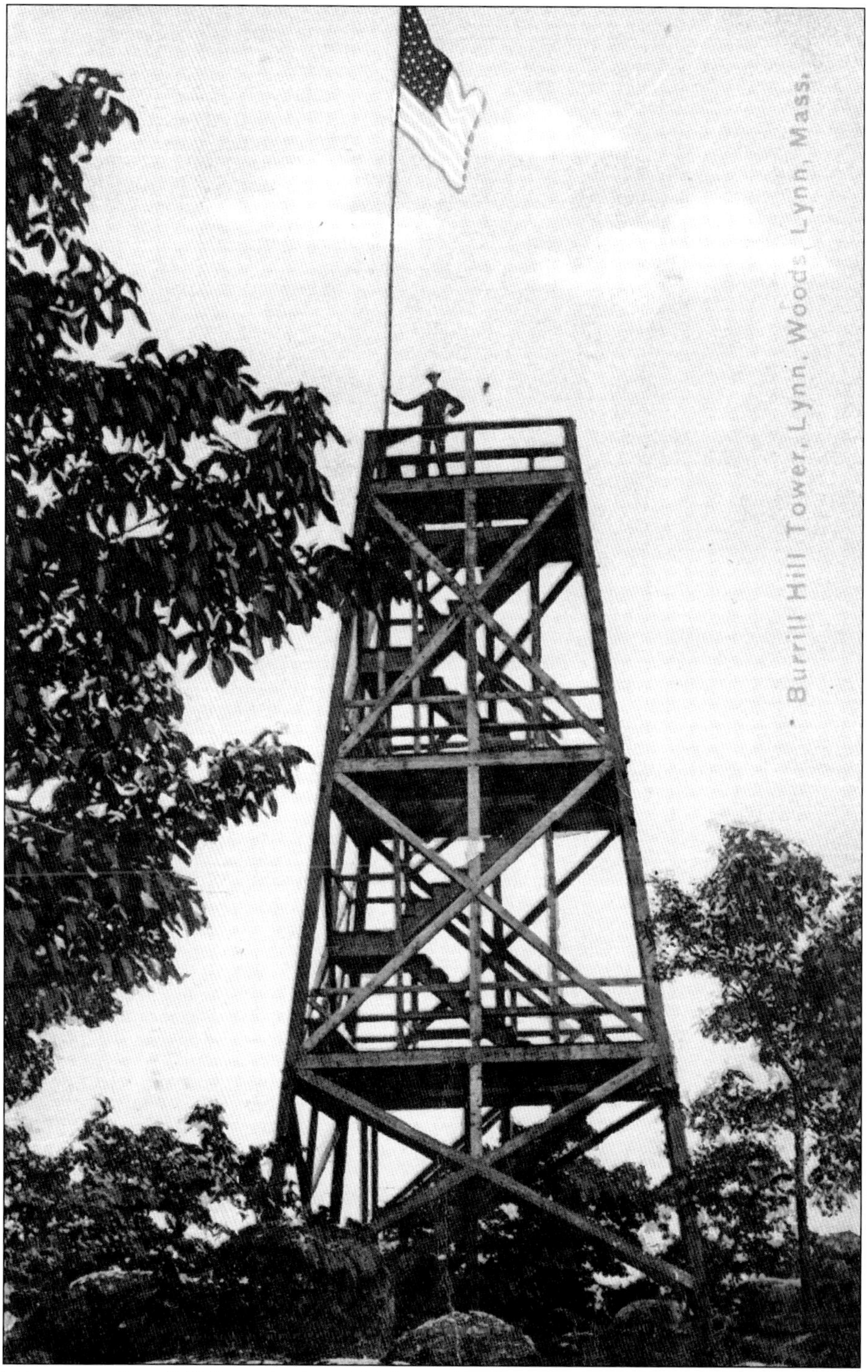

Steel Tower on Burrill Hill was built in 1895 to aid in fire detection, but it incidentally provided spectacular views of the surrounding towns. The highest point in Lynn at 275 feet above sea level, Burrill Hill was briefly known during the 19th century by the fanciful name of Mount Nebo. Its original name was later returned.

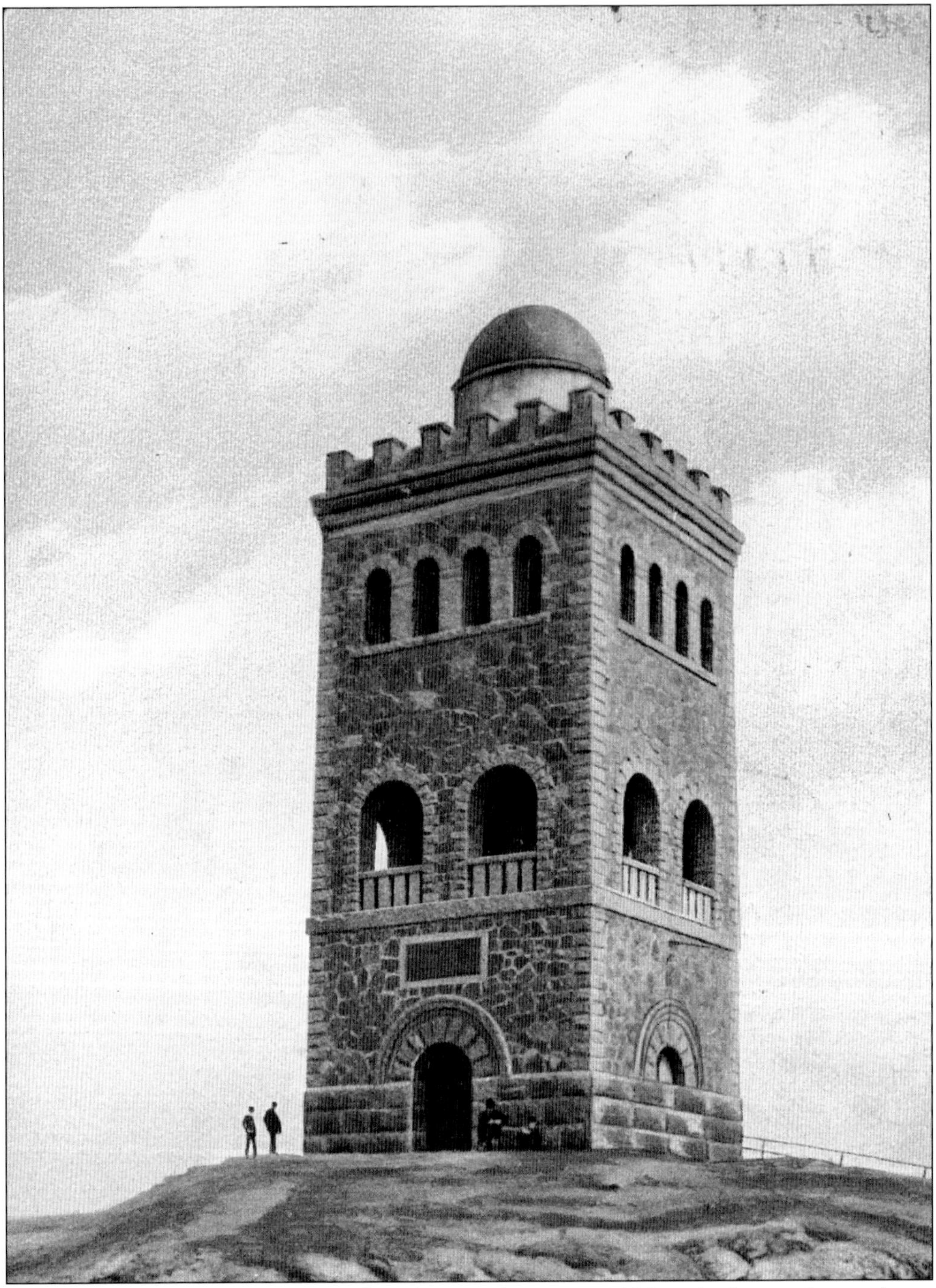

High Rock was donated to the city by John Hutchinson in 1904, with the stipulation that a tower with a telescope and observatory be built at its summit. This 1911 view shows the tower five years after its completion.

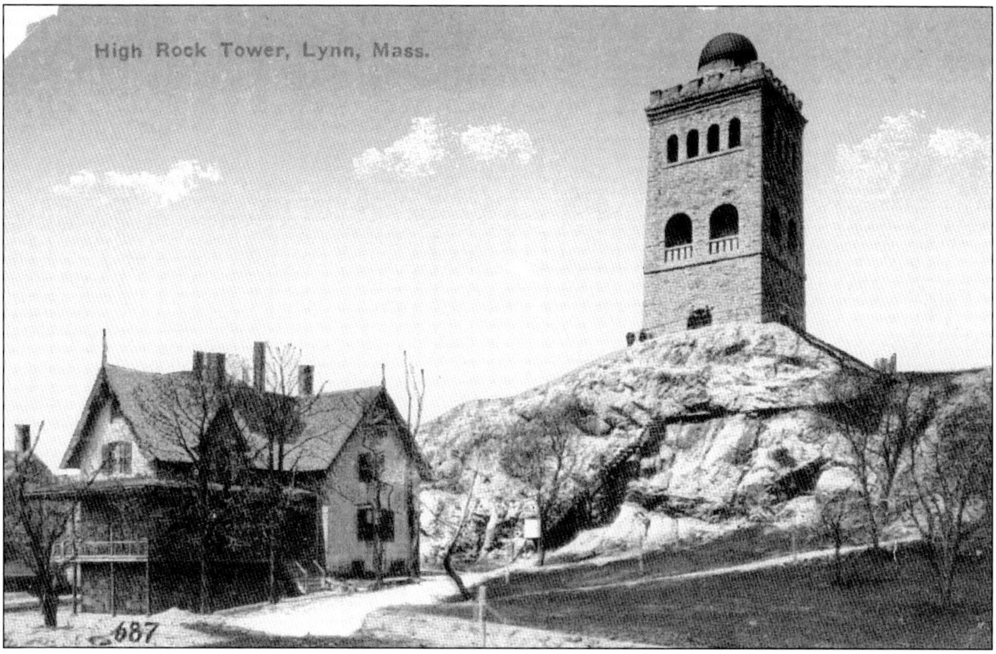

From the 1840s on, the area surrounding High Rock and the rock itself belonged to members of the Hutchinson Family, a group of crusading abolitionist singers who performed throughout the United States and Europe. Stone Cottage, in the foreground, is the only building left standing on High Rock that dates to their ownership. The original tower, made of wood, was sacrificed to a bonfire at the end of the Civil War.

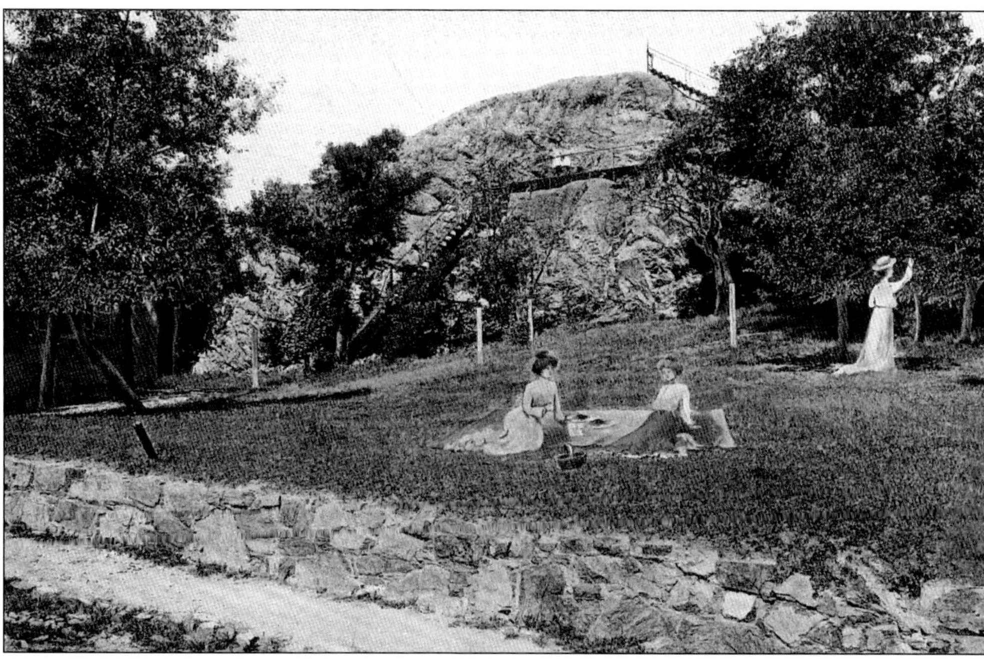

Picnicking took place on High Rock in 1905, before the construction of the new tower.

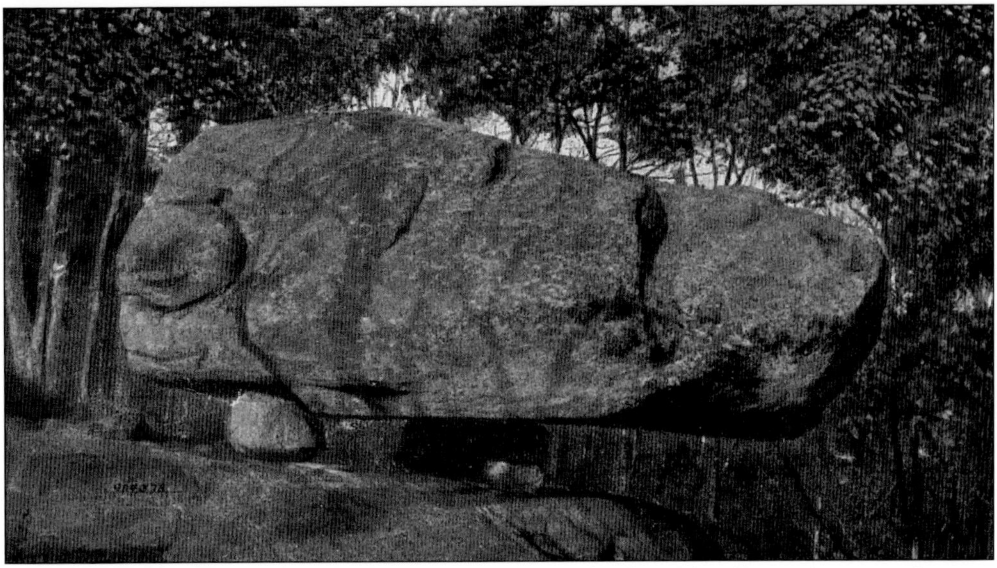

Phaeton, or Cannon, Rock, near the Lynn/Peabody line, has been the object of curiosity for most of Lynn's history. While some consider it evidence of a pre-Columbian European settlement in the area, others believe it is merely a prehistoric glacial formation, albeit an unusual one.

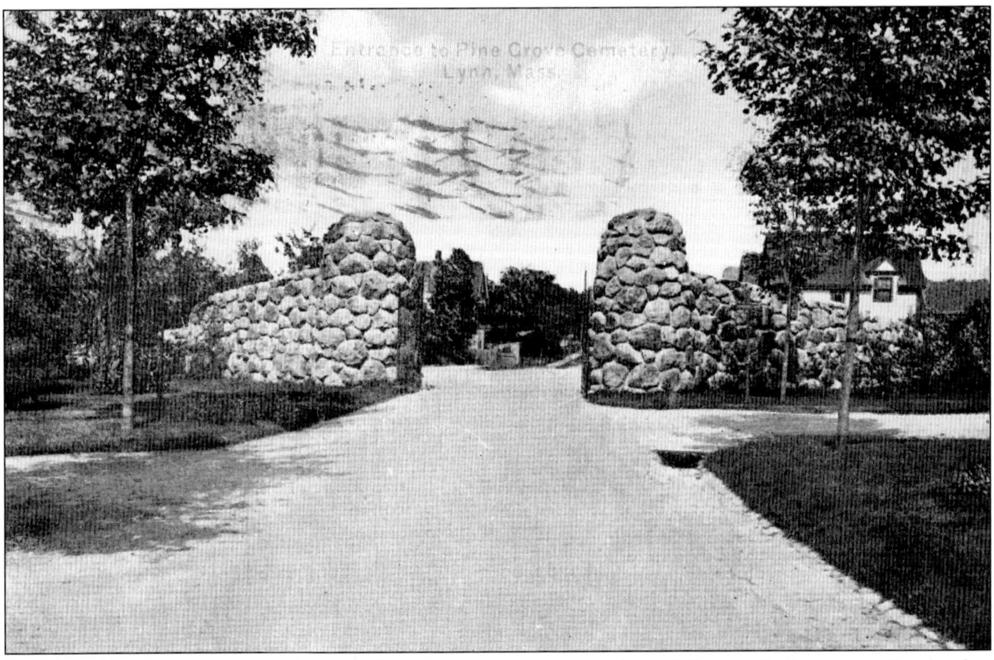

Pine Grove Cemetery was designed in the picturesque style of Mount Auburn in Cambridge in 1850 and was purchased by the city five years later. This c. 1905 view shows the Wyoma entrance from inside the cemetery.

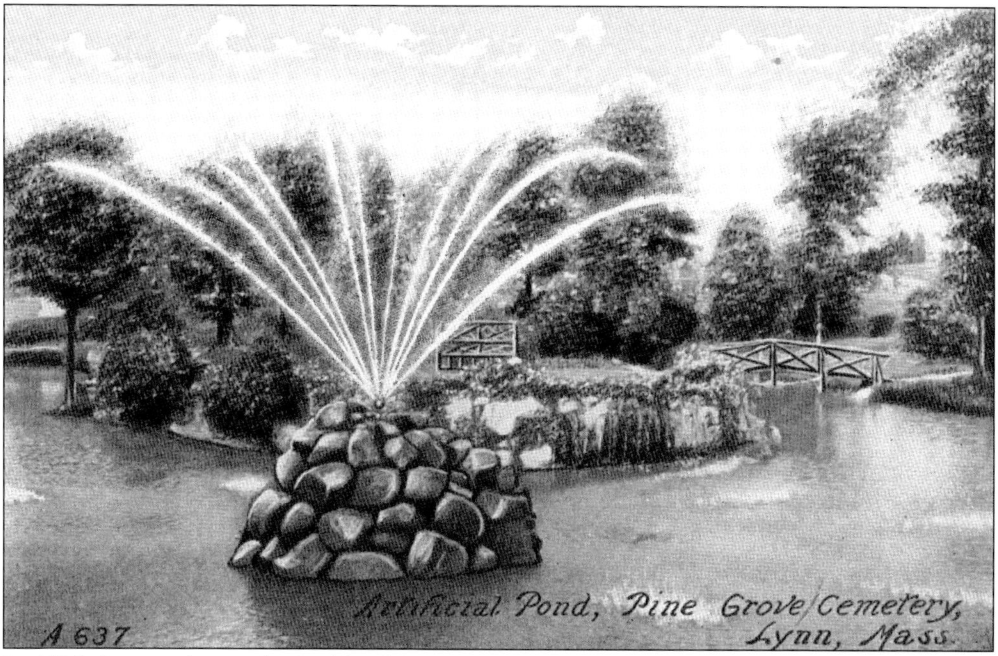

In 1905 this pond near the Parkland Avenue entrance was added as part of ongoing efforts to beautify Pine Grove. The "rustic little bridge" on the right and the fountain were much-praised features at the time.

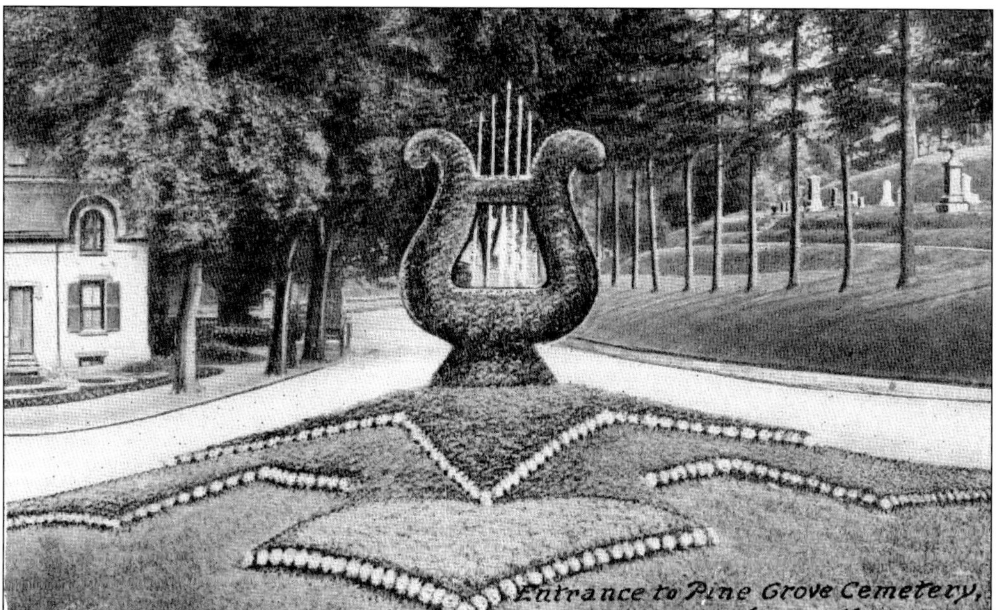

The formal flower bed and topiary at the main entrance to Pine Grove Cemetery are shown here in 1905. A greenhouse is still maintained on the premises to provide flowers for the gardens and perpetual care beds.

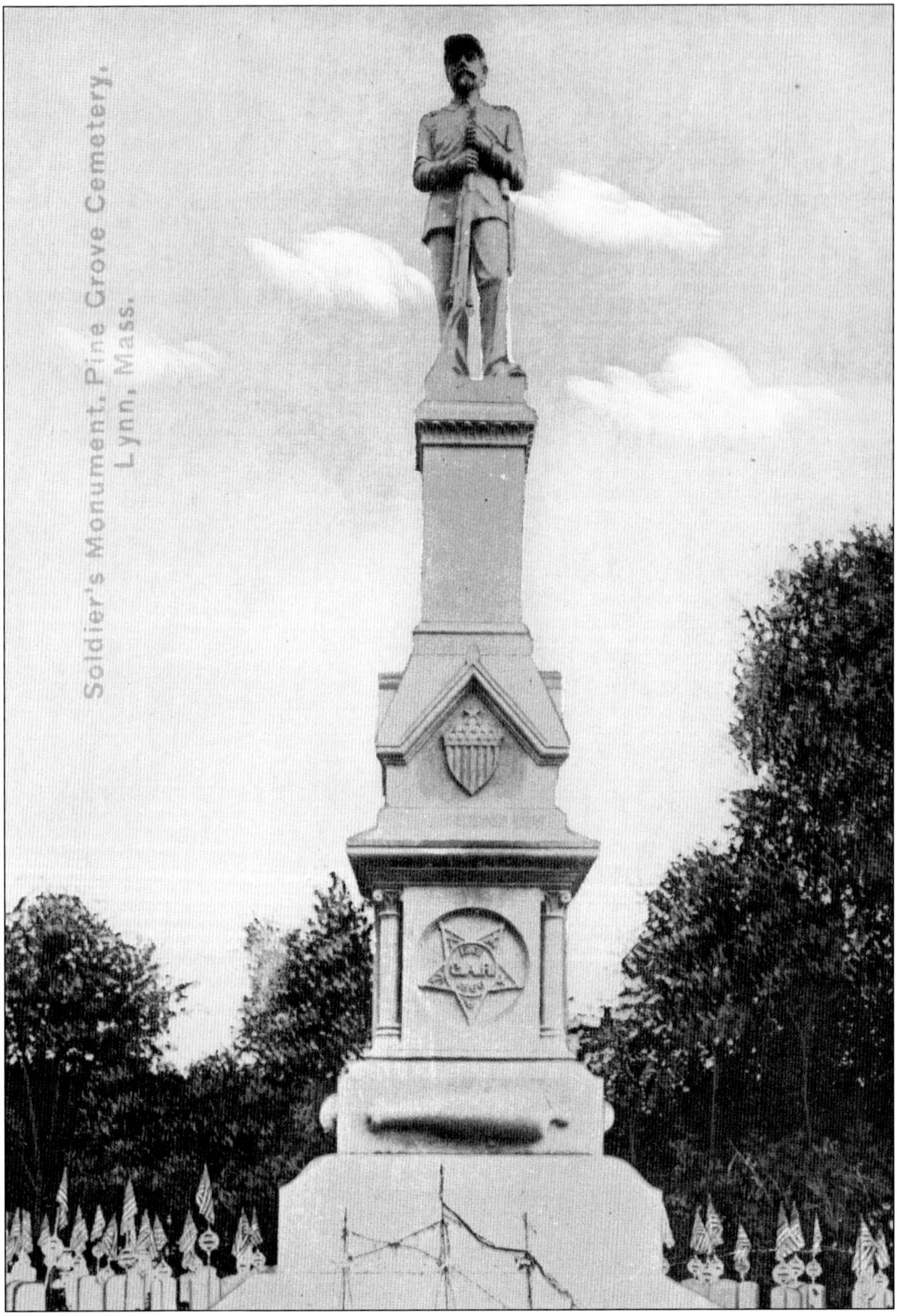

Lynn's Civil War veterans raised the money for the impressive soldier's monument now standing in the Grand Army lot. It was dedicated in 1905 and replaced a smaller, urn-topped monument that had stood for several decades. (Conway collection.)

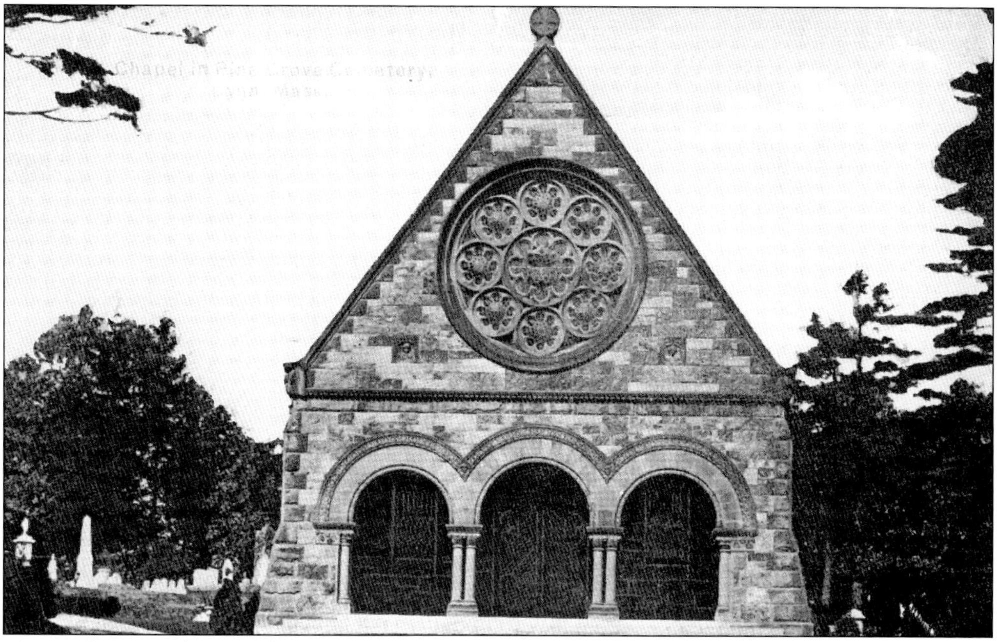

The architectural gem of Pine Grove is the Rhodes Chapel, built in 1890. A memorial to Amos Rhodes, a prominent Lynn banker, the chapel is a fine example of the Richardsonian Romanesque style, although today it has fallen into disrepair.

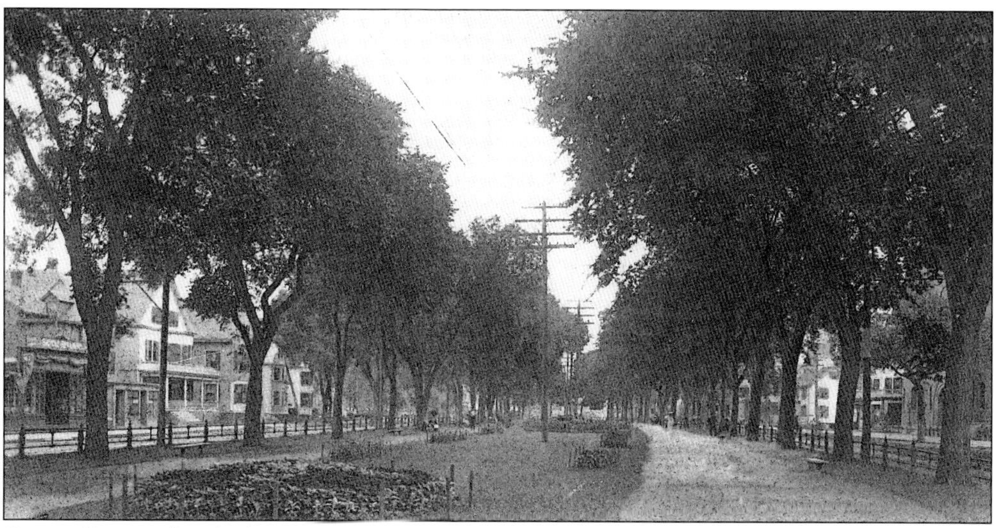

Originally woodland, the Common became the center of Lynn with the construction of the town's meetinghouse in 1682 on what is now North Common Street. Despite development around its borders, it remained "free to all cows and other animals" until the 1820s, when it was set aside as a park. This is a 1905 view looking toward city hall. The Lynn Gas and Electric utility poles, seen standing in a row down the center of the Common, were removed the following year to great approval.

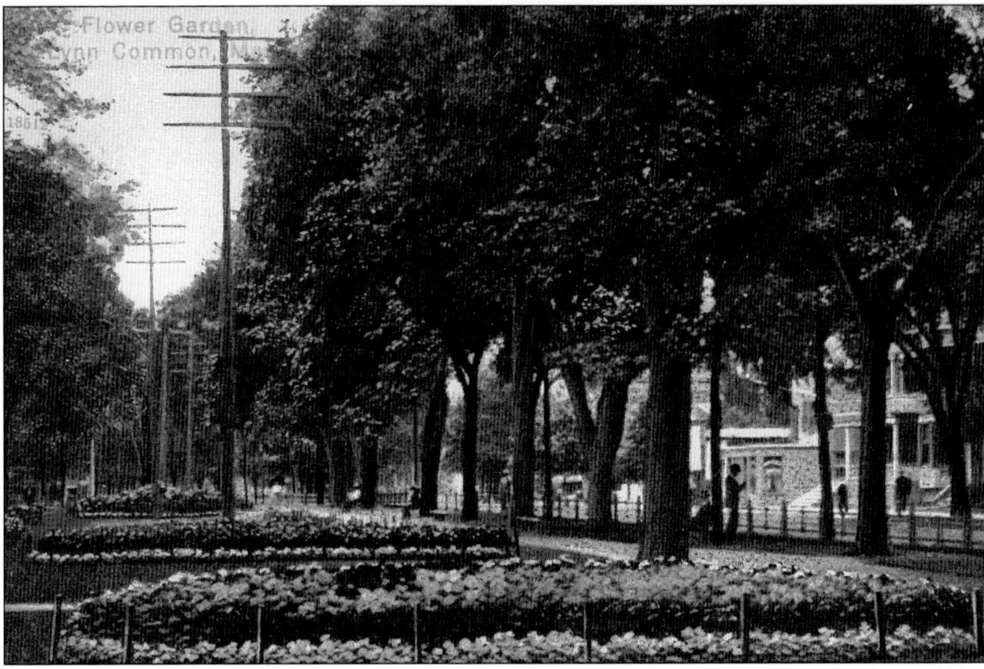

During the 19th century, the Common had been used for fireworks displays, military encampments, and balloon ascensions, as well as for high school football and baseball games. By the early 1900s there was a movement to reserve the park for more tranquil uses so that ladies and families might not be disturbed by "the antics of a profane mob of half-clad men aping the mythical sports of their uncouth forbears." In 1905 these flower beds were considered a showplace and indicated which sort of uses the city officially preferred.

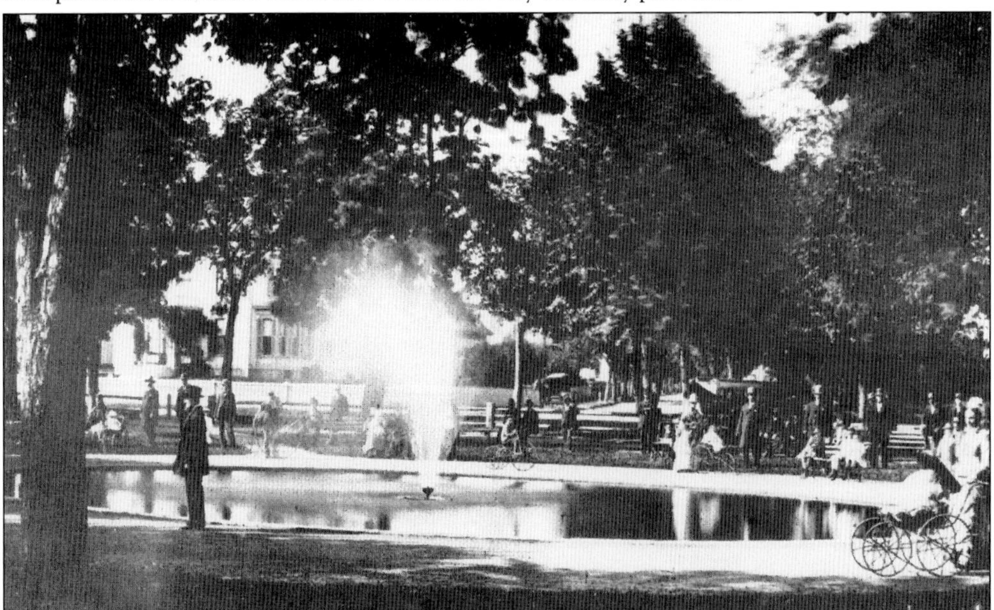

The frog pond was completed in 1870 and was later stocked with fish from Goldfish Pond. This is an 1879 view on a modern postcard.

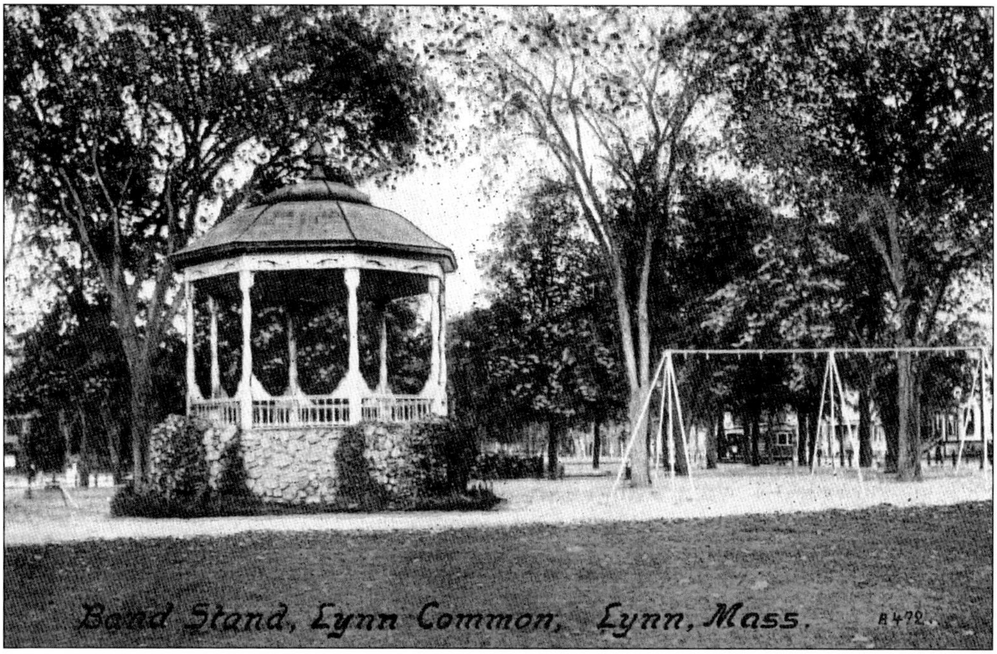

The bandstand, a requisite feature of any self-respecting New England common, was constructed in Lynn in 1887.

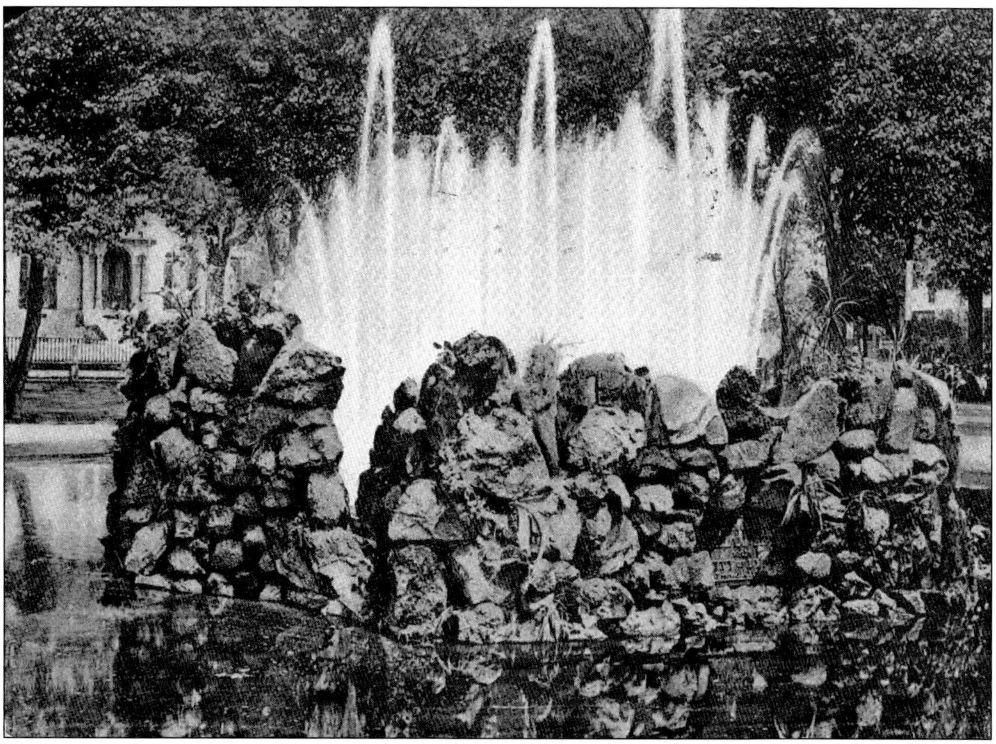

A crowd of 25,000 gathered to witness the dedication of the Common's electric fountain on October 5, 1893. It was one of only two in the country of its kind. Lynn philanthropist William Shute donated the $2,500 required for its construction.

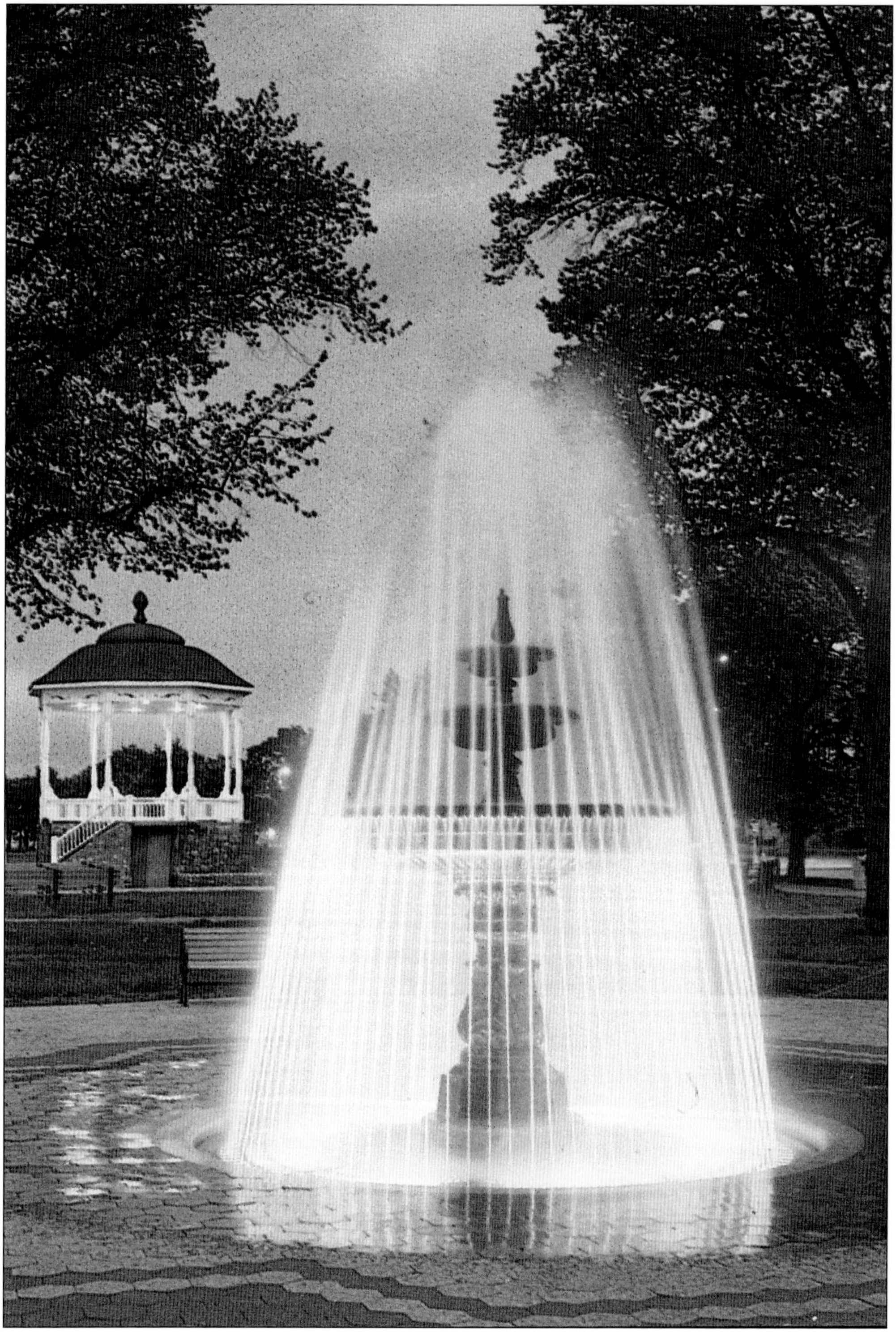

A new fountain was installed in the 1990s. In the background is the original bandstand, now restored.

Four

PUBLIC BUILDINGS, PUBLIC SERVANTS

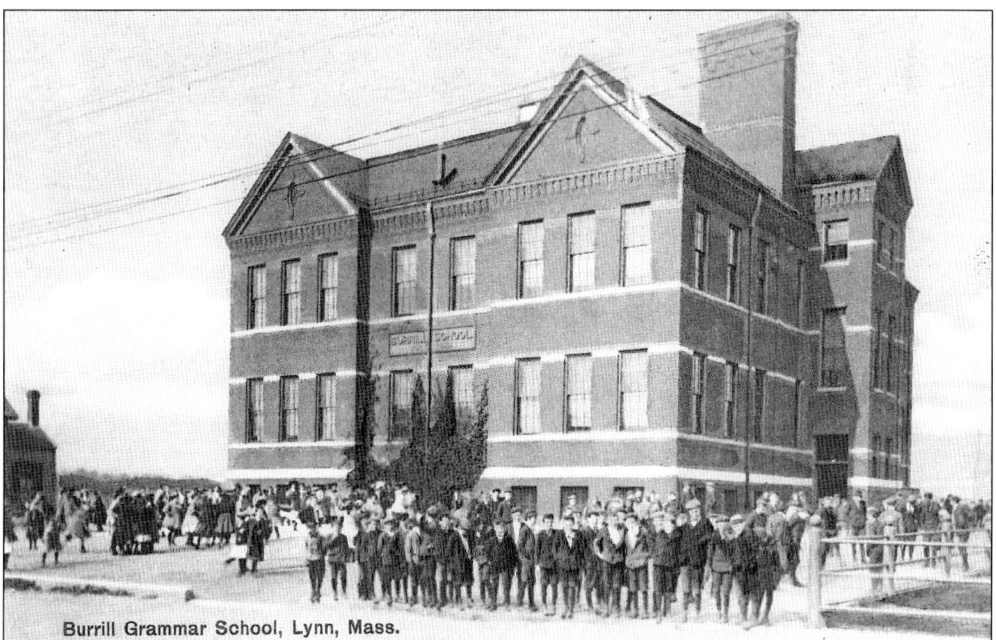

The second Burrill School was built in 1893 and named in honor of John Burrill, the first Lynn citizen to become Speaker of the Massachusetts House of Representatives. A large contingent from the boys' side of the school yard lined up for the camera in 1909.

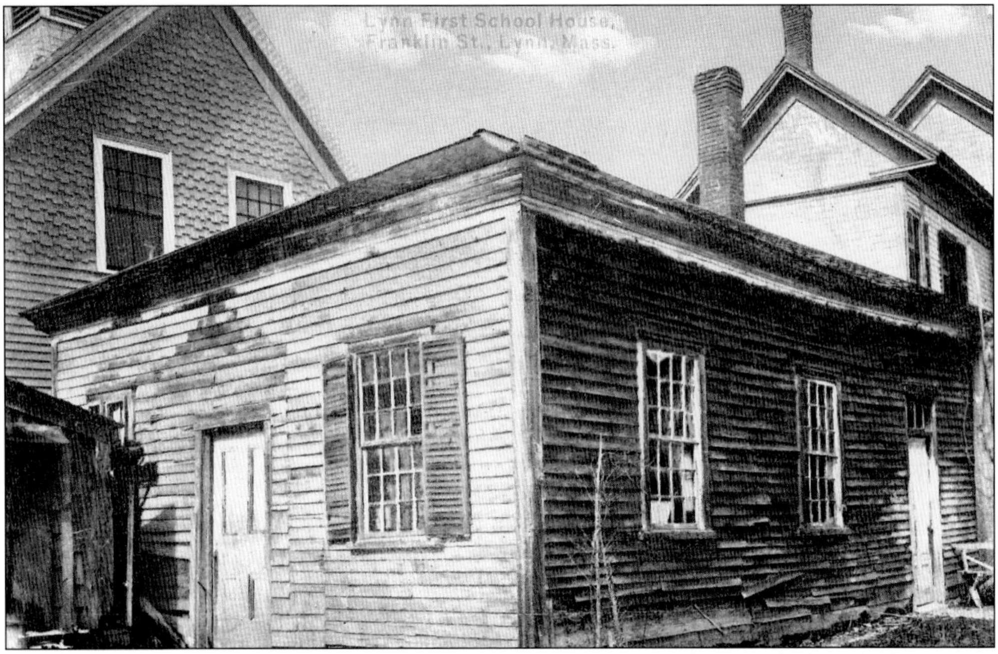

This less-than-impressive edifice was home to many generations of Lynn scholars. Built in 1728, it stood on Franklin Street until 1921, when it was replaced by the O'Keefe School.

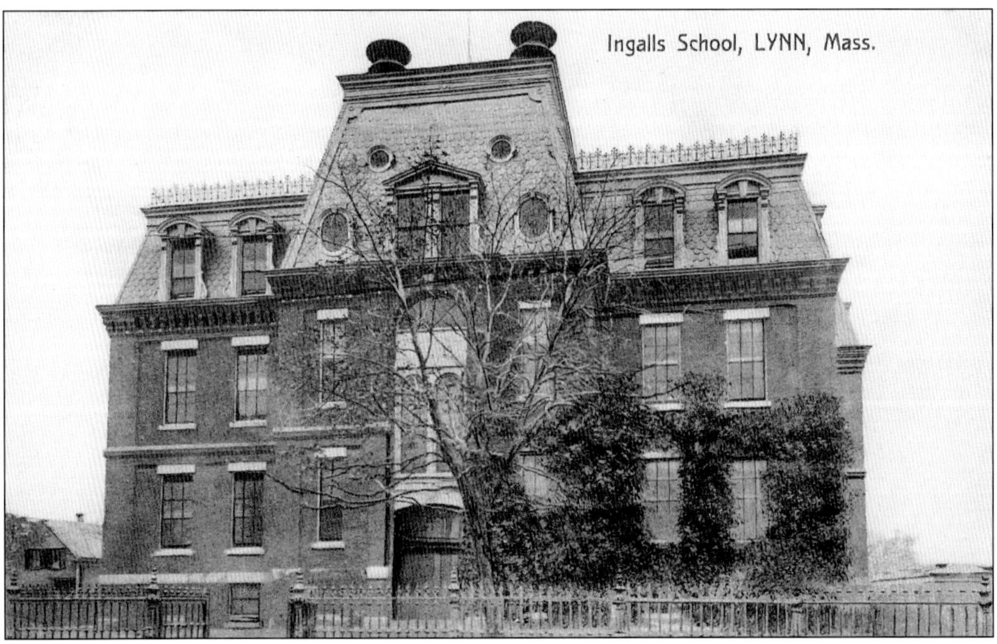

The old Ingalls School on Essex Street housed both grammar and junior high schools in the course of its 80-year history. A replacement for the original Ingalls School on Parrott Street, it in turn was replaced by a new building in 1953.

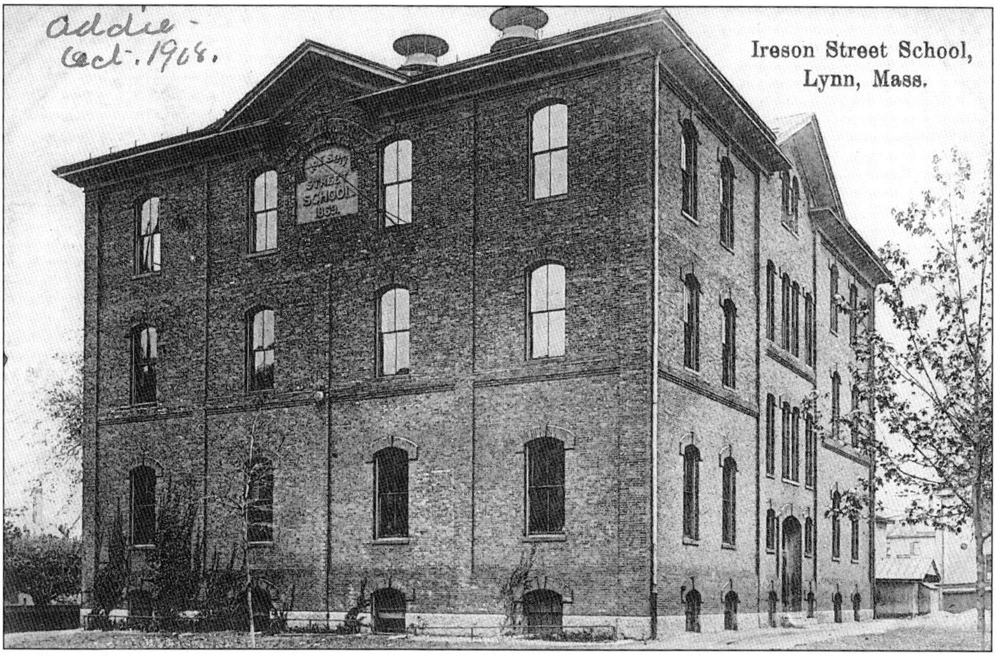

Dedicated in 1869, the Ireson Street School almost immediately changed its name to the Whiting School in honor of the first pastor of the First Church of Lynn. The building was razed in 1940 and shortly thereafter Ireson Street was renamed Joyce Street.

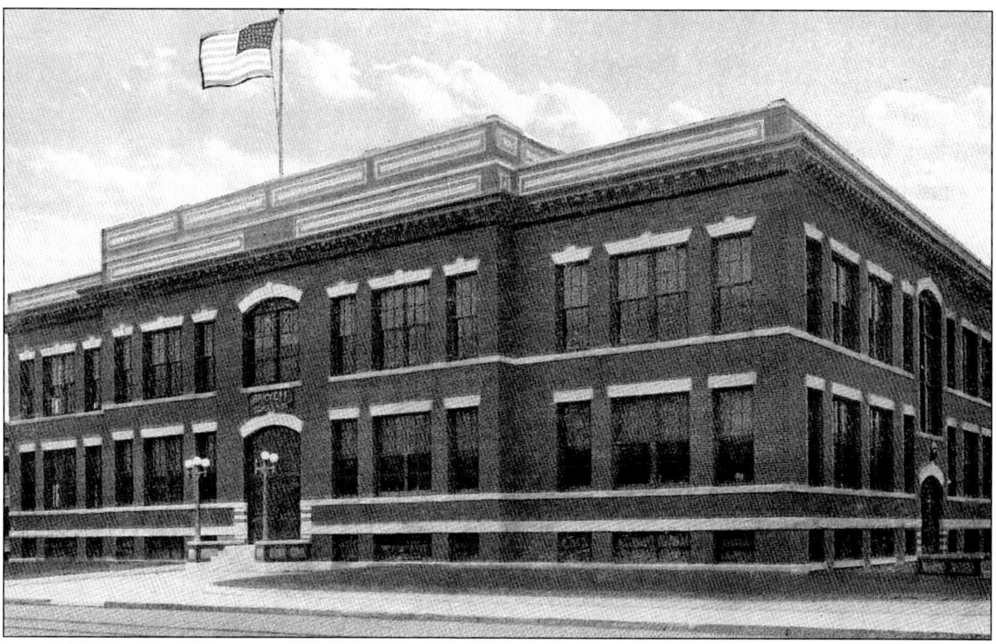

Described at the time of its construction in 1912 as "a thoroughly modern school building of the best type," the Brickett School is still in use.

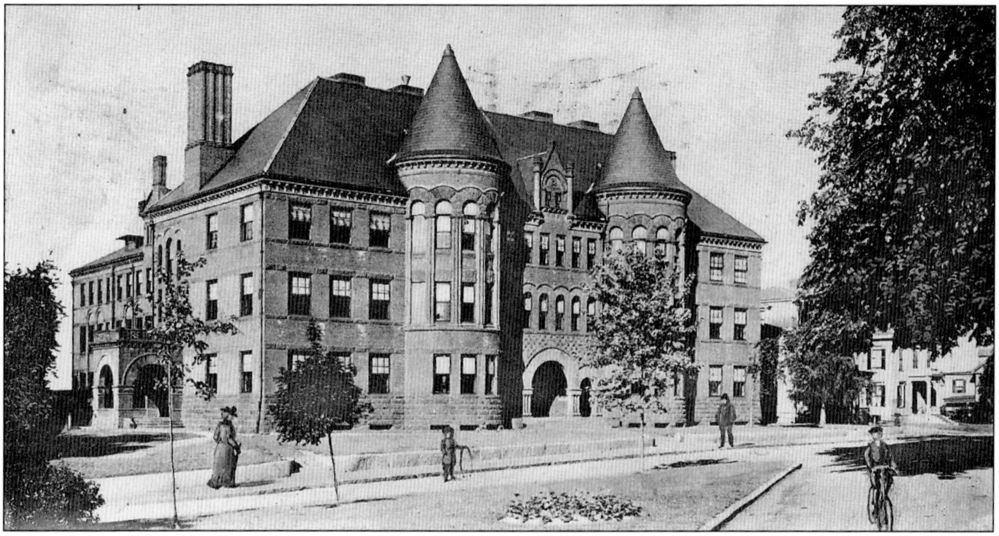

The old Lynn English High School was actually home to Classical as well from 1891 to 1911. A fire in April of 1924 destroyed much of the building. With extensive remodeling, it was reclaimed for use as Cobbett Junior High.

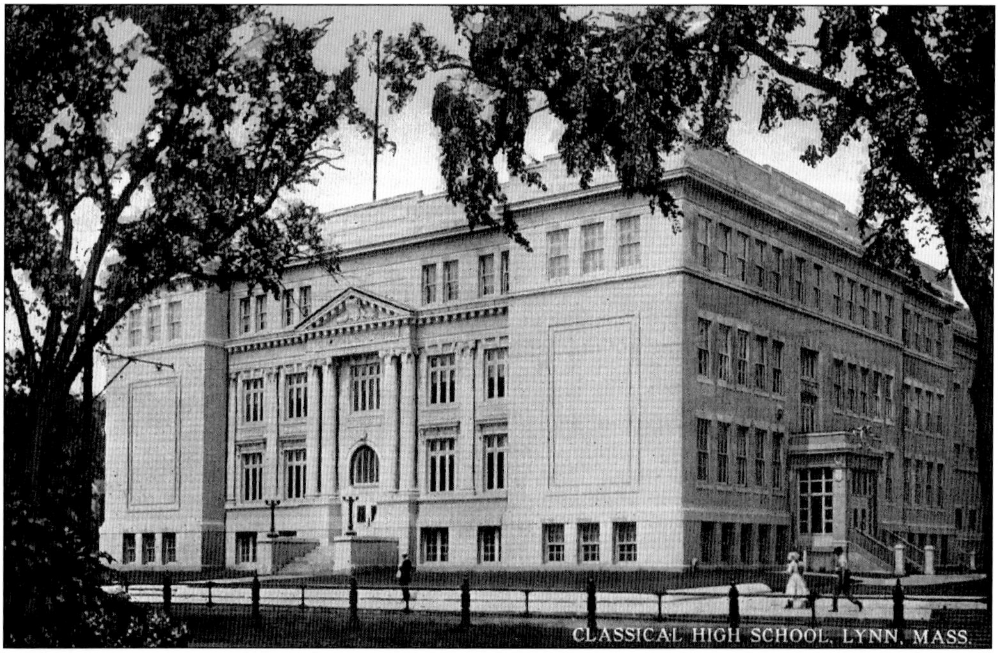

Throughout the late 19th and early 20th centuries, Lynn struggled with the familiar problem of overcrowded schools. The construction of Lynn Classical in 1911, "a beautiful and commodious building . . . one of the best high school plants in the state," solved the problem for many years, at least at the high school level.

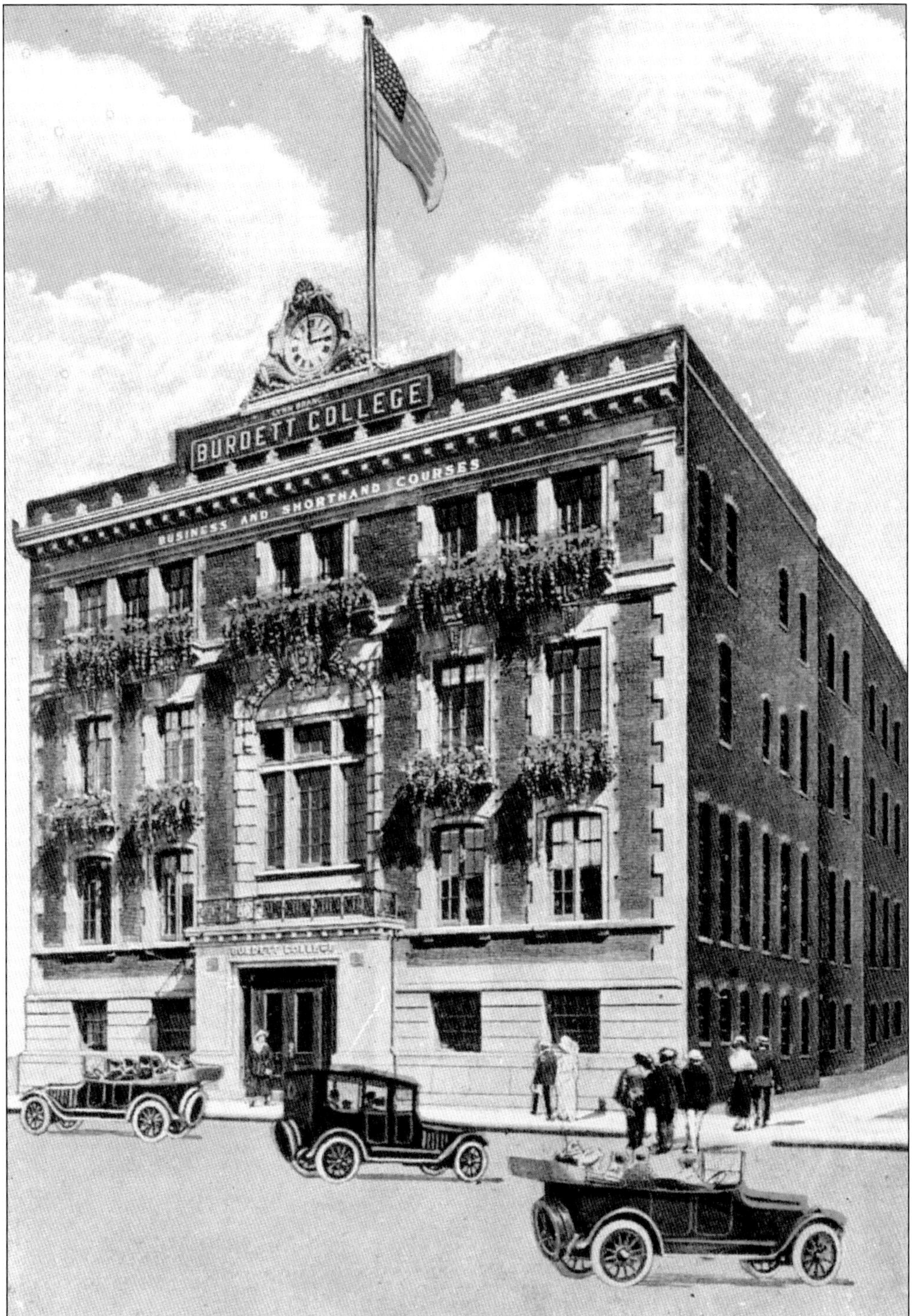

This is a *c.* 1920 view of the Burdett building on Mount Vernon Street. From 1904 to 1968, Burdett College offered business courses to students from all over New England. It was demolished in 1970 to make way for a parking lot. (Conway collection.)

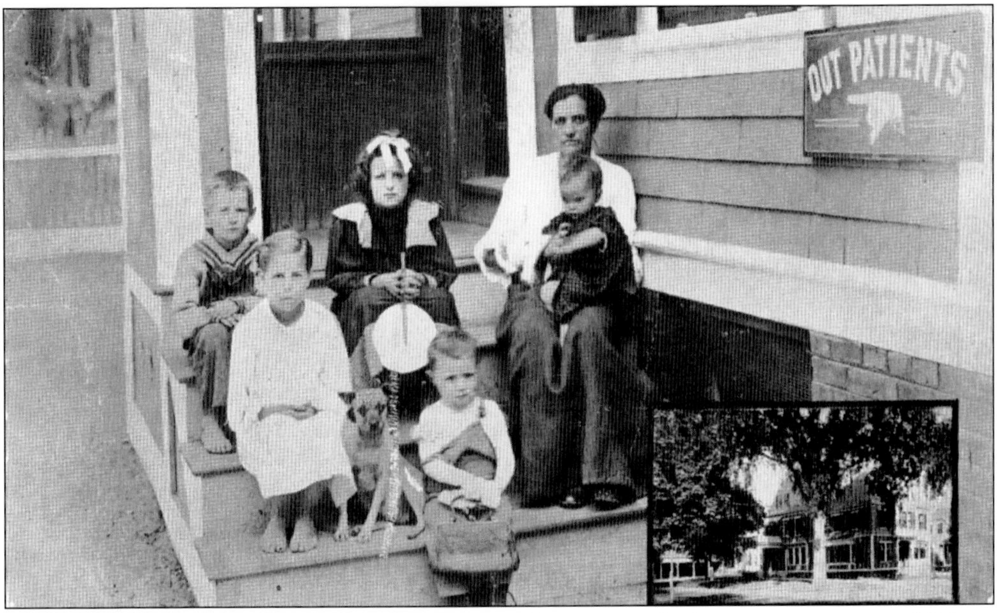

Lynn's first hospital lasted only four years, but its closing provoked a movement to establish an institution that would truly meet the needs of the growing city. Lynn Hospital received its first patient on March 12, 1883, and the outpatient department was opened later that same year. This is a 1910 view. (Conway collection.)

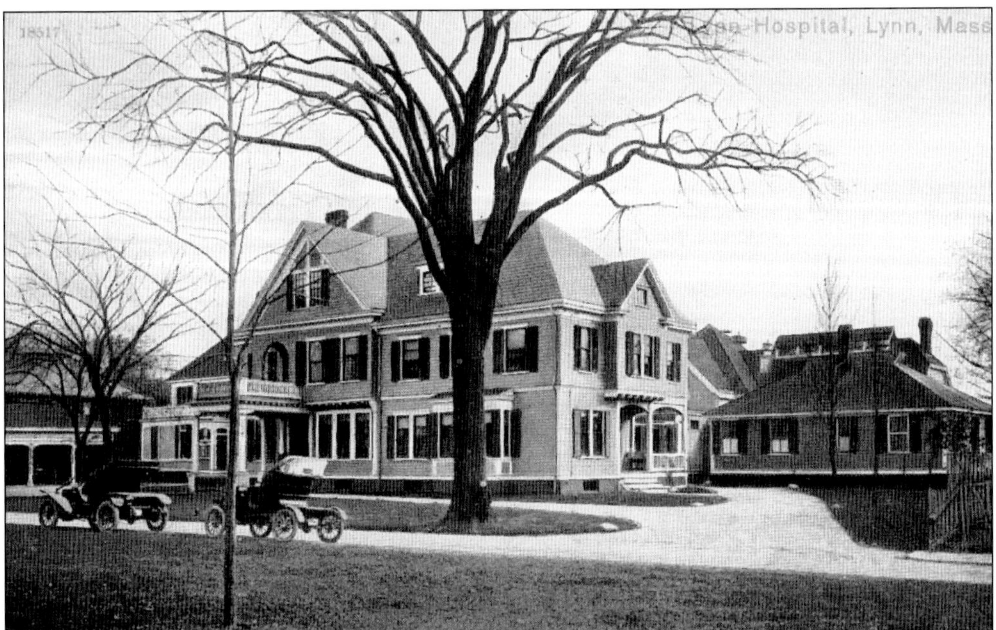

Lynn Hospital is shown here in 1910. The buildings shown here, from left to right, are the outpatient department, the administration building, and hospital ward A. Strawberry Brook ran directly in front of this site until it was finally covered entirely in the 1930s.

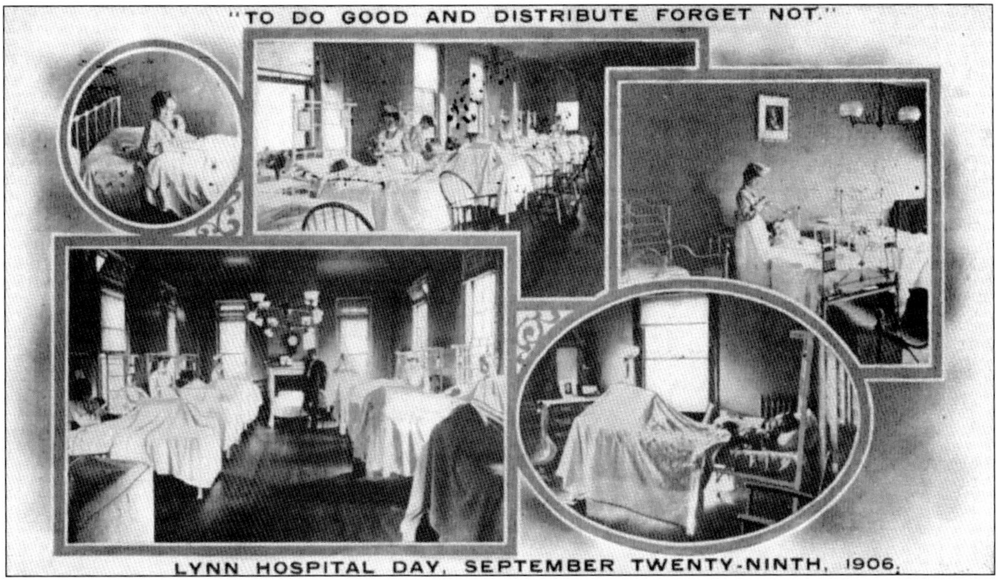

This 1906 souvenir card proudly showcases the interior of several wards at Lynn Hospital, which seem intolerably crowded to modern sensibilities. (Conway collection.)

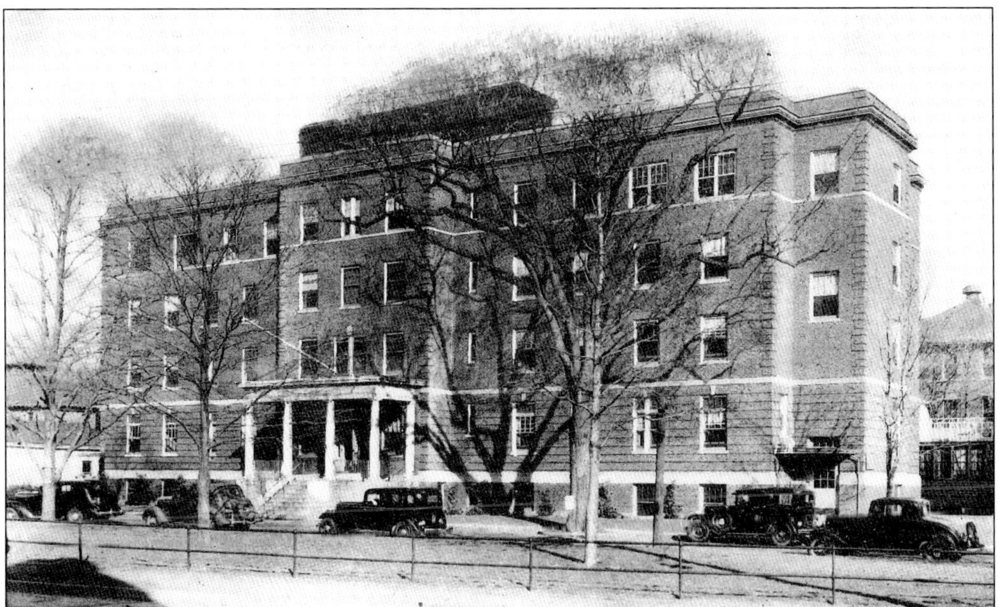
The new administration building of Lynn Hospital, built in 1926, was a Boston Street landmark for 70 years until it was razed along with the rest of the hospital in 1996. (Conway collection.)

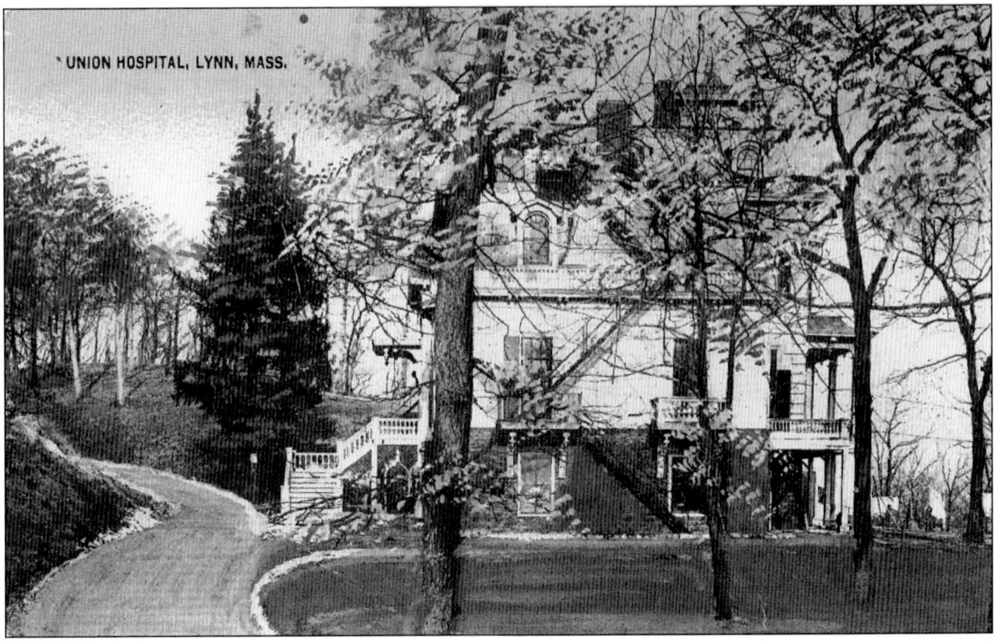

In 1901 the former home of leather manufacturer Phillip Tapley, on Pine Hill, was converted into Union Hospital. The hospital remained at the Tapley Mansion until its new home, the present Atlanticare facility, was built on Lynnfield Street. (Conway collection.)

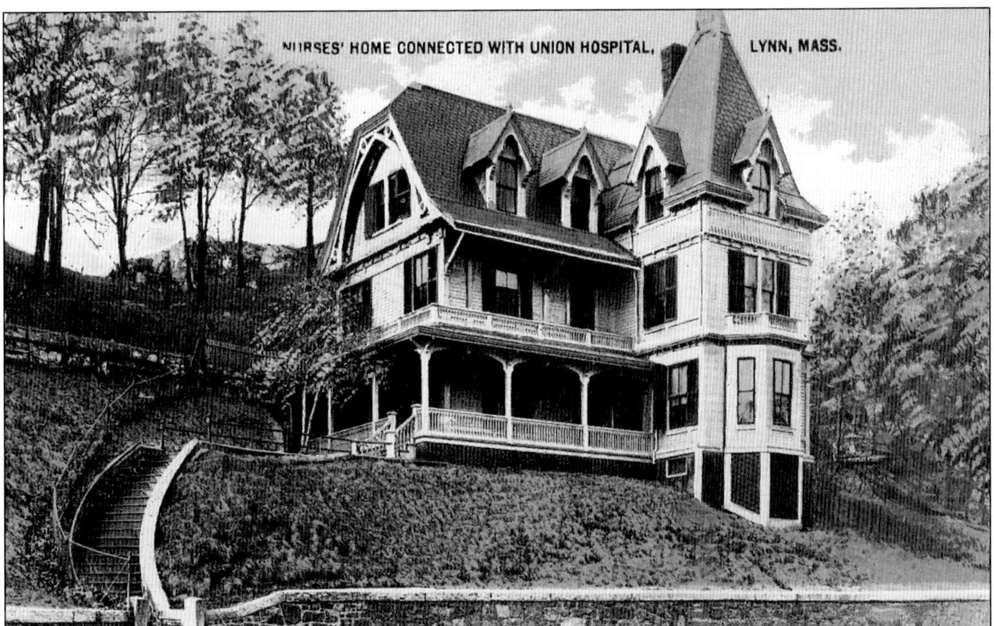

Just down the hill from Union Hospital, on Forrest Street, was the Mary Grant nurses' residence. (Conway collection.)

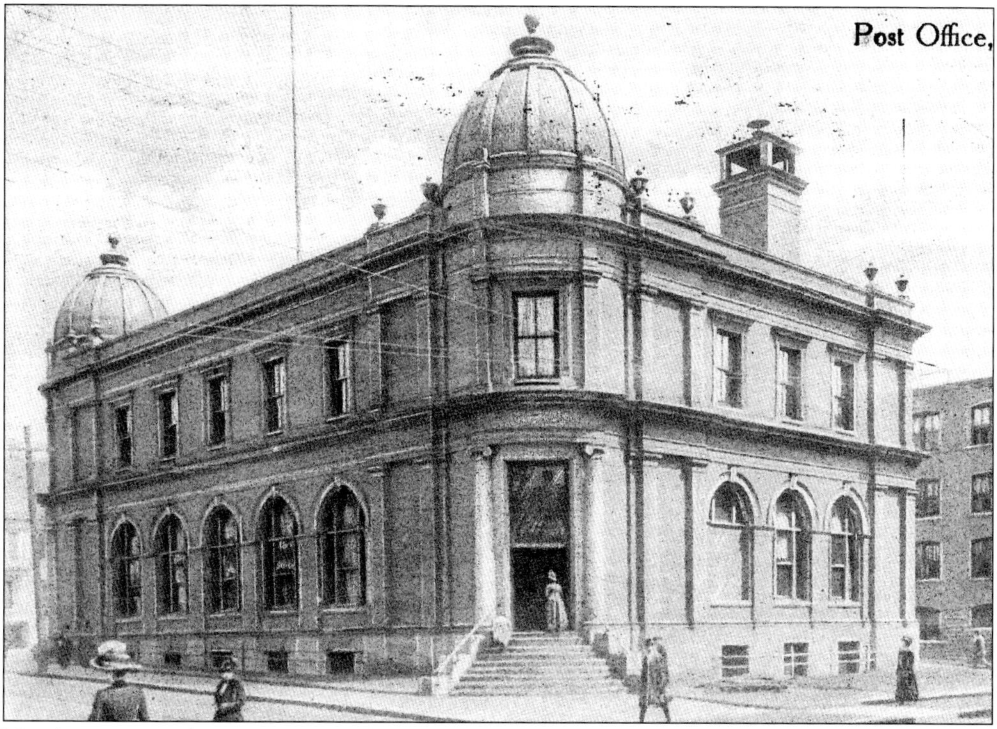

Nearly 14 years after it was originally proposed in Congress, Lynn's federal post office building opened for business in February 1898. This is a 1912 postcard printed by the North Shore Novelty Company of Lynn.

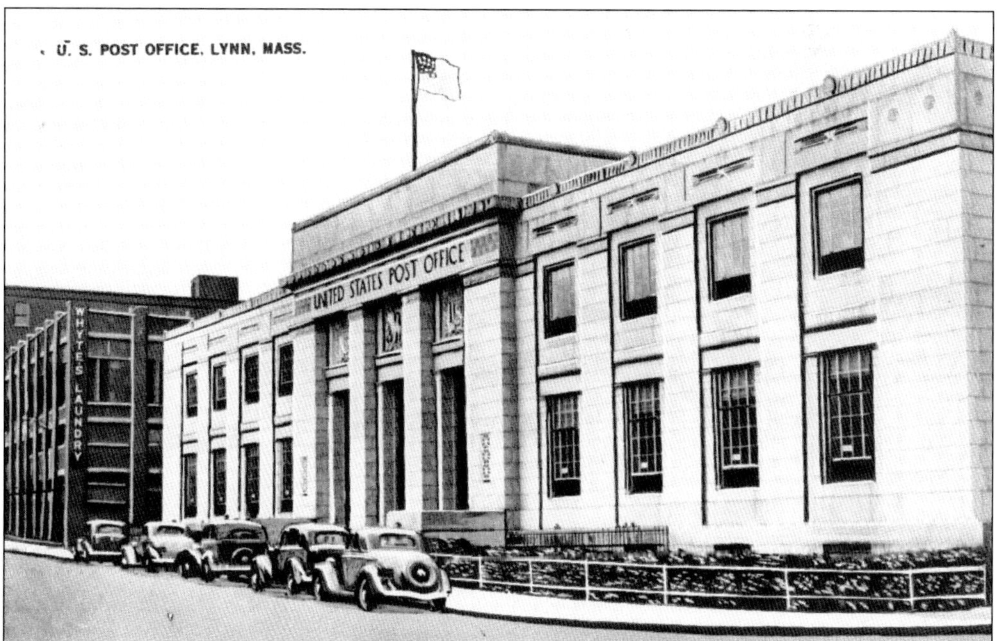

By the 1930s, Lynn had outgrown its old post office and the current facility on Willow Street was built as a Work Progress Administration project. (Conway collection.)

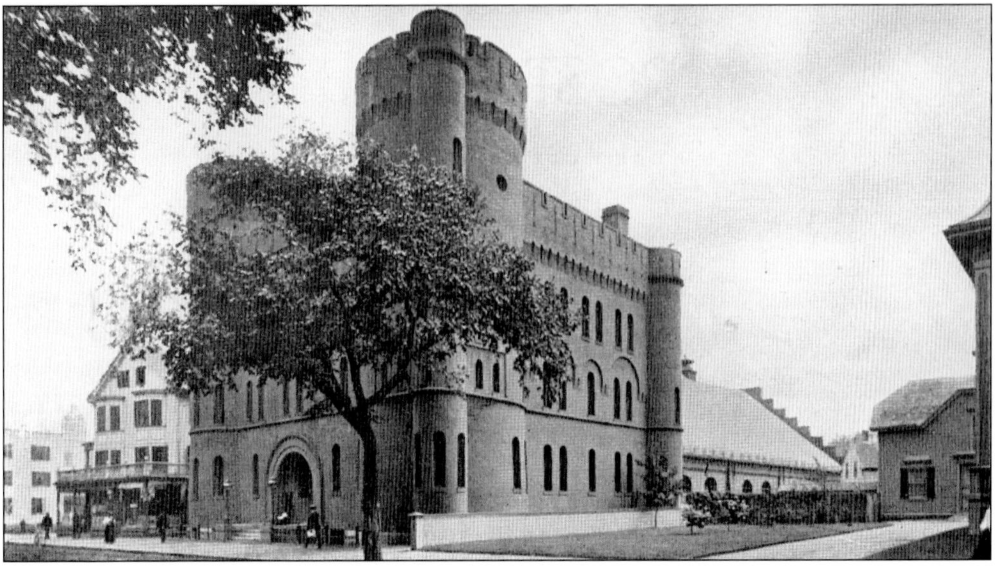

In 1900 the National Guard Armory on South Common Street was headquarters to Company E of the Naval Brigade and Company D (the Lynn Light Infantry) and Company I (the Woolridge Cadets) of the Massachusetts Volunteer Militia.

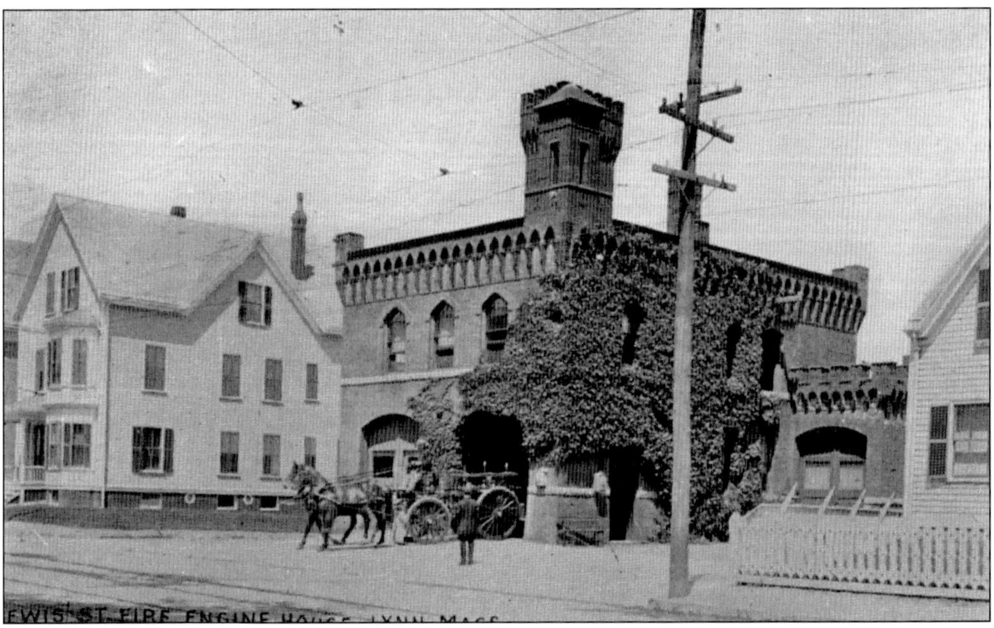

The Lewis Street fire station, erected in 1892, originally housed Chemical No. 4 and was later home to Engine 12. The company was disbanded in 1965 and the station demolished two years later. This was one of several fire stations built on virtually identical plans.

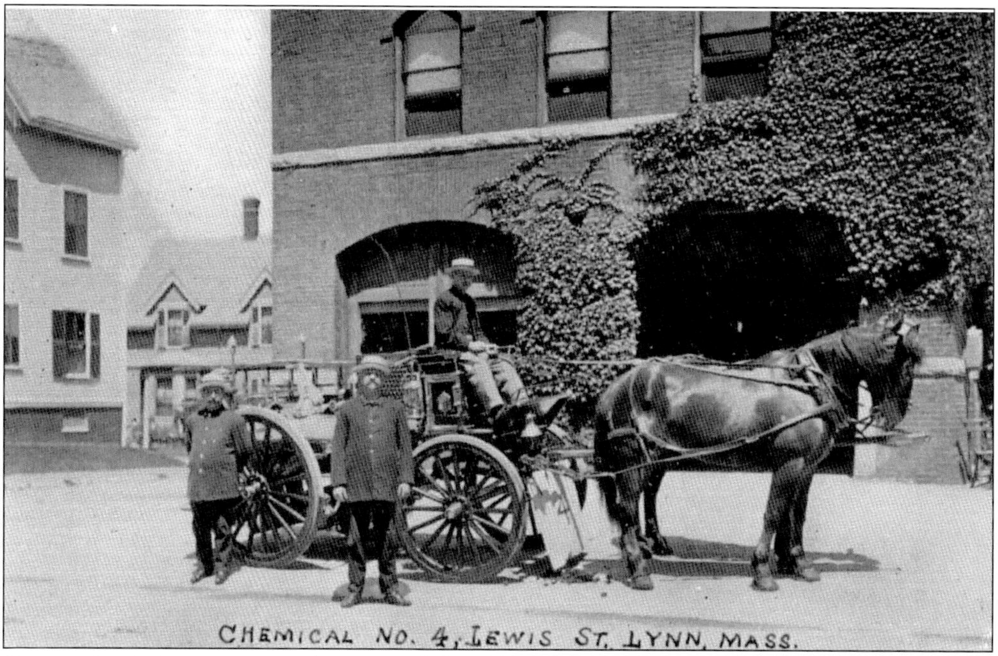

Captain Paul Downer (center) poses with his Chemical No. 4 crew in 1907.

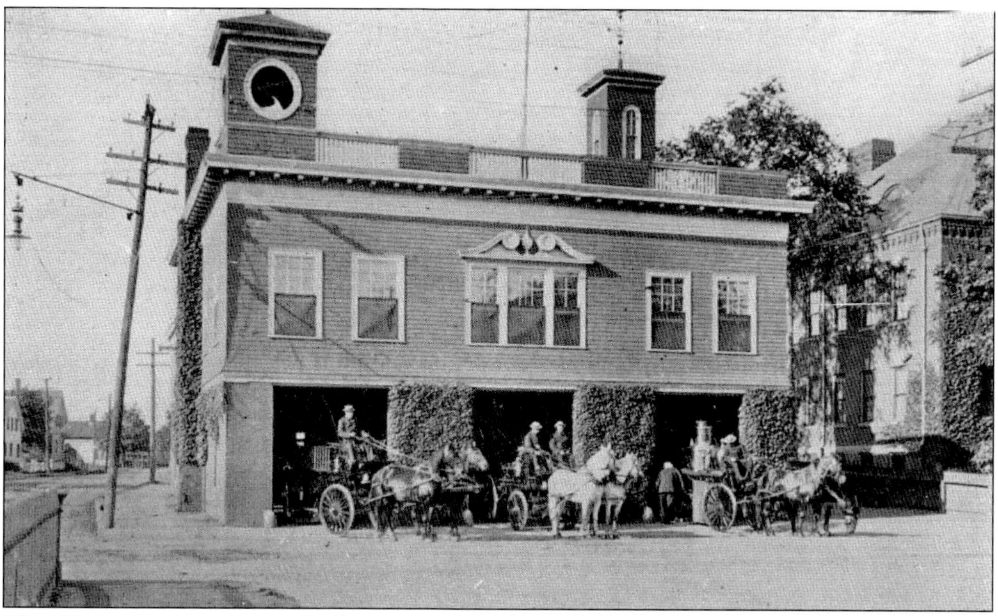

The Glenmere station was also known as the Chestnut Street station. By 1910 the process of motorization had begun and horse-drawn engines such as these were refitted.

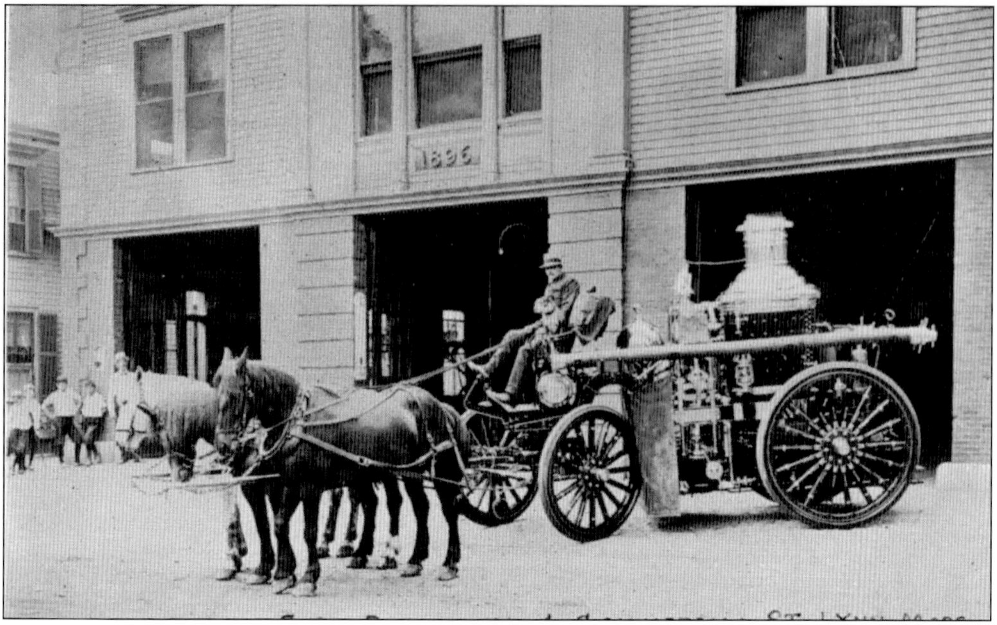

Fire Engine No. 1 made its home at the Commercial Street station, erected in 1896. The deputy chief was also headquartered here.

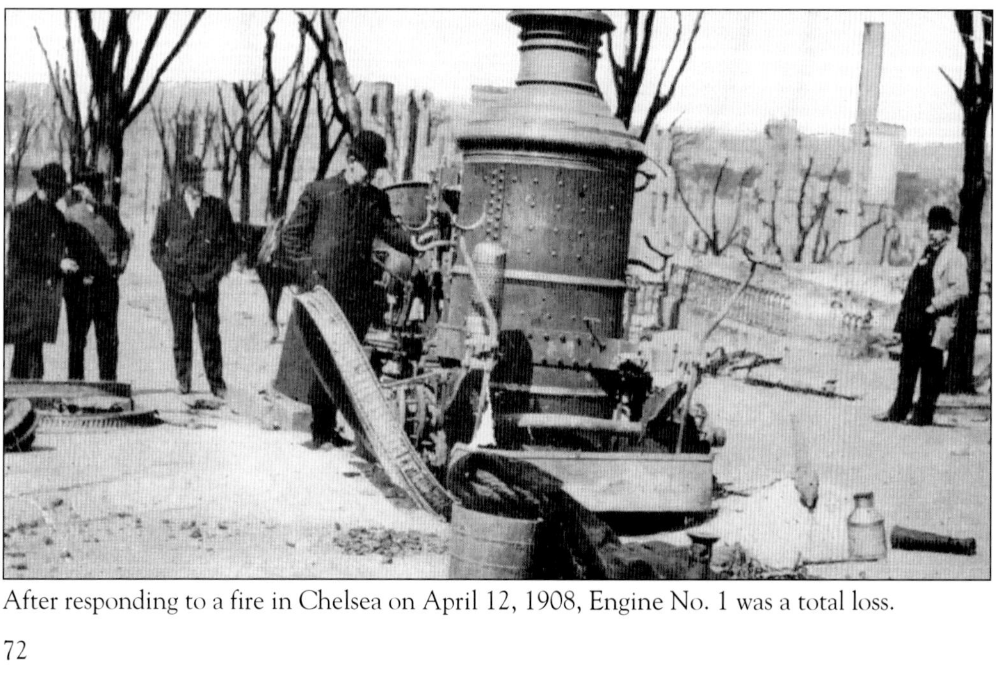

After responding to a fire in Chelsea on April 12, 1908, Engine No. 1 was a total loss.

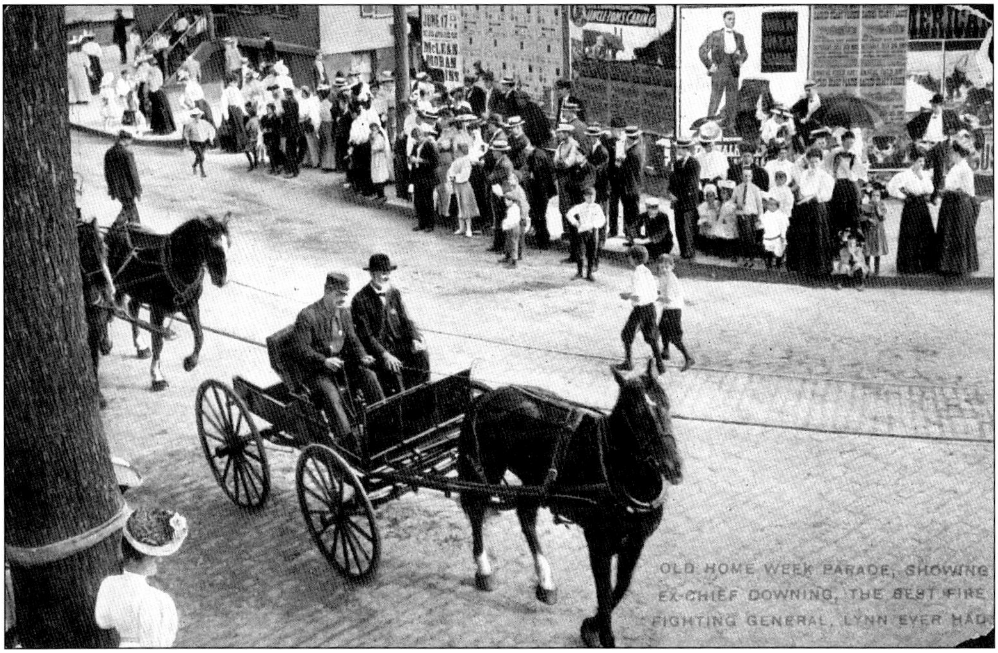

A popular guest in Lynn's Old Home Week parade in 1907 was Fire Chief Charles Downing, described as "the best fire fighting general Lynn ever had." Downing served from 1905 to 1913.

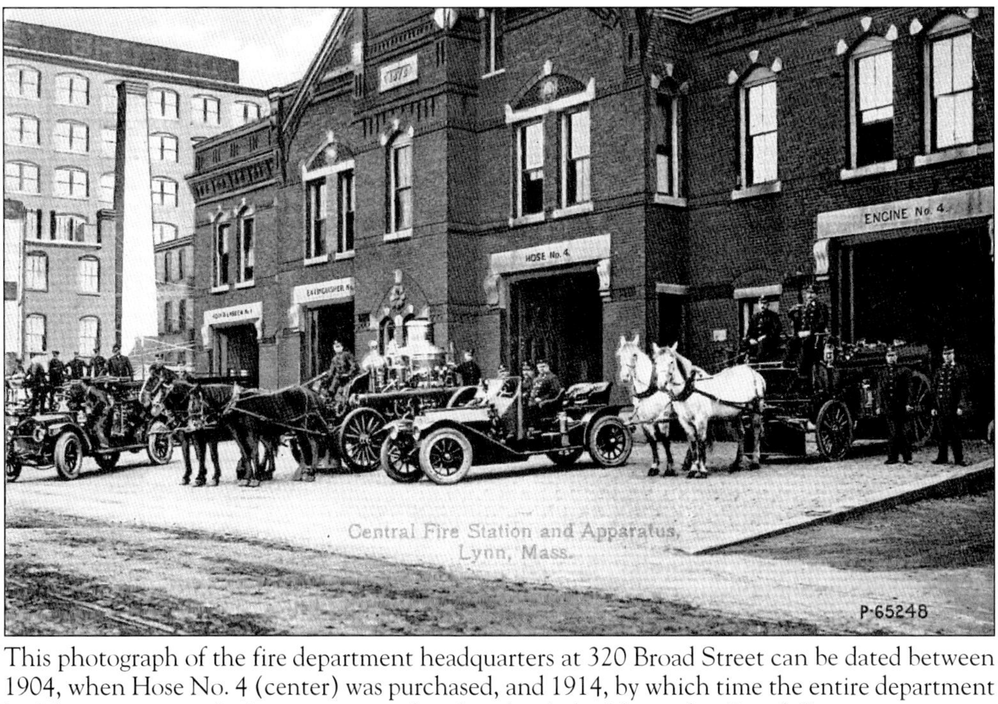

This photograph of the fire department headquarters at 320 Broad Street can be dated between 1904, when Hose No. 4 (center) was purchased, and 1914, by which time the entire department had been motorized. An impressive four-bay brick building, the Broad Street station was consigned to the wrecking ball in 1973 after nearly one hundred years of service.

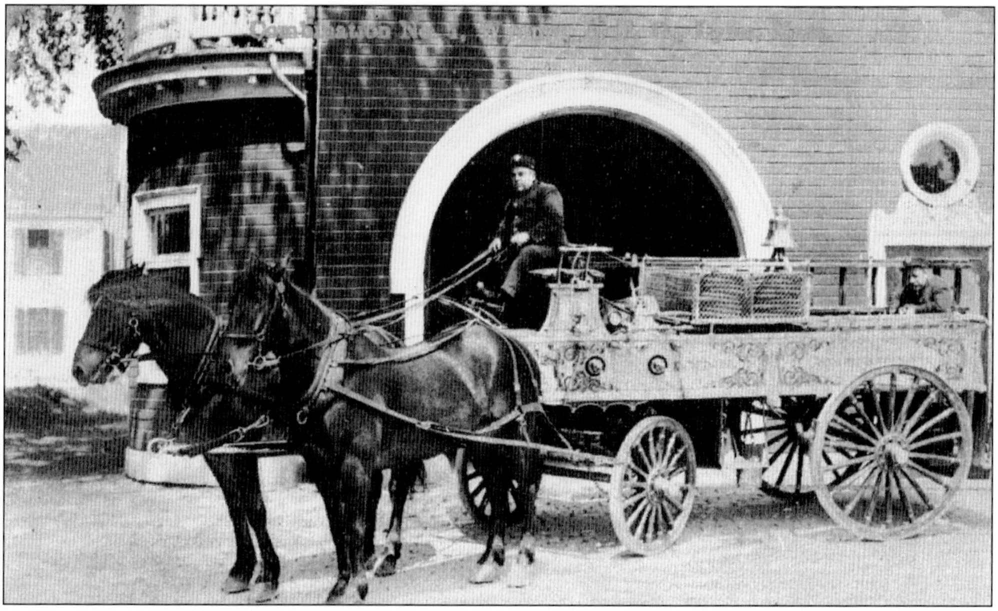

William Durkee (front) and S.H. Johnson pose with Combination No. 1, nicknamed the "White Angel," in front of the Wyoma station on Broadway in 1905.

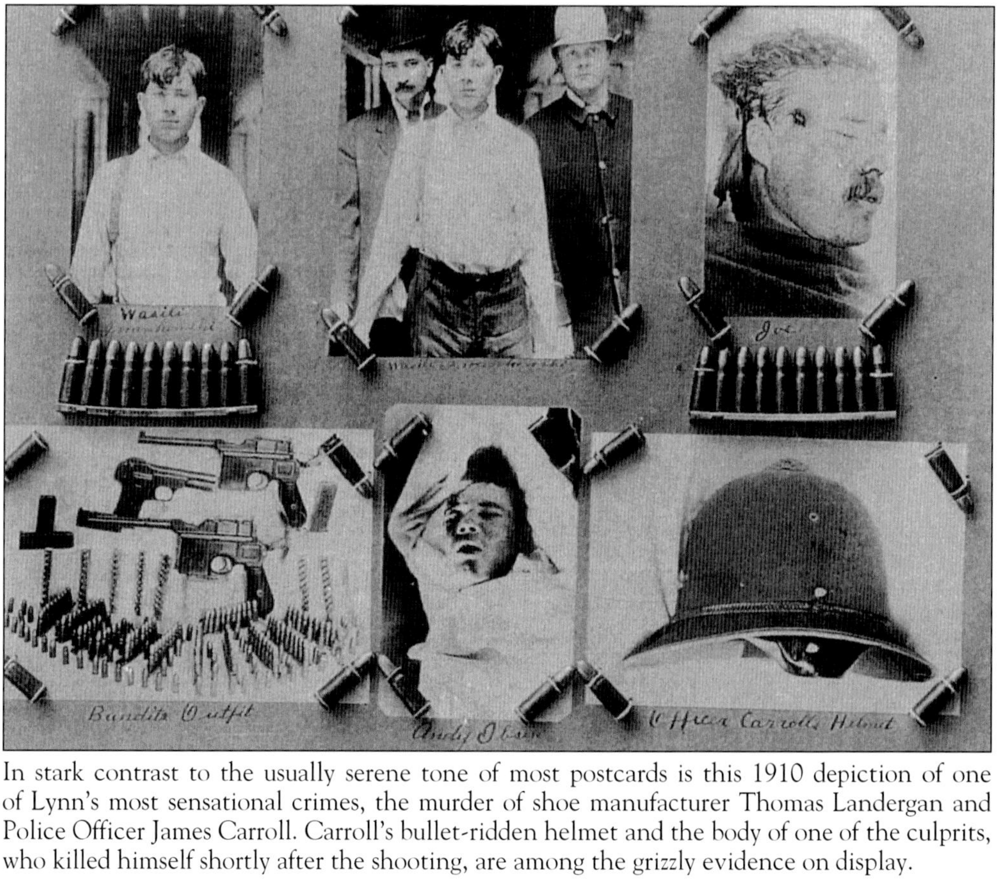

In stark contrast to the usually serene tone of most postcards is this 1910 depiction of one of Lynn's most sensational crimes, the murder of shoe manufacturer Thomas Landergan and Police Officer James Carroll. Carroll's bullet-ridden helmet and the body of one of the culprits, who killed himself shortly after the shooting, are among the grizzly evidence on display.

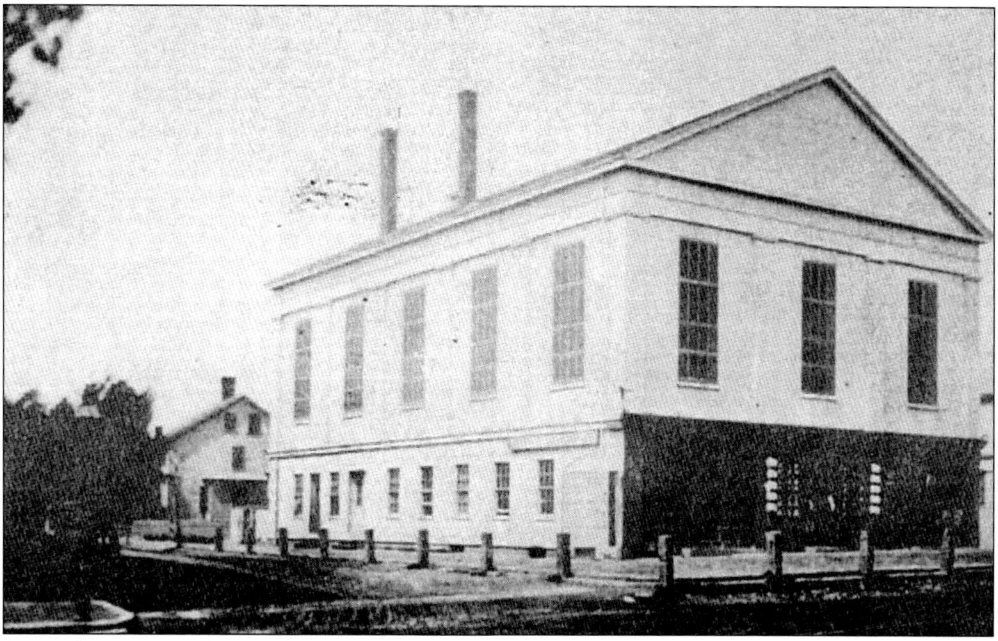

One of Lynn's earliest and most significant meeting halls was the Lyceum at the corner of Market and Summer Streets. Many of the greatest figures of the 19th century lectured or performed here during its relatively brief life. It burned in a spectacular blaze on Christmas Day in 1868. This early view was reproduced on a much later postcard.

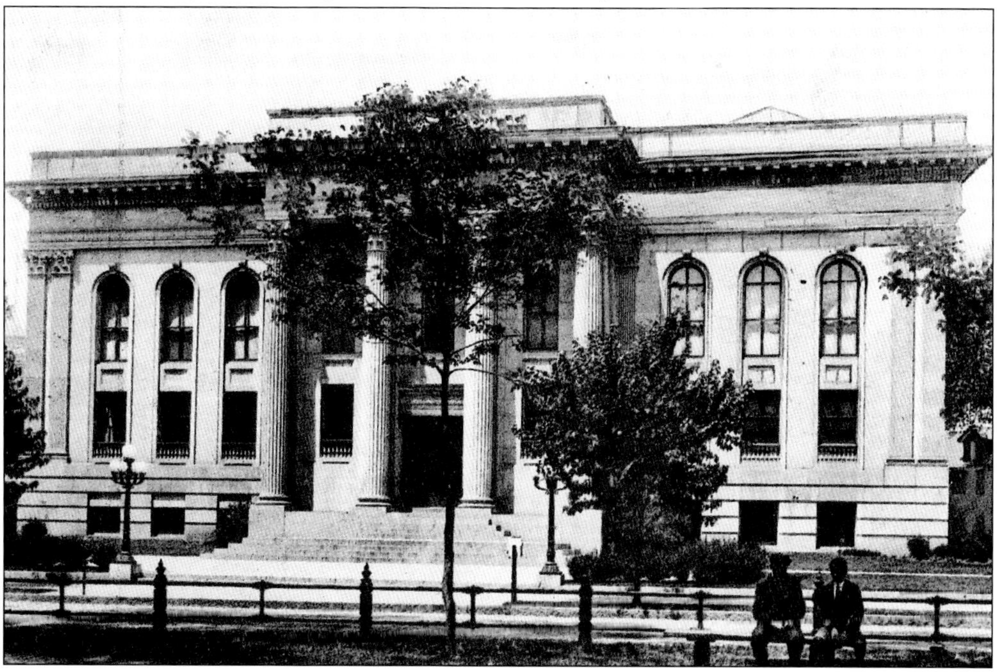

A bequest of $100,000 was given to the City of Lynn in 1893 by Elizabeth Shute for the purpose of building a public library in memory of her husband, morrocco manufacturer William Shute. After a somewhat acrimonious competition, Boston architect George Moore's plans were chosen. The attractive Renaissance Revival design is shown in this 1908 image.

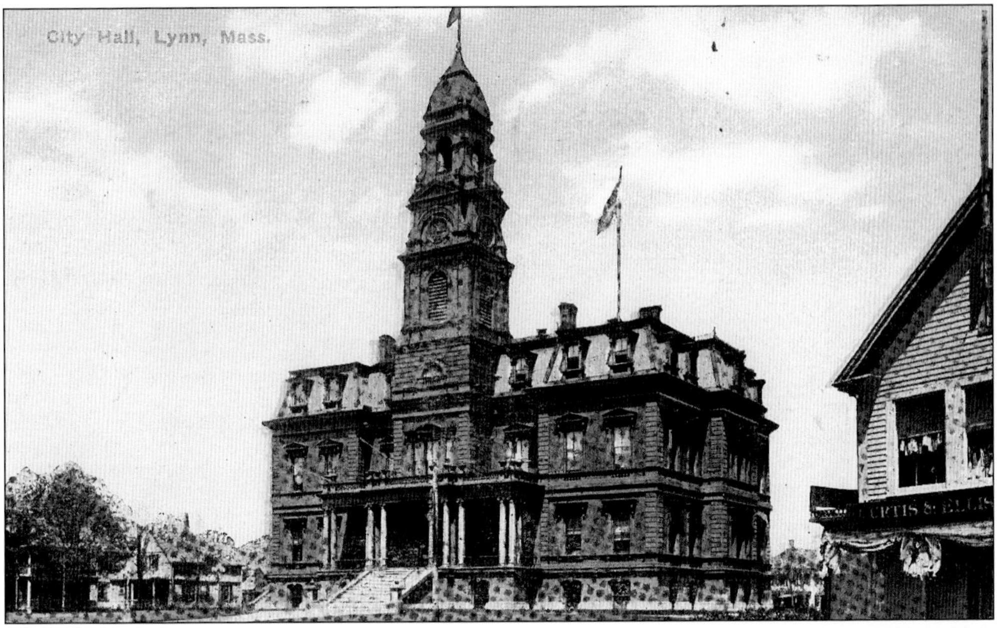

Lynn's old city hall was razed to make way for the present structure in 1948. This photograph was taken after the ornamental gates that once stood in front had been removed to Pine Grove Cemetery.

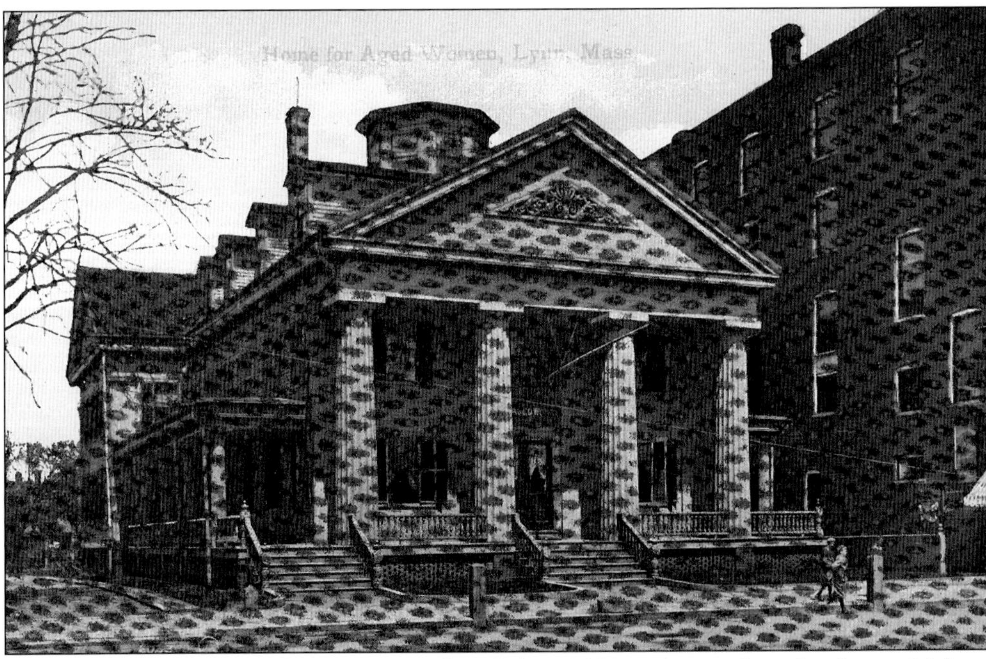

The Lynn Home for Aged Women was founded in 1872 and moved to the former Nahant Bank building on North Common Street in 1877. Its stated object was to "provide an asylum for aged women of worthy character, whatever their social condition may have been, and who find themselves, in their advancing years, bereaved of friends and means of support." Four of the home's residents lost their lives when fire destroyed the building in 1920.

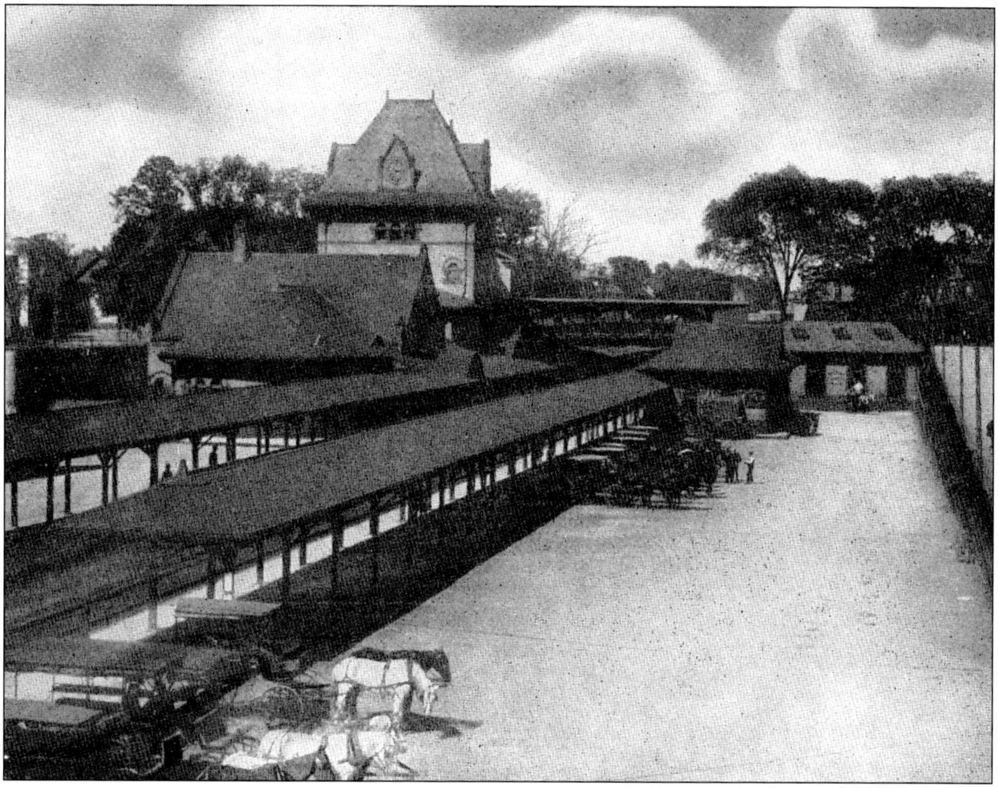

Boston & Maine Railroad's Central Square Station is shown *c.* 1910 (above) and in 1914 (below), after the elevation of the tracks.

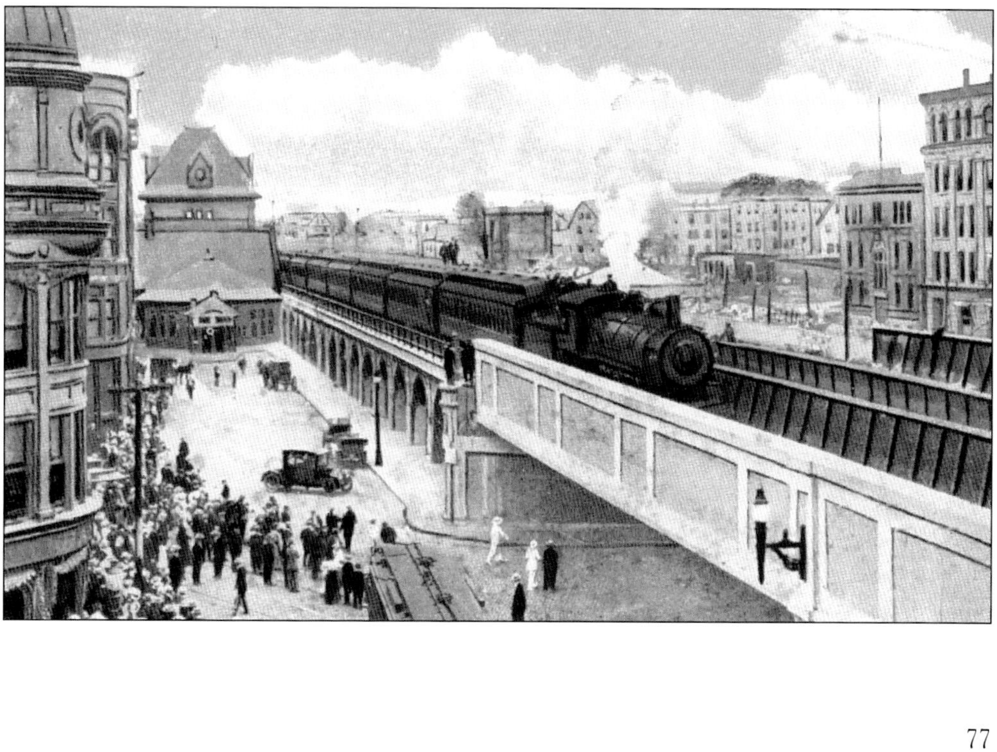

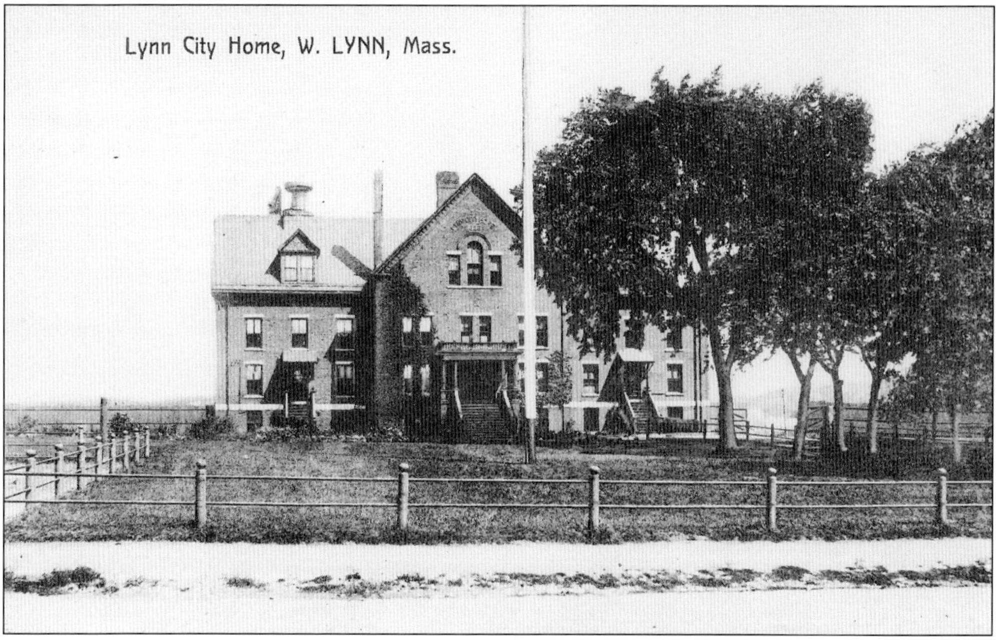

The City Home and Infirmary on Tower Hill, built in 1895, was the successor to the almshouse, or poor farm, which had been operated at various locations since the 18th century.

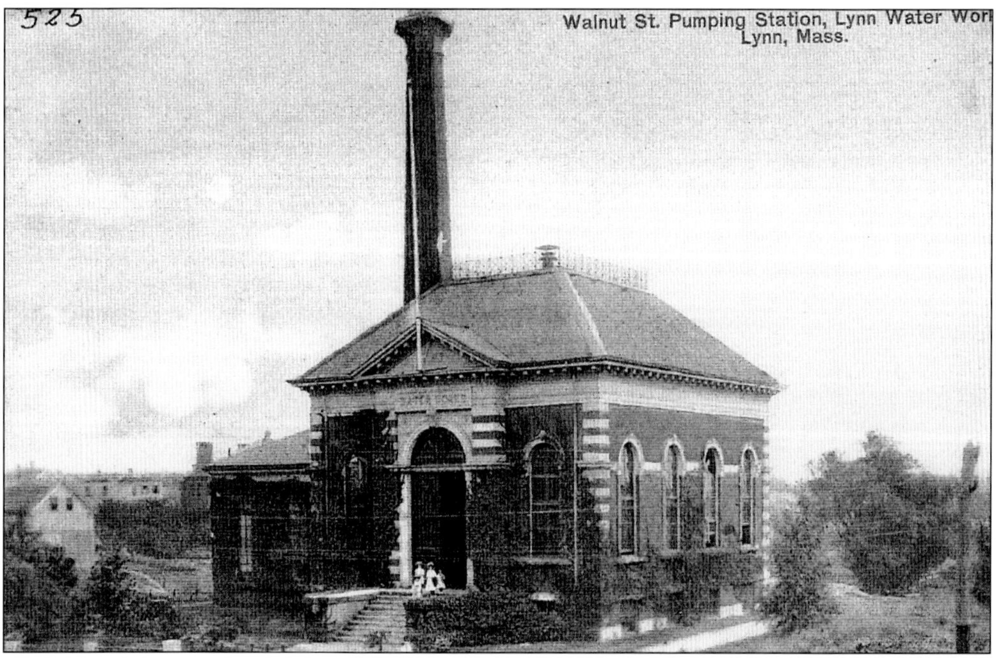

The beautiful Colonial Revival pumping station on Walnut Street was designed by N.J. Bradley of Boston in 1871. It remained in use until the construction of a new plant in the 1990s and is still standing.

Five

Homes and Neighbors

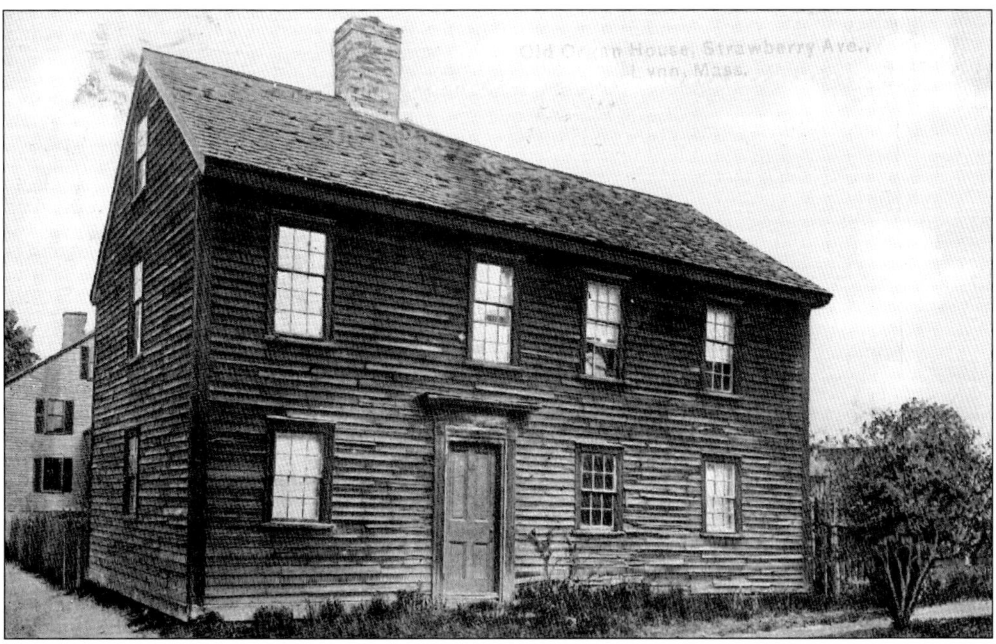

Although it had been demolished in 1891, the Organ house was featured on this 1905 card in keeping with the contemporary popularity of all things deemed quaint and Colonial. Isaac Organ, who lived in this house, had been a drum major in the American Revolution.

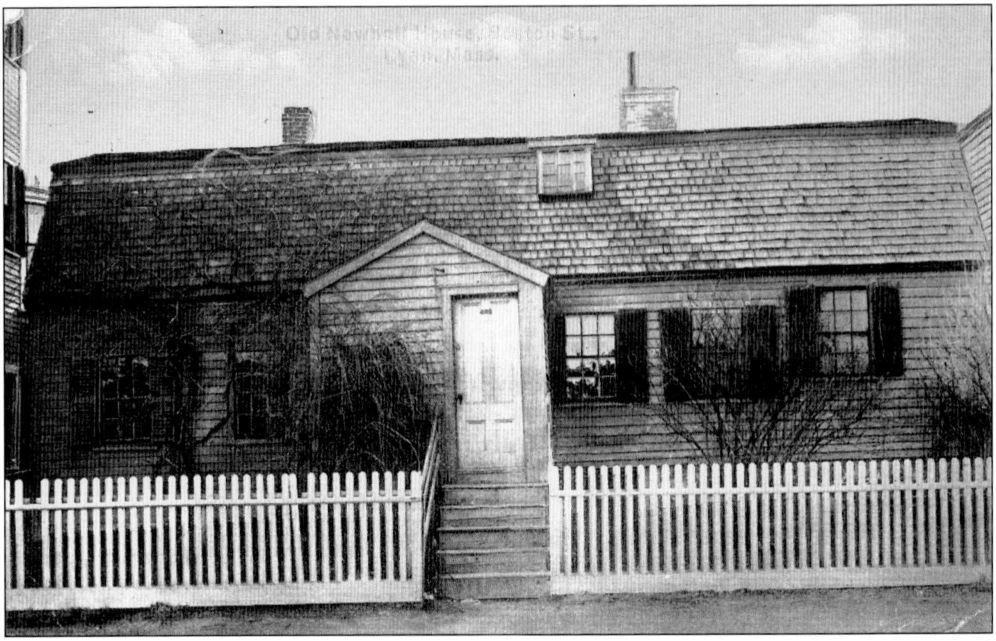

This small, gambrel-roofed house on Boston Street was still standing when this 1912 postcard was printed. It belonged to Jedediah "Uncle Jed" Newhall, a minuteman at Lexington and Concord. It was razed in 1914.

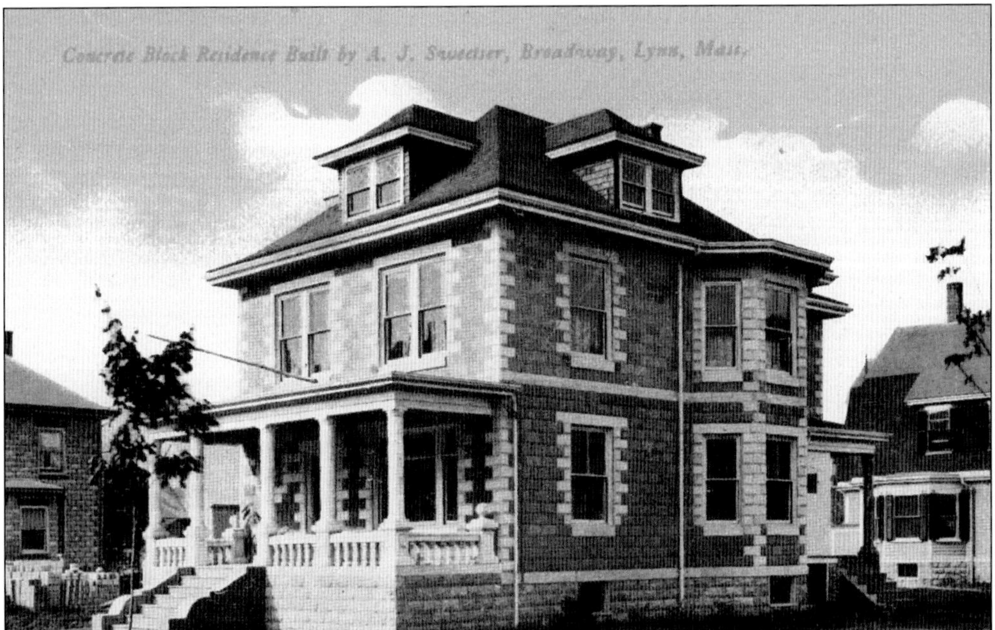

Andrew J. Sweetser claimed to own "the largest concrete plant in New England." Not surprisingly, he built his home out of concrete blocks, a fact considered novel enough for the Glenmere Company to print this card in 1910. (Conway collection.)

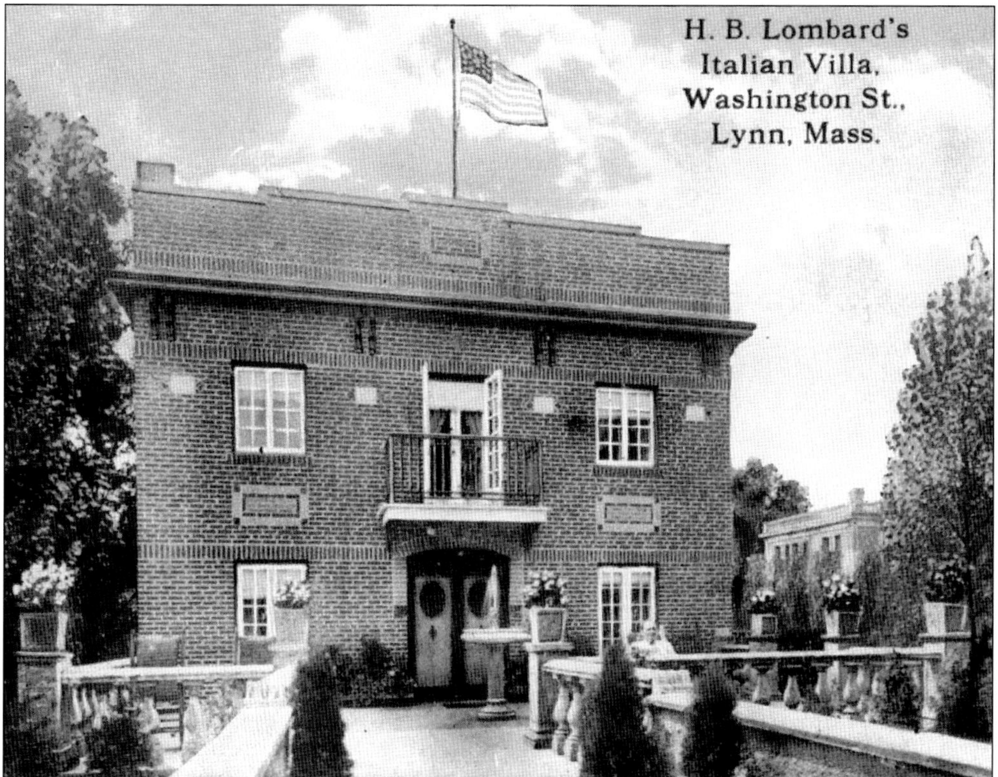

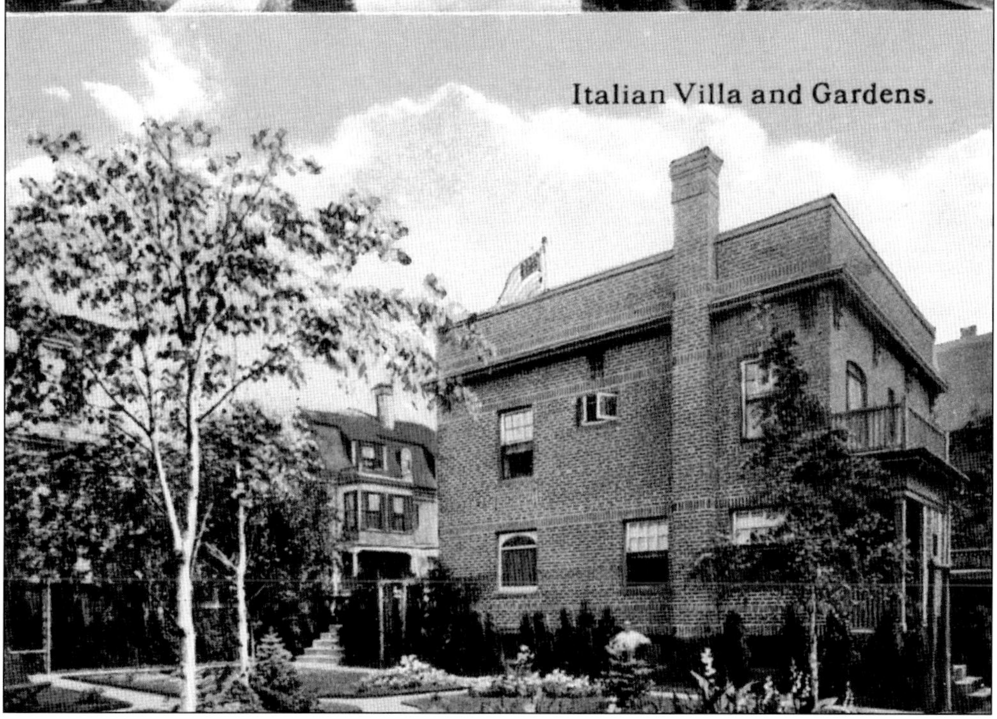

Wig manufacturer Henry B. Lombard built and briefly occupied this attractive home on Washington Street next to the Home for Aged Couples in the 1920s. (Conway collection.)

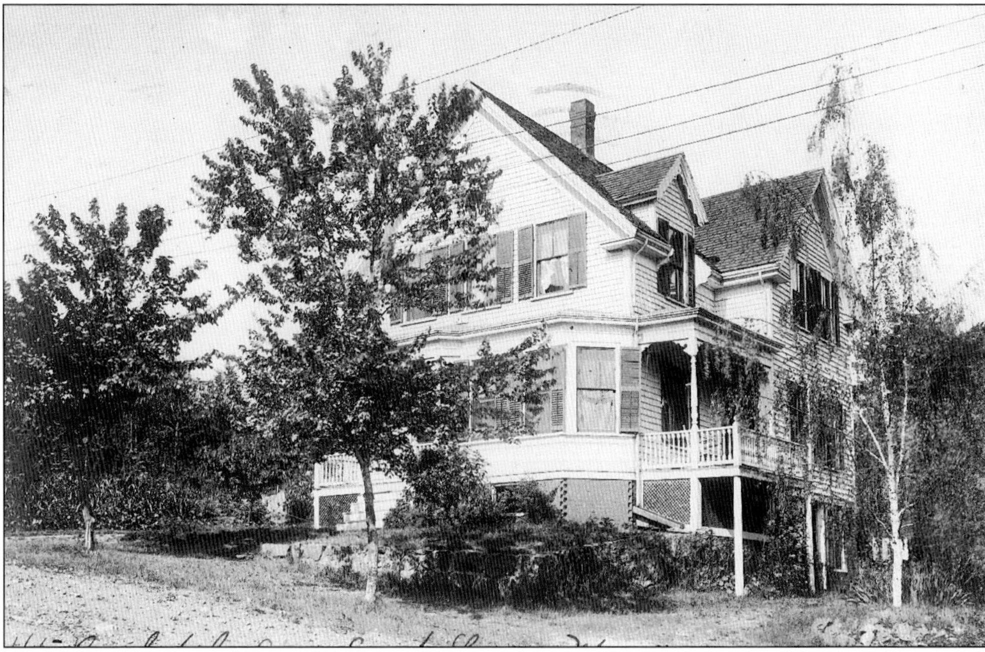

The area around Wyoma and Lakeside was the center of residential development in the early 20th century. This fine home on Rockdale Avenue was built for Alma Medilius *c.* 1905. (Conway collection.)

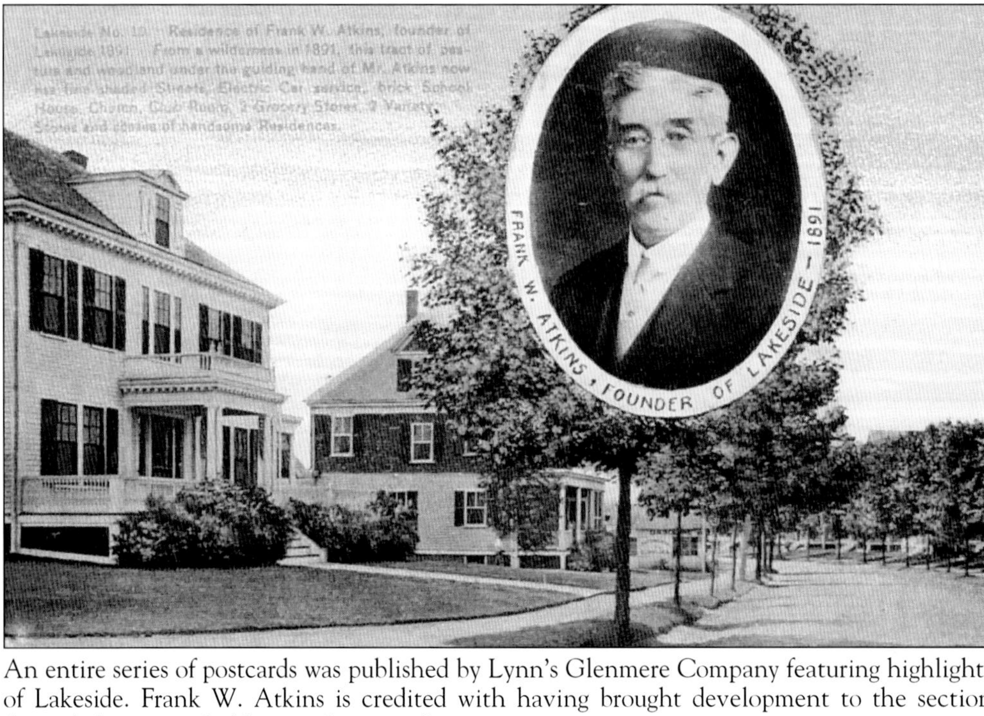

An entire series of postcards was published by Lynn's Glenmere Company featuring highlights of Lakeside. Frank W. Atkins is credited with having brought development to the section formerly known as "seldomgood pasture."

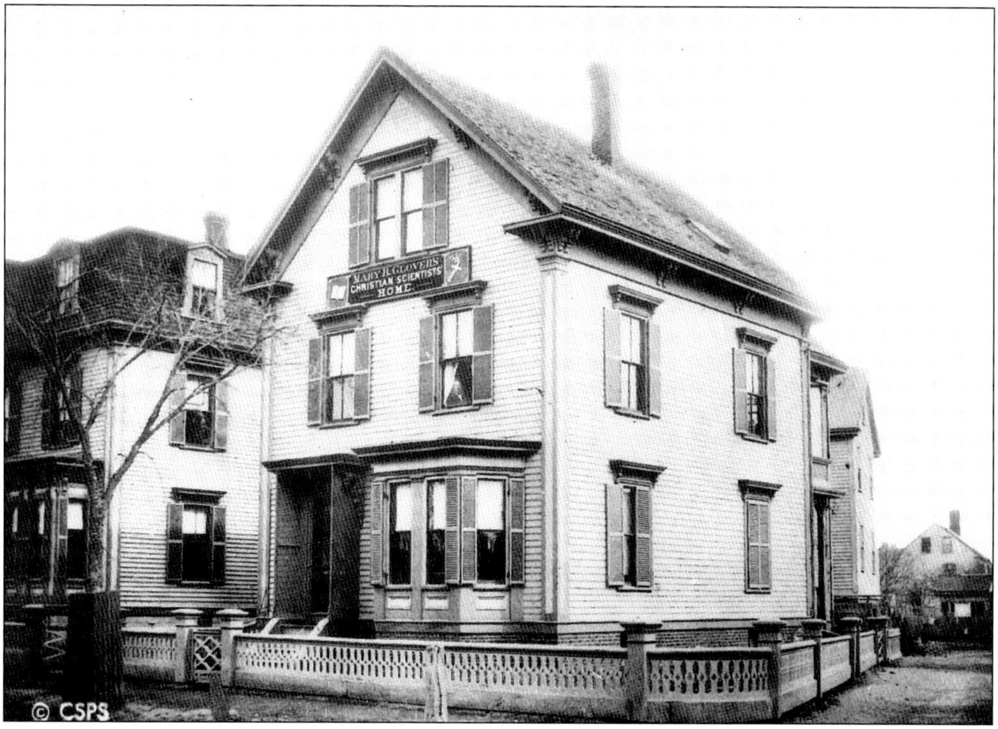

Science and Health was written at the Mary Baker Eddy House at 12 Broad Street. Note that the sign in front reads "Mary B. Glover Christian Science Home," reflecting the fact that this picture was taken before she married Asa Eddy in 1877. The postcard, however, was published in 1931.

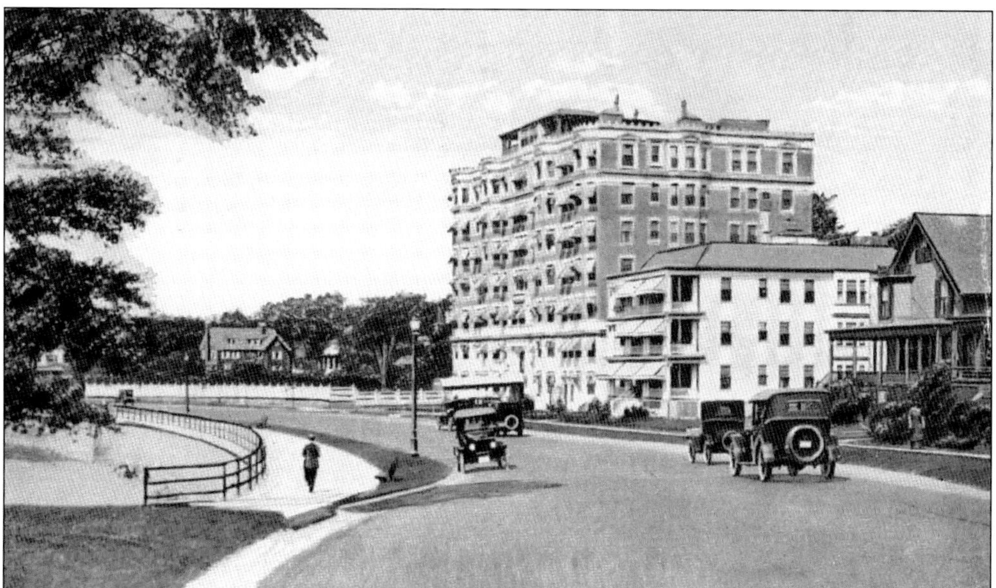

One of Lynn's largest and most distinctive apartment buildings remains the Breakers on Lynn Shore Drive. The seven-story Neoclassical design was created by Lynn architect Dana Sanborn. This view dates to c. 1924.

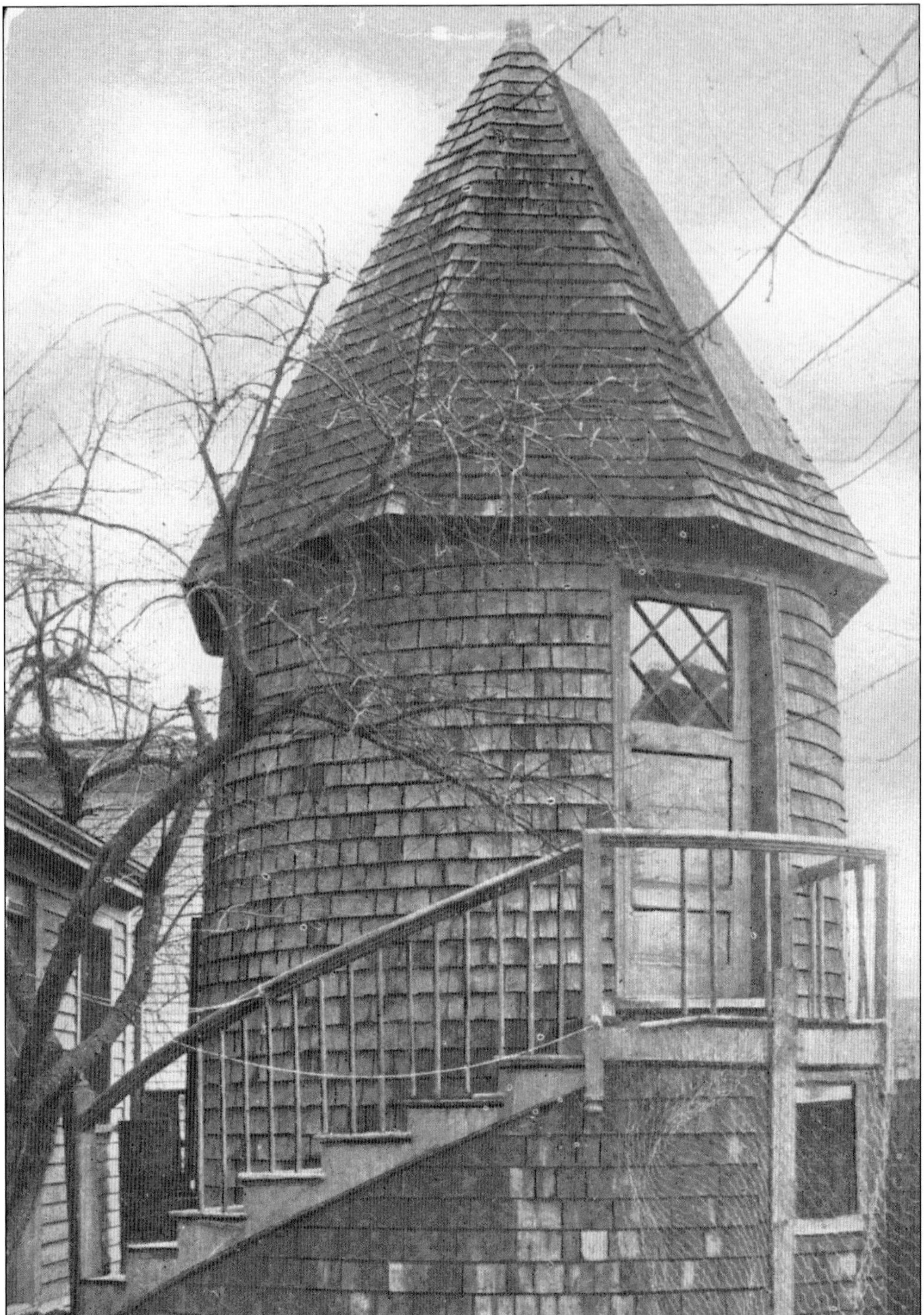

Astronomer Maria Mitchell, the first woman admitted to the American Academy of Arts and Sciences, in her later life lived with her sister, Mrs. Owen Dame, at 111 Green Street in Lynn. She had this small observatory built in the backyard.

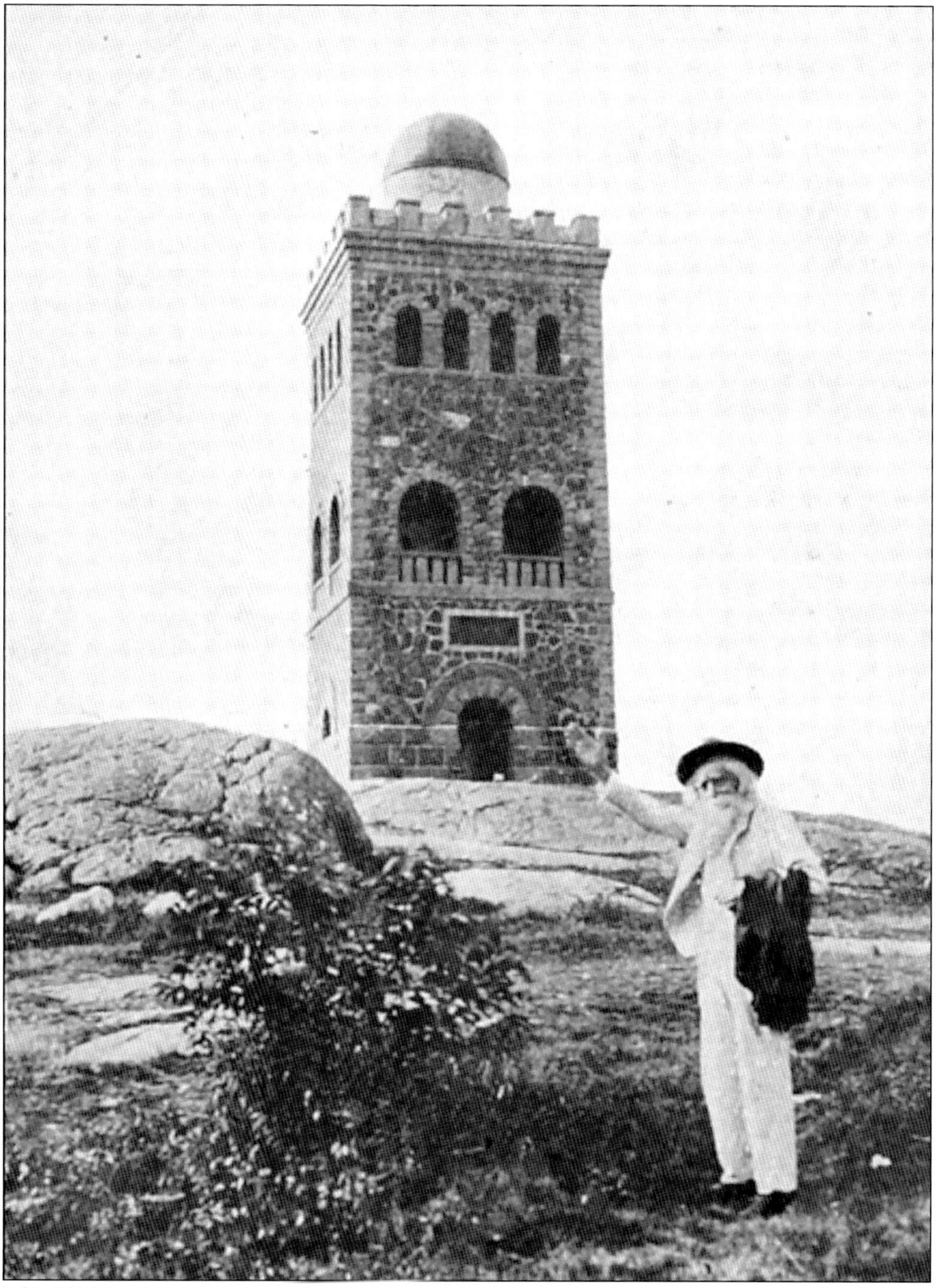

John W. Hutchinson poses in front of the newly constructed High Rock Tower two years after he donated the land to the City of Lynn. An eccentric, generous, and not infrequently prickly character, Hutchinson had kept the city waiting so long and attached so many strings to his bequest that he was never formally thanked for his efforts.

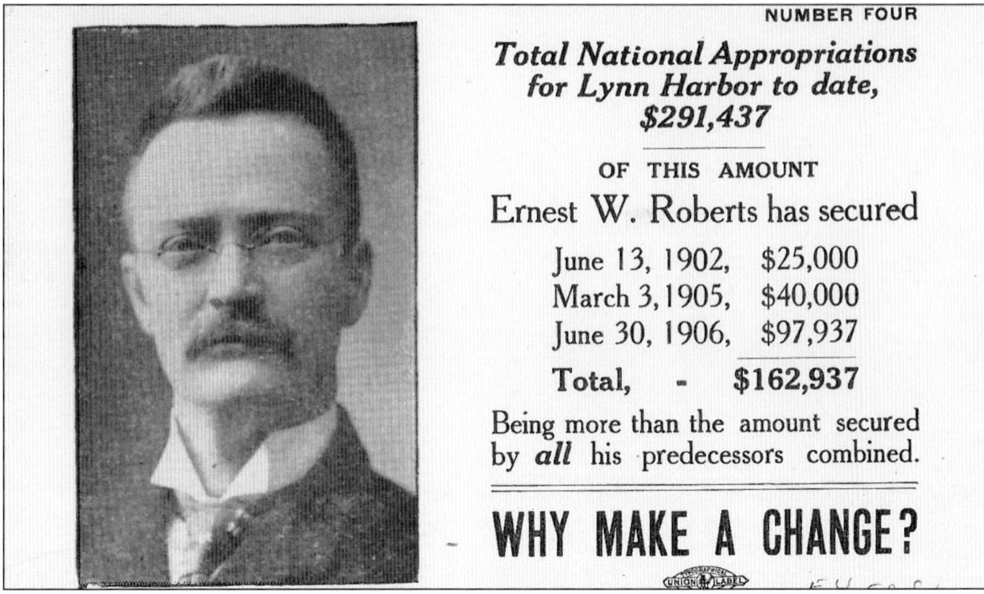

Politicians were quick to take advantage of the inexpensive campaign opportunities postcards afforded. Congressman Ernest W. Roberts of Chelsea sent out a whole series of cards aimed directly at the voters of Lynn, emphasizing all he had done for the largest city in his district and asking, "Could a Lynn man do more?"

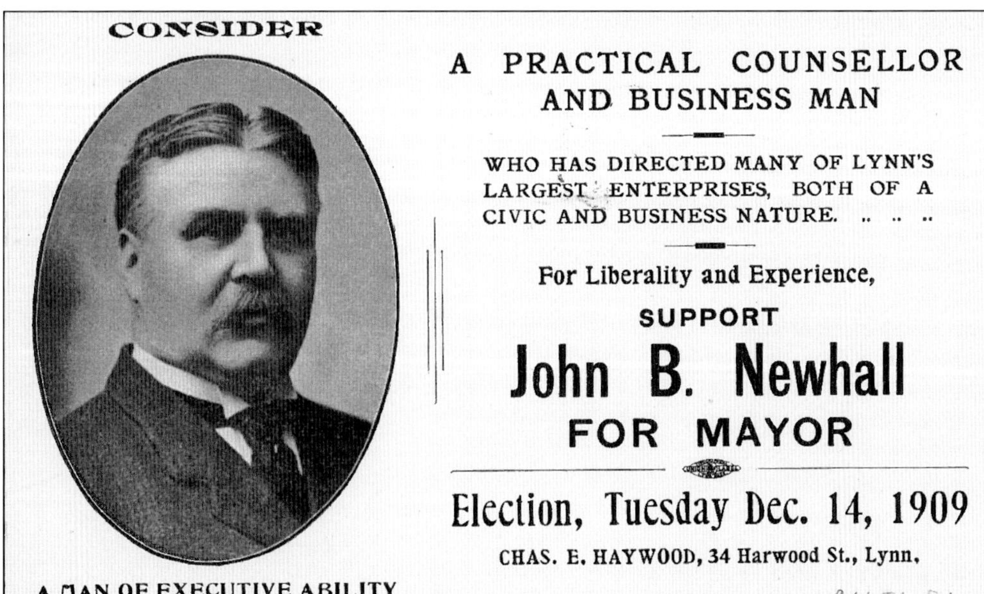

John B. Newhall was a prominent Lynn attorney, active in both business and politics. Nonetheless, he was defeated by James Rich in the 1909 mayoral election.

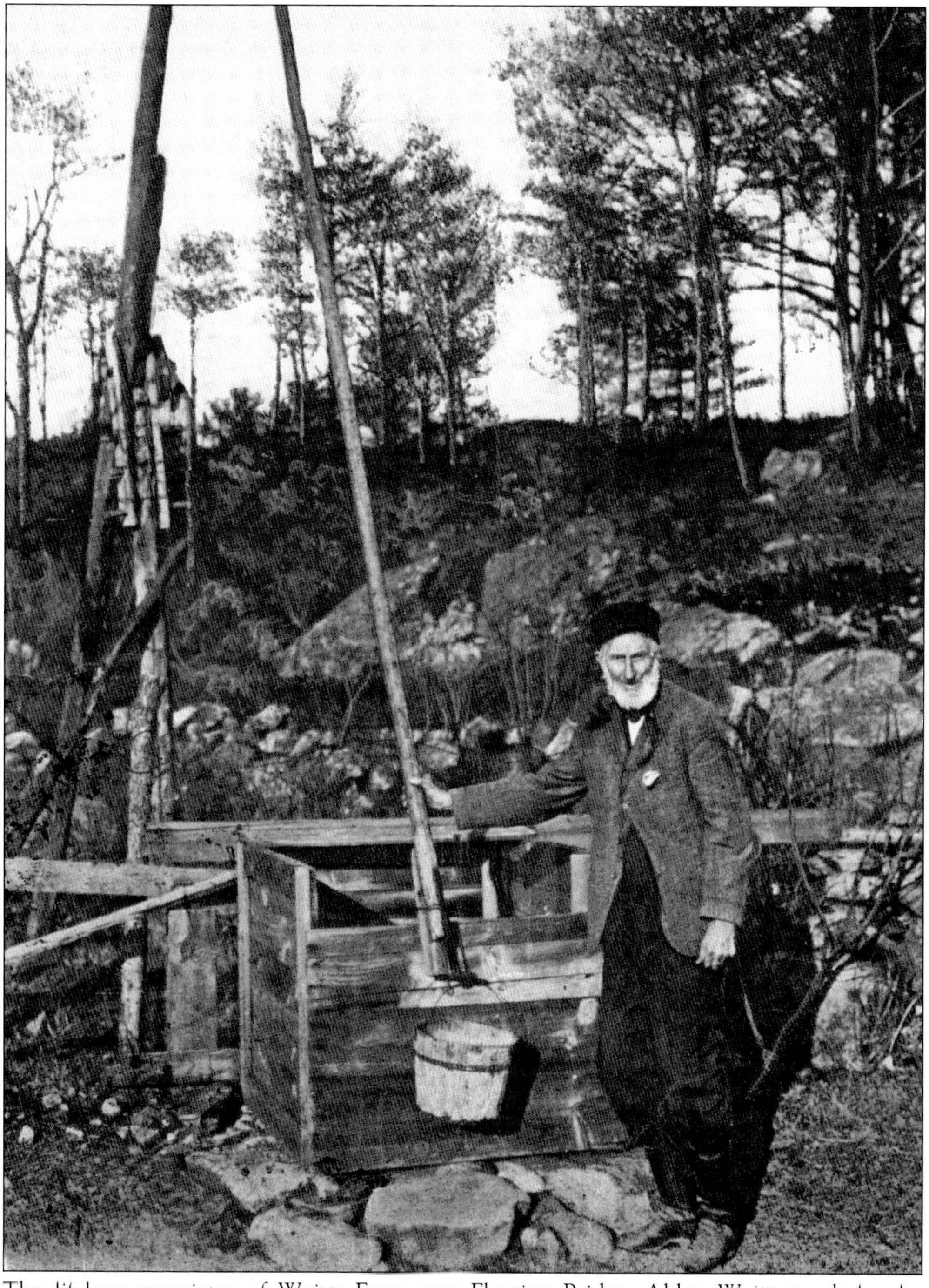

The lifelong proprietor of Waitts Farm near Floating Bridge, Alden Waitt stands by the Colonial-era well that was still operable in his day. Waitt's appearance, which coincided so perfectly with the popular image of a Yankee farmer, and the picturesque quality of the setting combined to make this view and others like it very popular with artists of the day. At the time of his death in 1909, it was reported that Waitt had slept away from his home only two nights in 82 years.

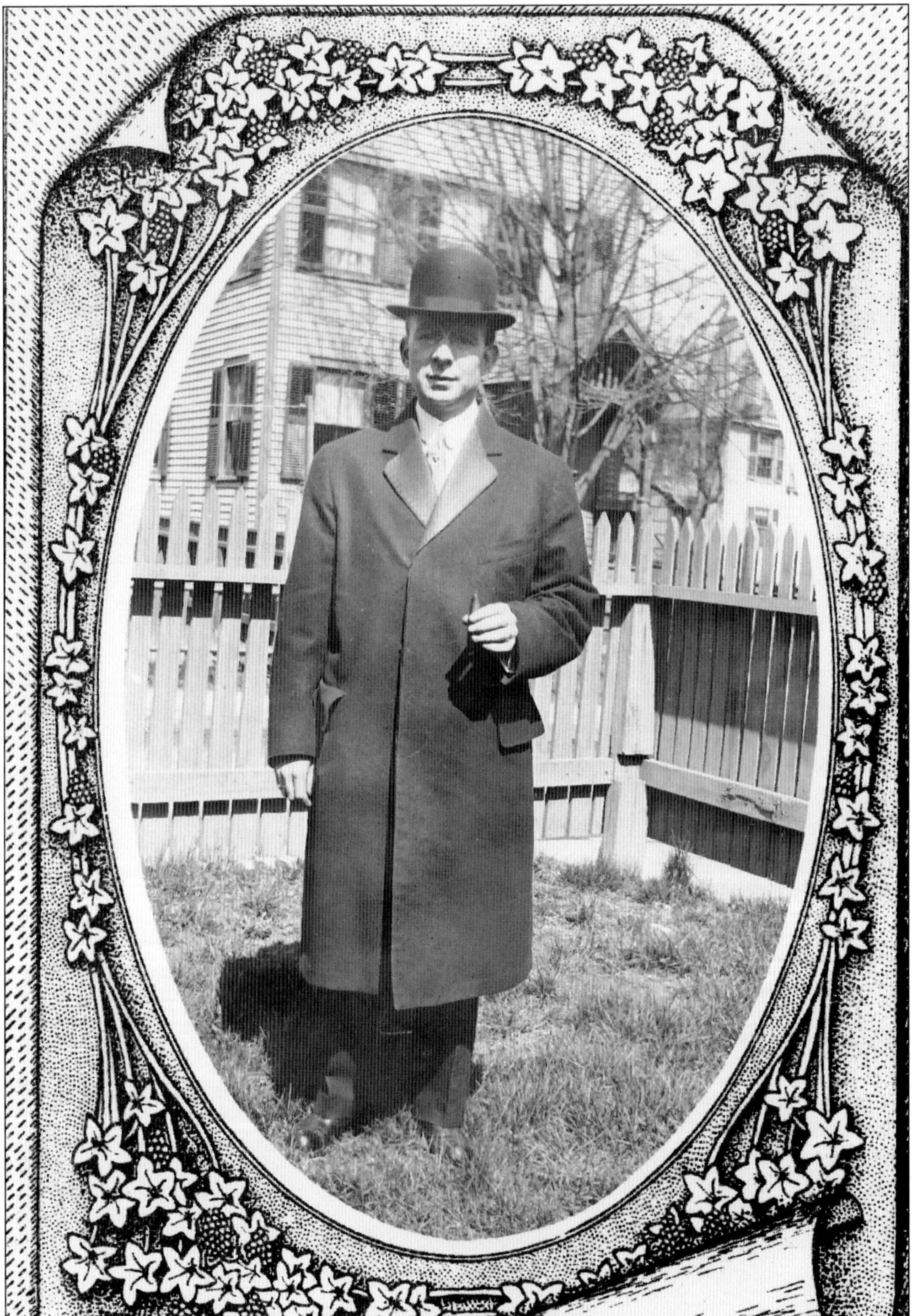

One need not have been famous nor particularly colorful to have his or her image on a postcard. Many photographic studios routinely printed their customers' portraits in this form. This dapper gentleman posing in his backyard is identified only as Mr. St. Onge.

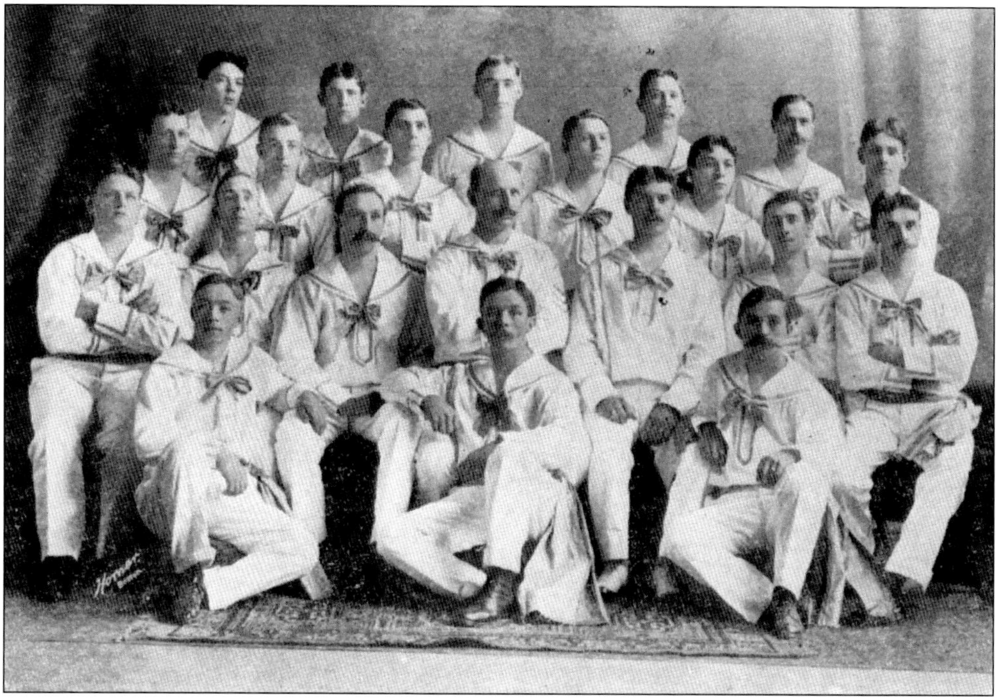

Not much is known about the Swedish Athletic and Gymnastic Club, but judging from this undated card their activities must have appealed to men of a wide age span.

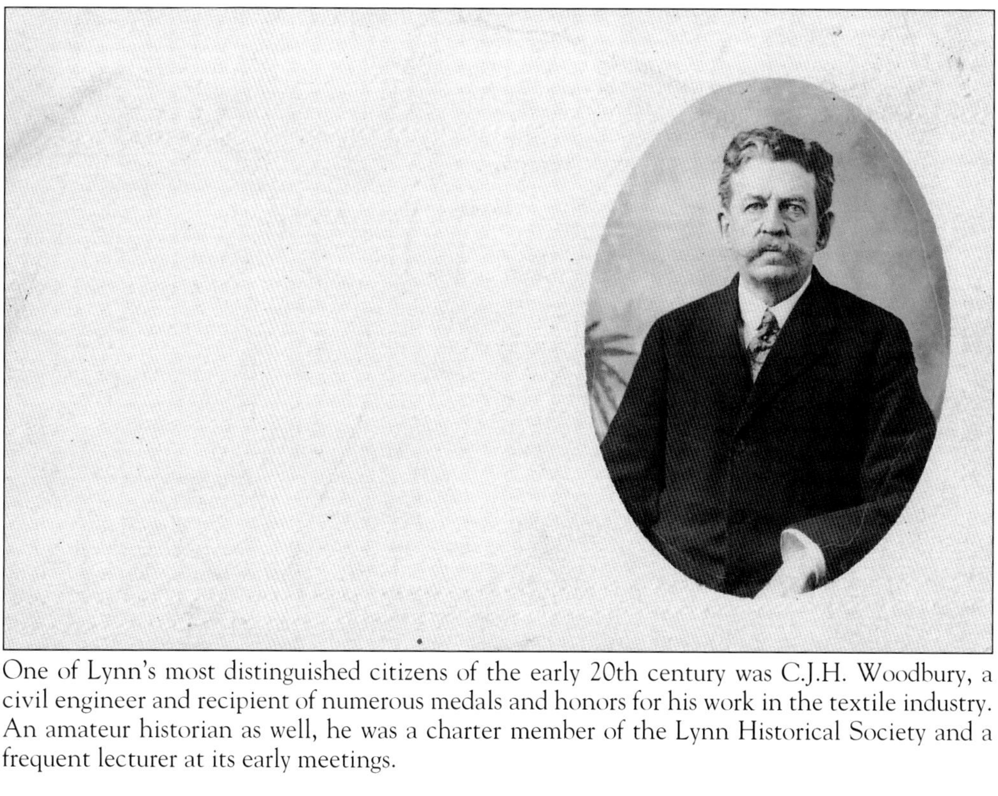

One of Lynn's most distinguished citizens of the early 20th century was C.J.H. Woodbury, a civil engineer and recipient of numerous medals and honors for his work in the textile industry. An amateur historian as well, he was a charter member of the Lynn Historical Society and a frequent lecturer at its early meetings.

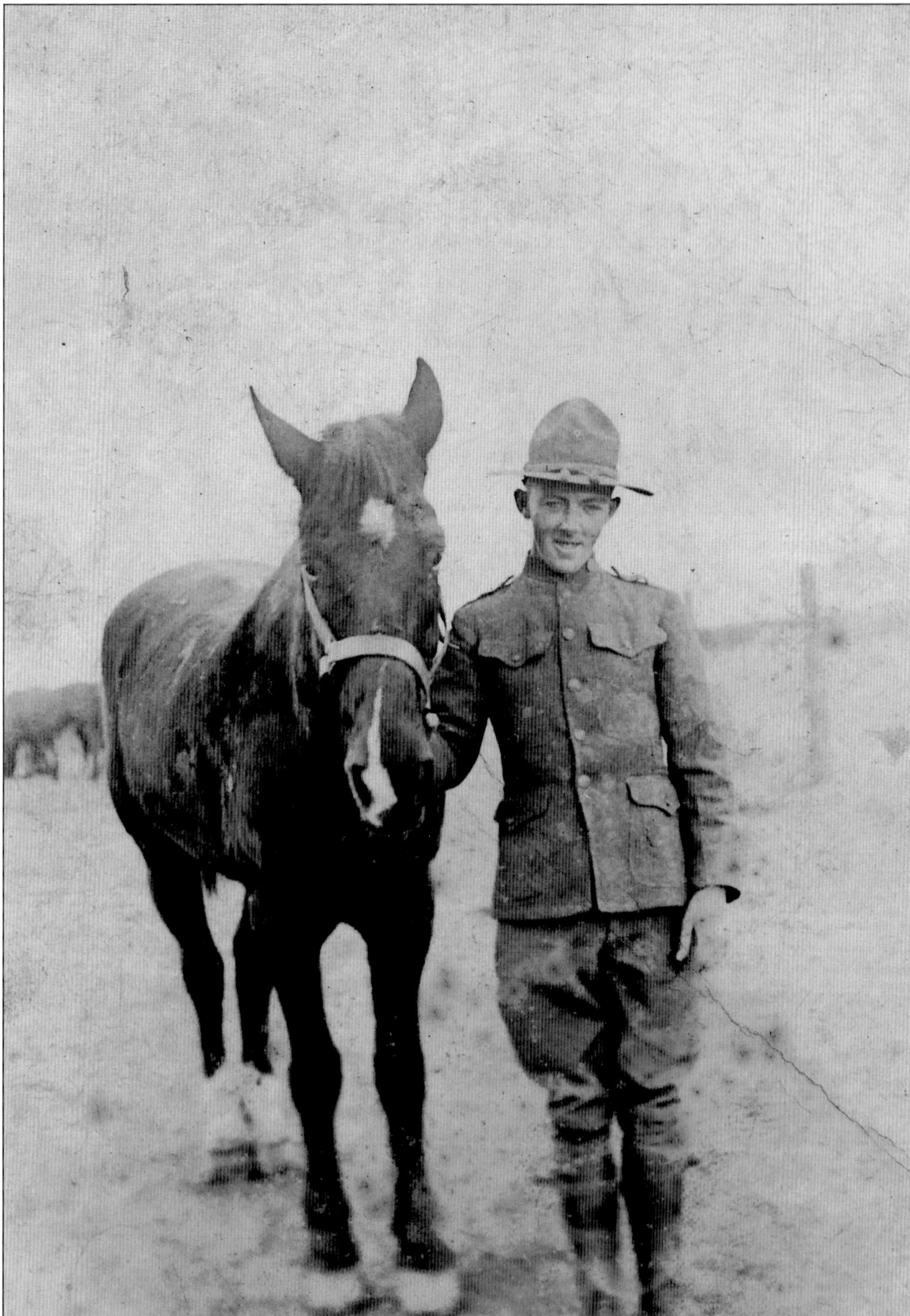

Peter J. O'Connell was one of over six thousand Lynn men who served in the armed forces during World War I. Postcards such as this were no doubt meant to reassure the folks at home that all was well.

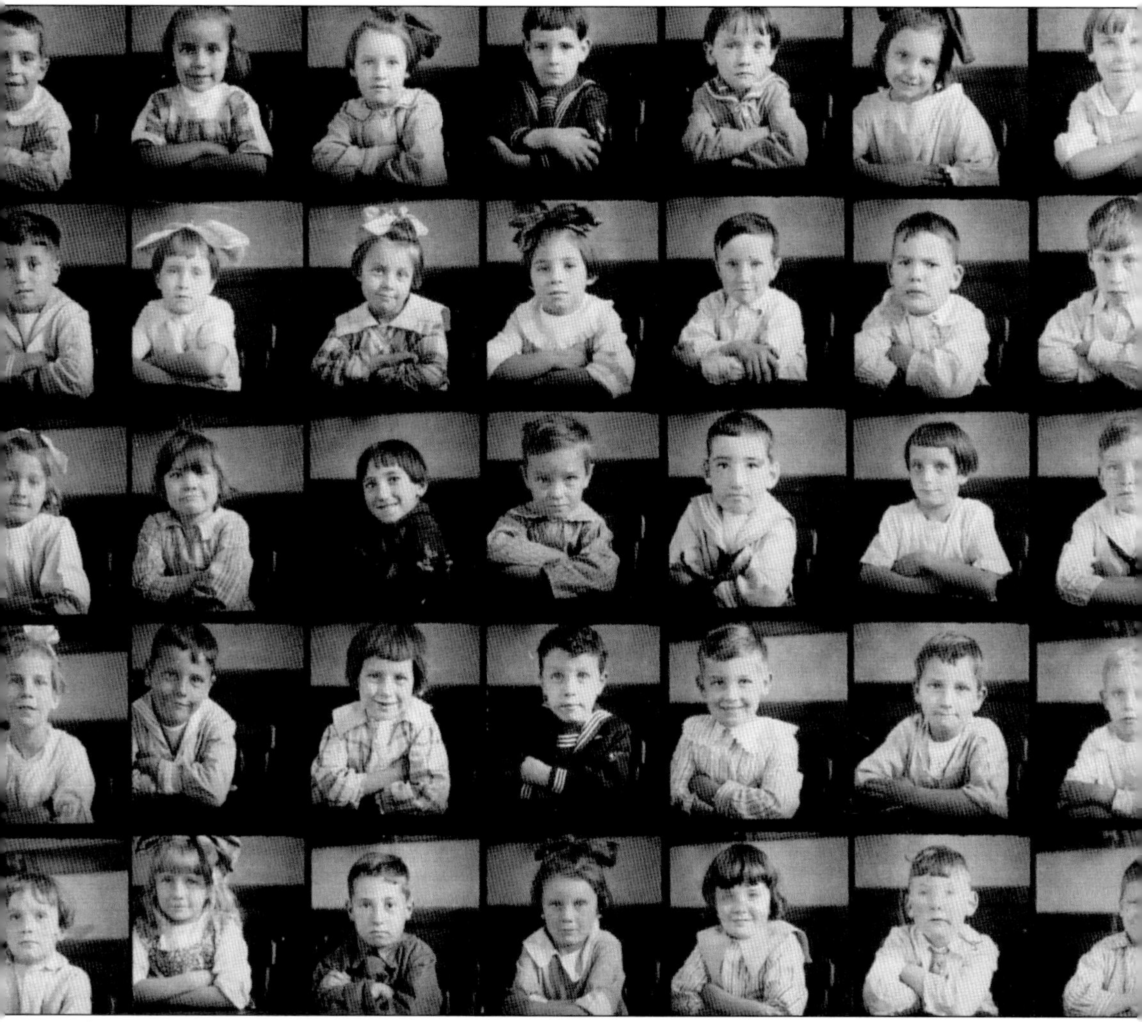

A first-grade class from an unidentified Lynn school faced the camera in 1921.

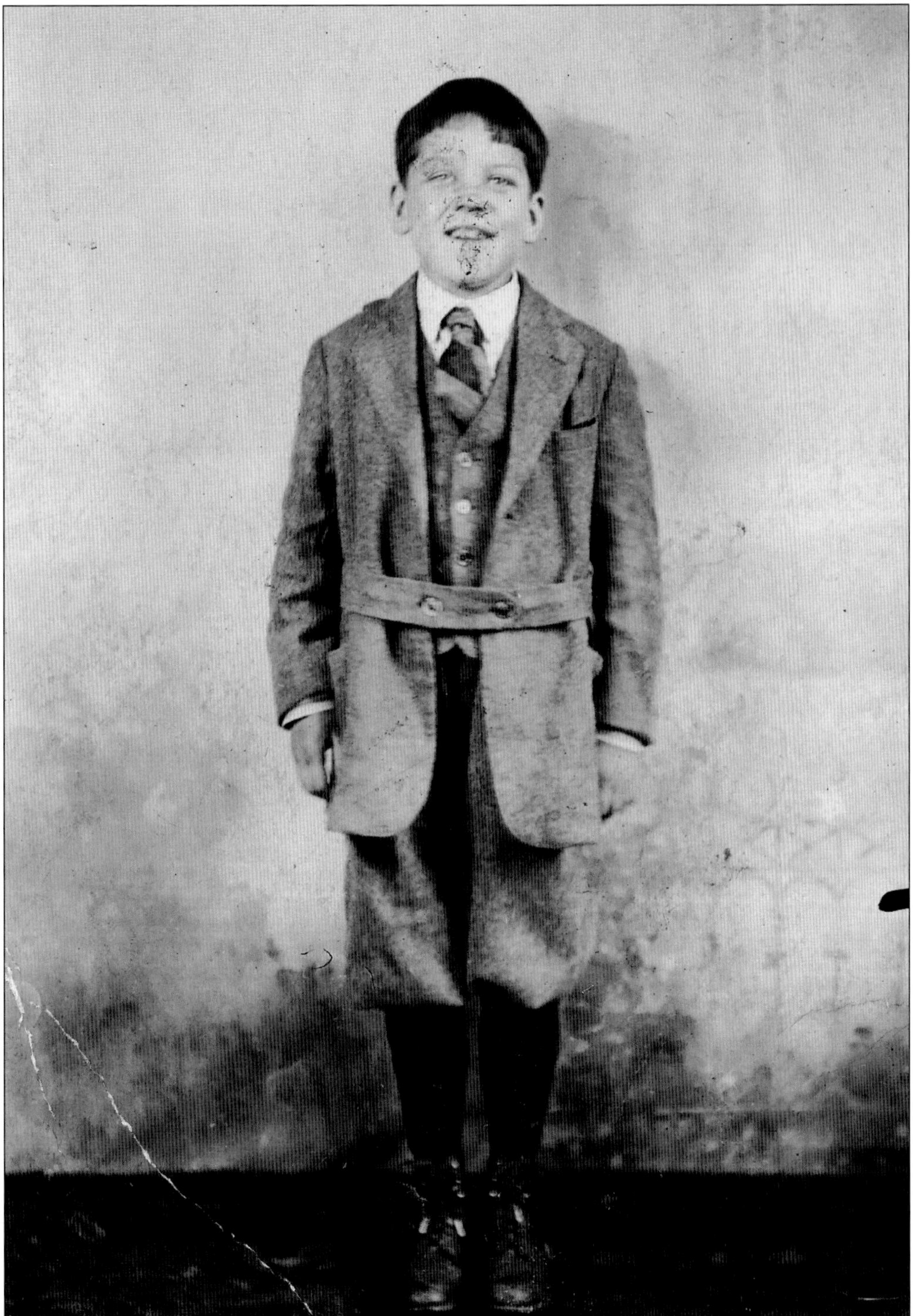

Joseph Schier, a former Lynn policeman, recalled having this photograph taken at Lynn Photo Studio on Market Street about 1924 for no other reason than that he had a new suit of which he was very proud. (Courtesy Stephen Schier.)

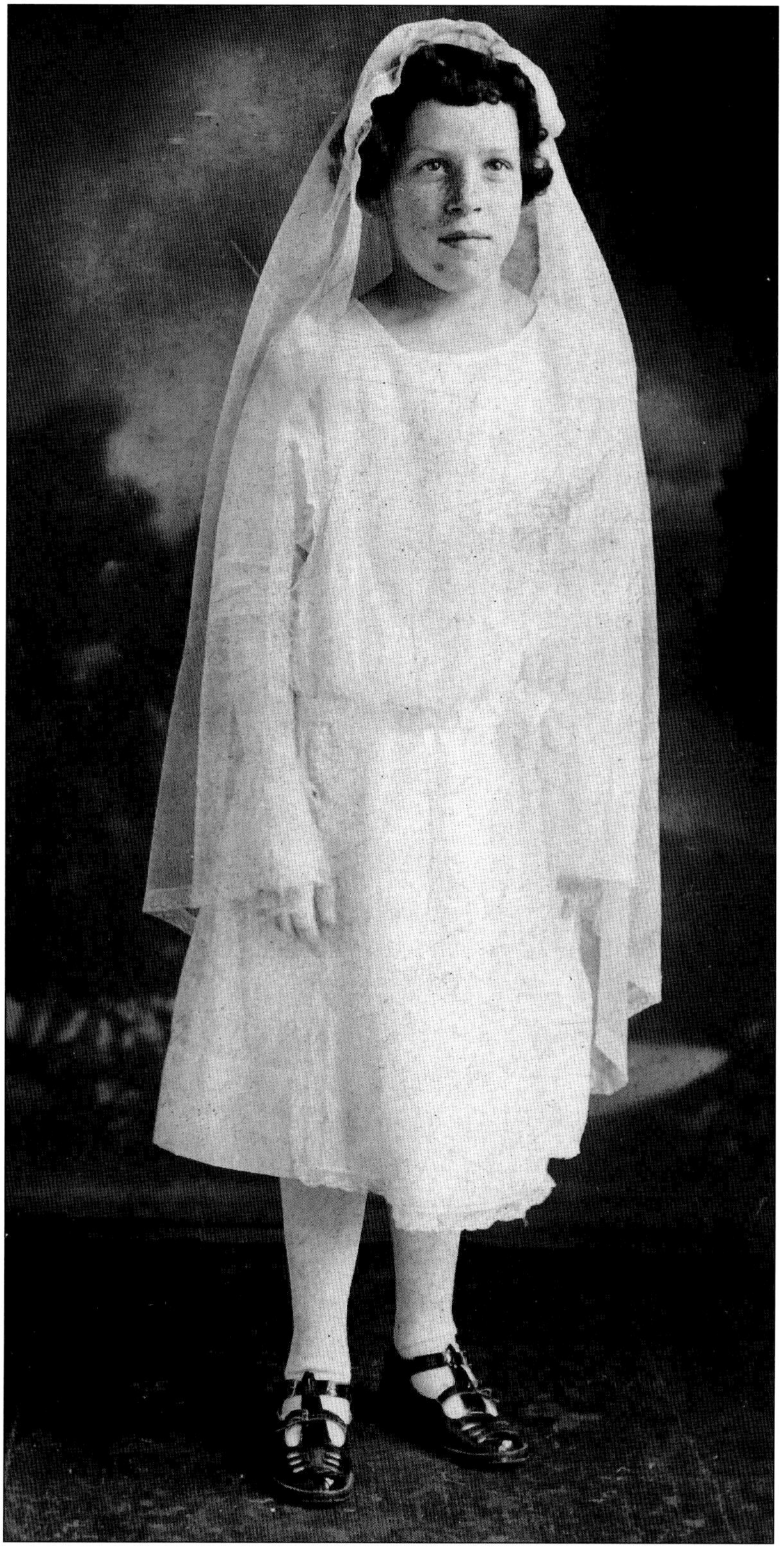

Joseph's sister, Margaret Schier (later Blodgett), wore her first-communion finery in 1922. She attended St. Mary's Grammar School.

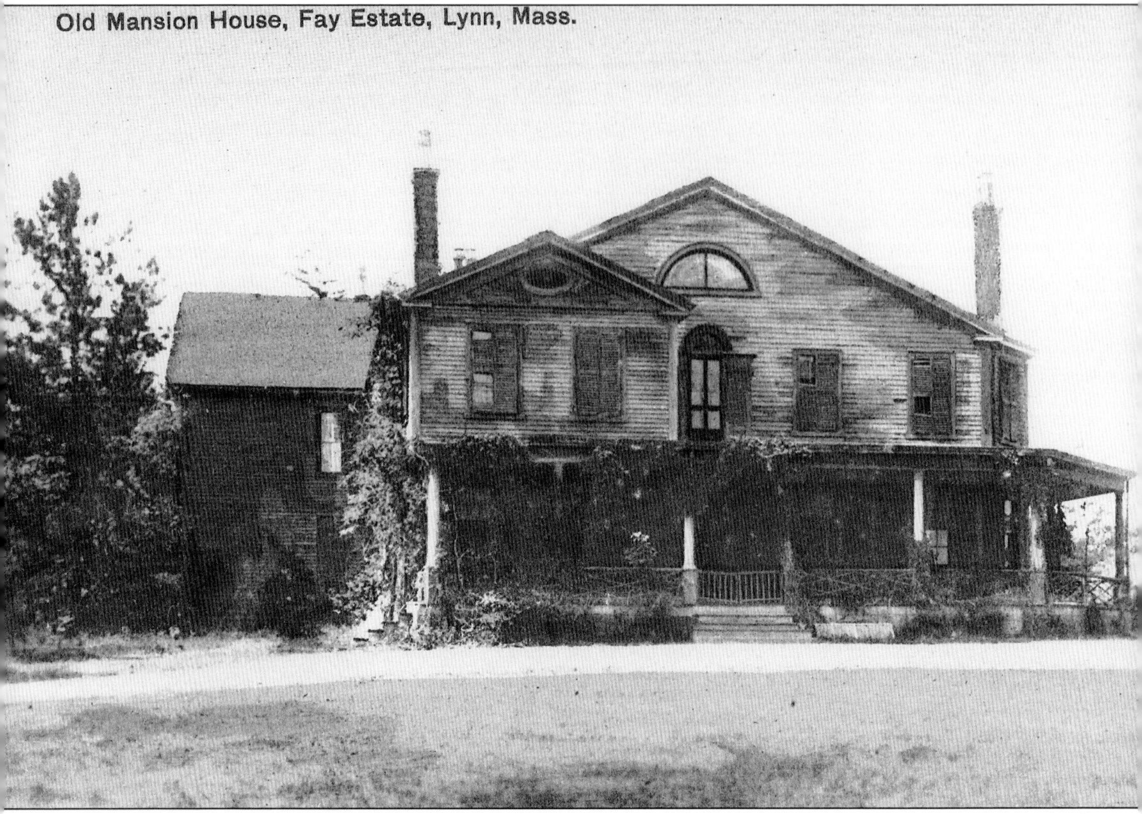

The Mineral Spring Hotel, built in 1810 in Glenmere, was purchased by Richard S. Fay and remodeled into one of the city's most elegant homes. Mr. Fay indulged his passions for gardening, ornamental trees, and sheep farming on his 500-acre estate. The home is seen in its declining years after the death of his widow, Madame Fay. It was torn down in 1916.

Six

CHURCHES AND CLUBS

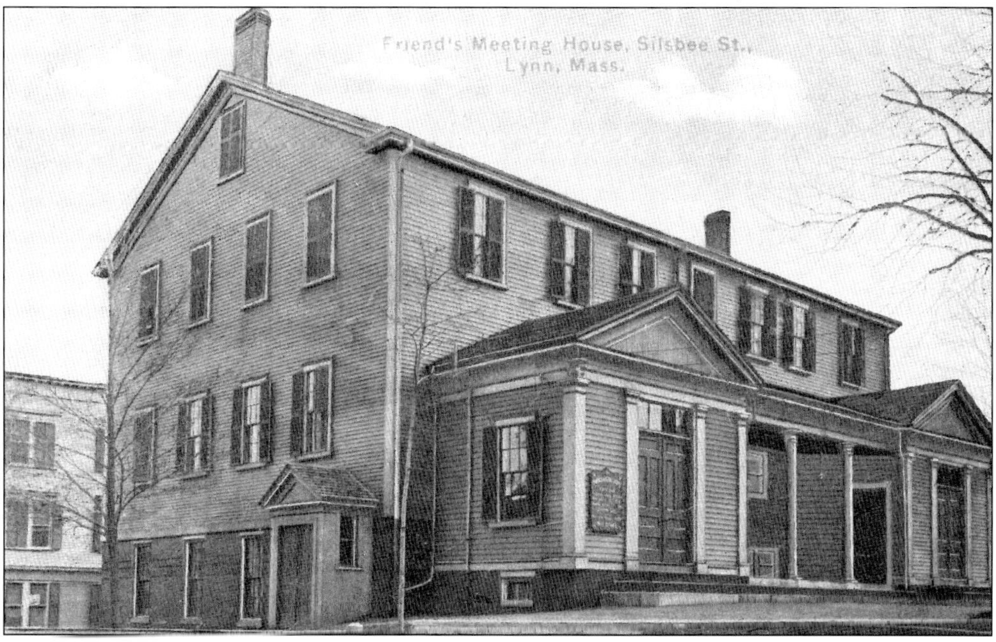

The Society of Friends, or Quakers, established their first meetinghouse in Lynn in 1728 on Broad Street. The building shown here was built in 1816 and used until 1955. During the 19th century, many of Lynn's most prominent businessmen and political leaders belonged to the Friends and the tenets and beliefs of the Society played an important role in Lynn's becoming a center of abolitionism and social reform during the period.

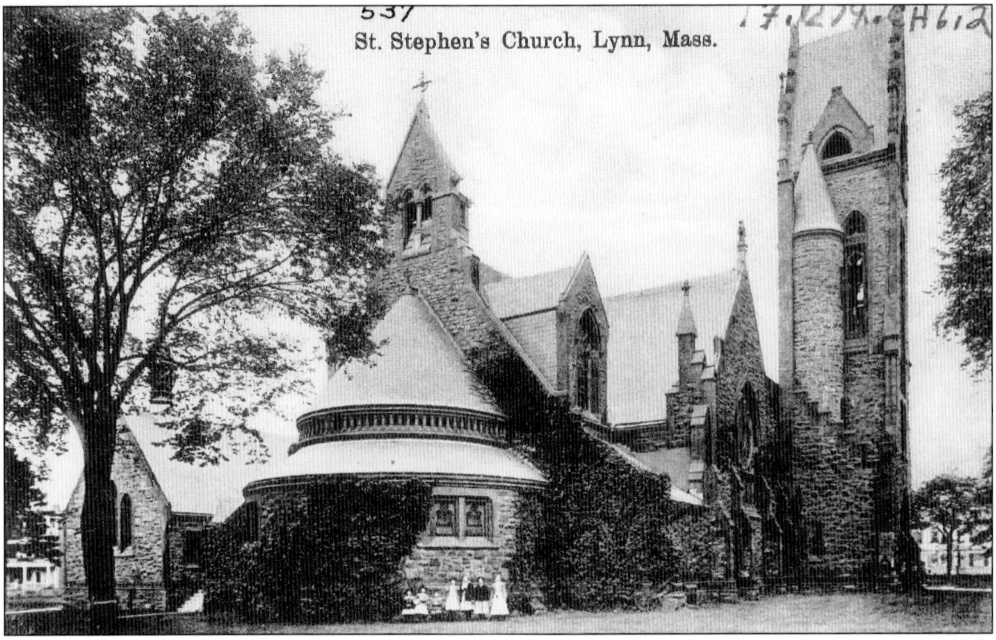

One of Lynn's finest architectural treasures is St. Stephen's Memorial Church. Enoch Reddington Mudge commissioned the building for the parish as a memorial to his son, Lt. Col. Charles R. Mudge, killed at Gettysburg. It was designed by Henry Van Brunt of Boston and is listed on the National Register of Historic Buildings.

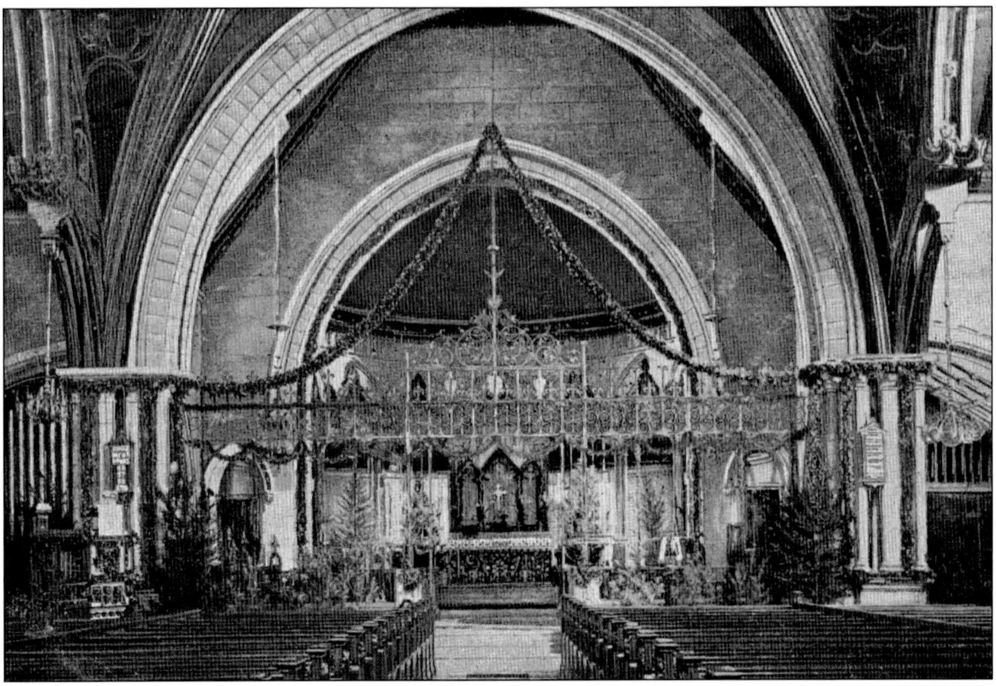

The interior of St. Stephen's is shown decorated for Christmas in 1906. The Episcopal Church was a relatively late comer to Lynn, not establishing regular services here until the 1830s.

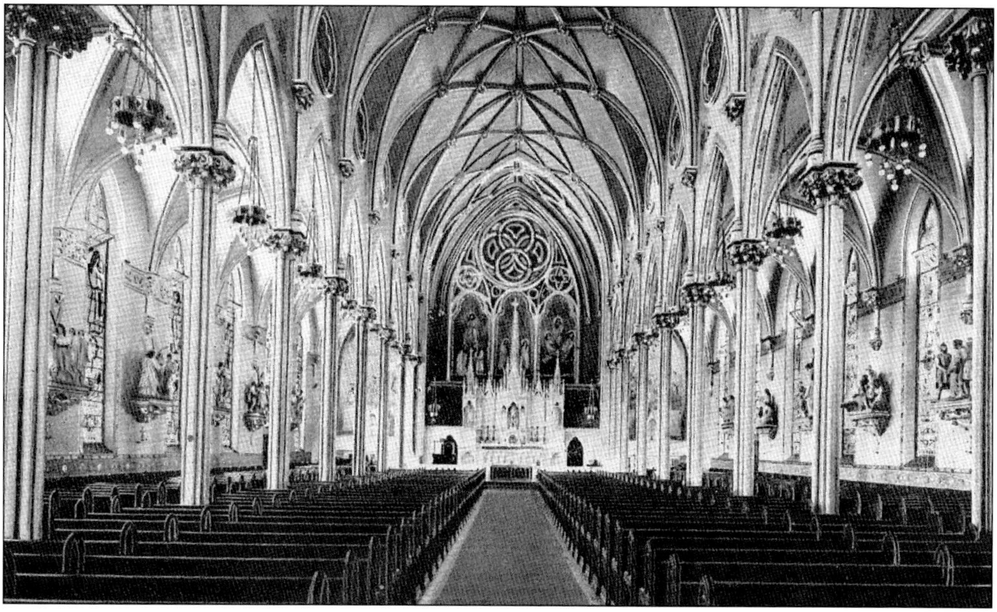

Lynn's first Catholic residents, present at least as early as the 1790s, had to attend services either in the Salem church or in private homes until St. Mary's parish was founded in 1862.

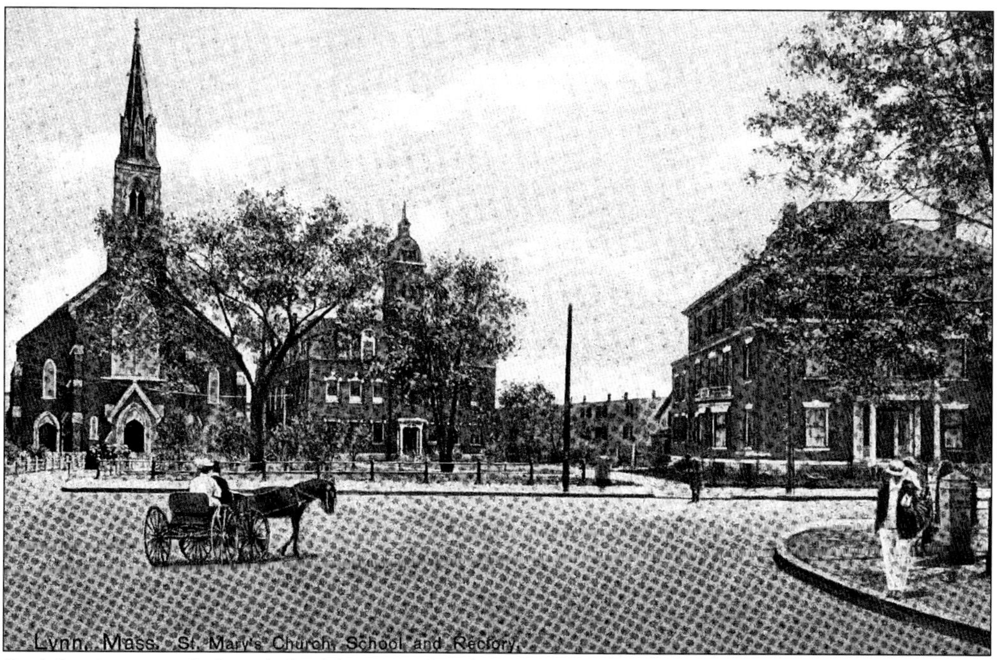

St. Mary's original church building on South Common Street was destroyed by fire in 1941. The present church sits on the same site. The school, to the right, opened in 1880.

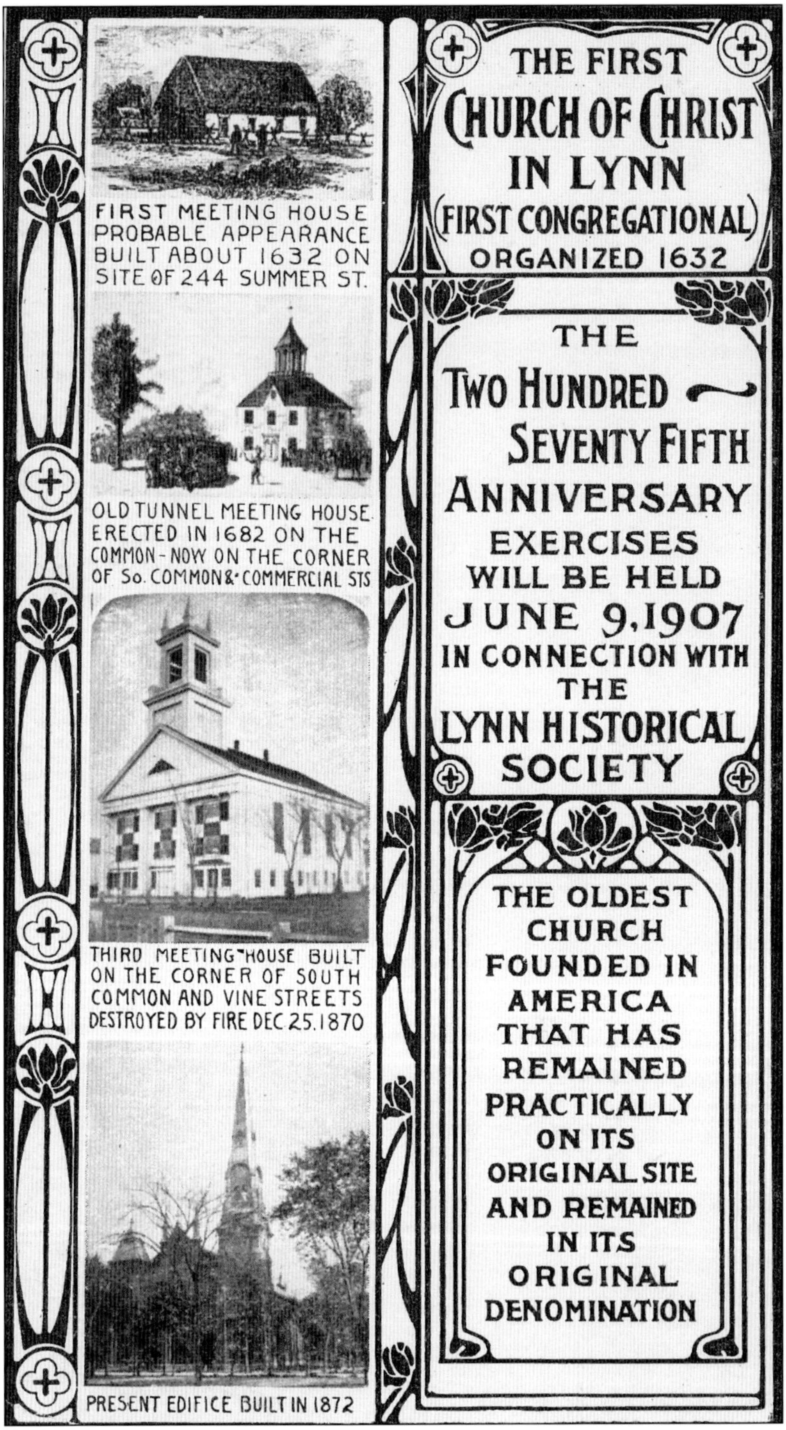

When the meetinghouse of the First Church was built in 1632, it was the site of town meetings and militia drills as well as religious services. This souvenir card from 1907 illustrates the different homes the society has occupied. It is likely that no contemporary likeness was ever made of the first building and the sketch of it is conjectural.

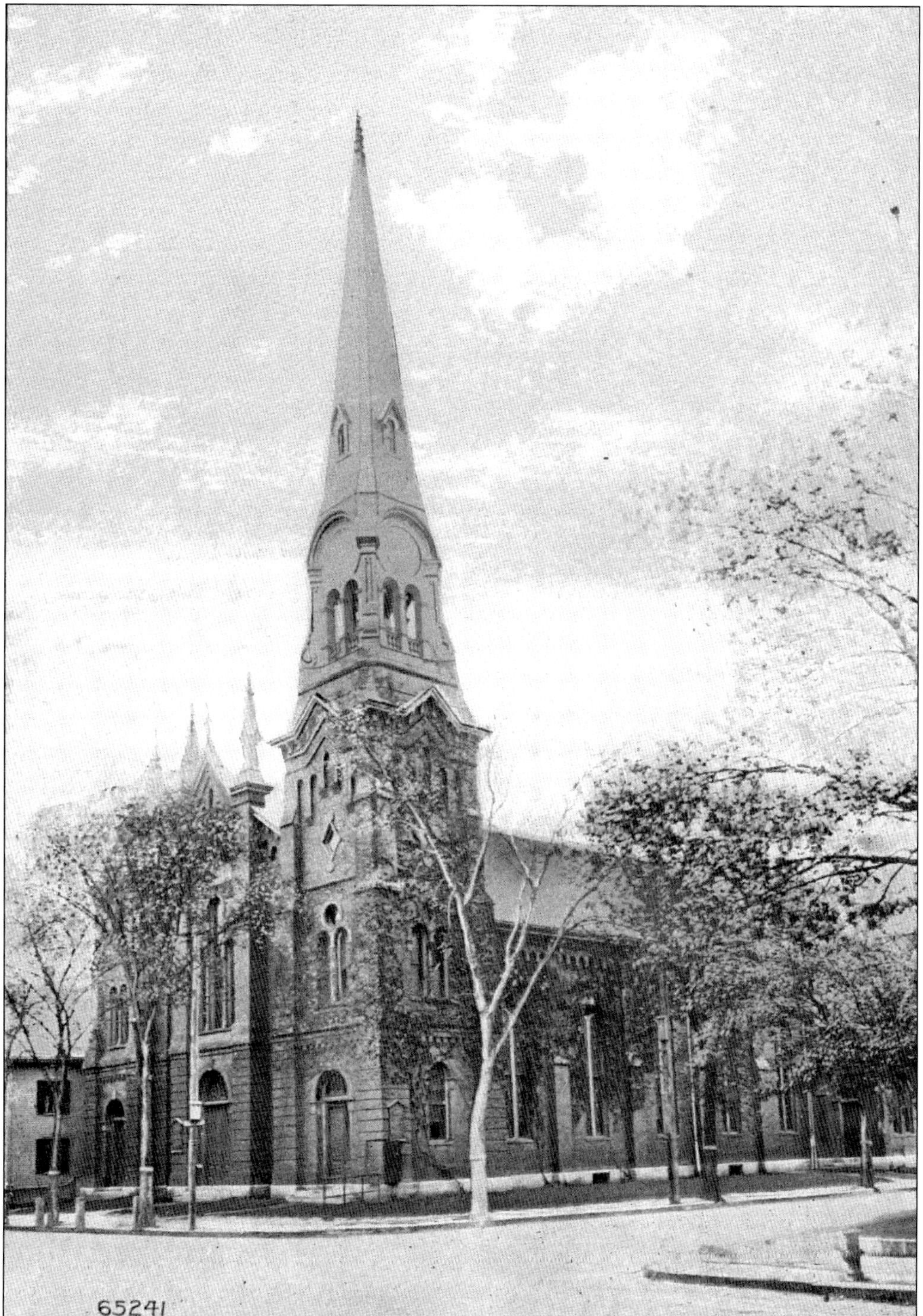

The First Congregational Church at South Common and Vine Streets was built in 1877 after its former edifice burned on Christmas Day in 1870. It served until 1944, when the parish merged with the North Congregational Church. It is headquartered on Lynnfield Street today.

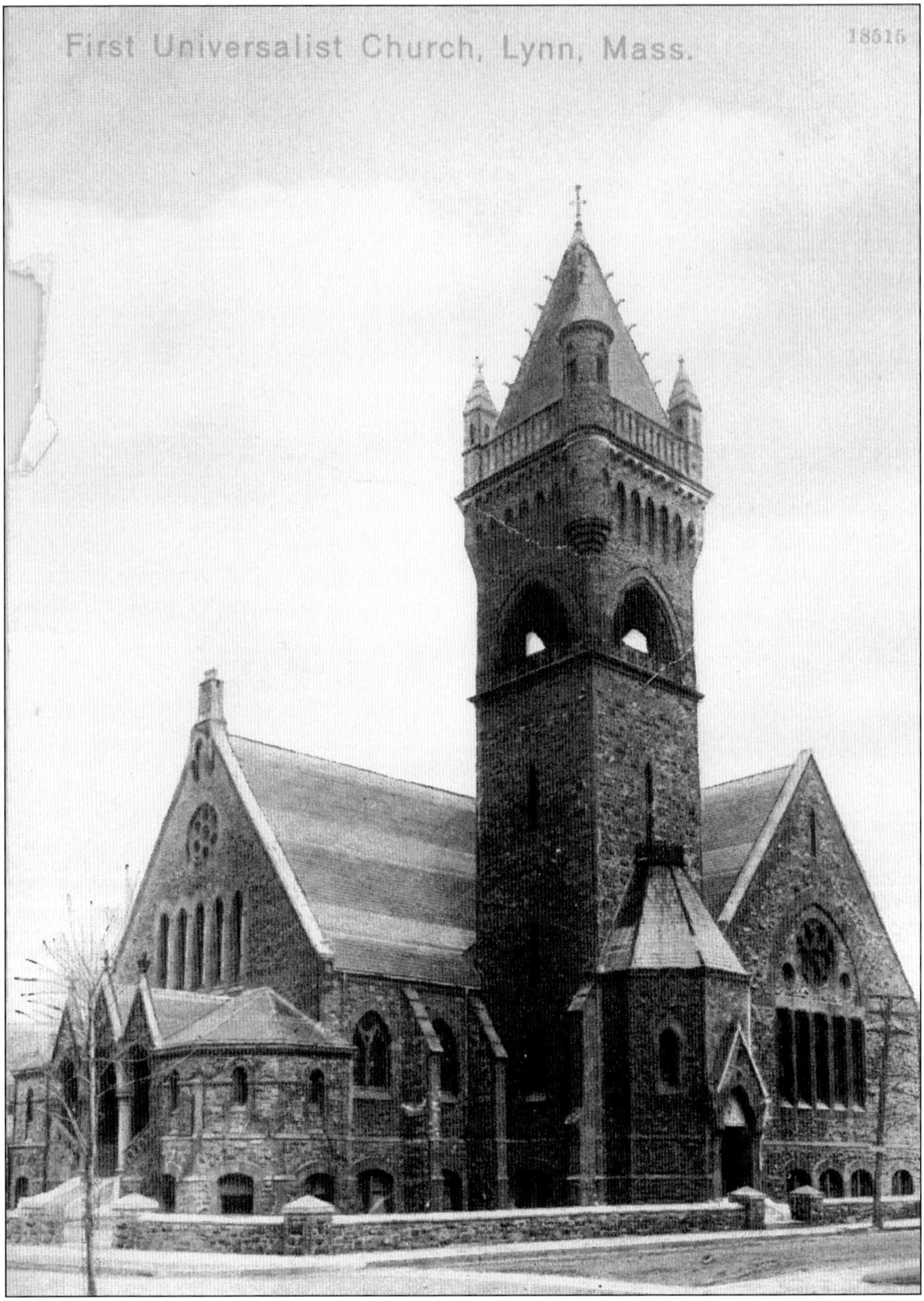

The First Universalist Society was founded in 1833 and was originally located on Union Street. In 1873 this new building on Nahant Street was built, with the tower added in 1887. The society joined with the Universalist Church of Swampscott in 1964 and the Unitarian Church of Lynn in 1966 to form the Unitarian-Universalist Church of Lynn. When the Nahant Street church burned in 1976, the congregation moved to Swampscott.

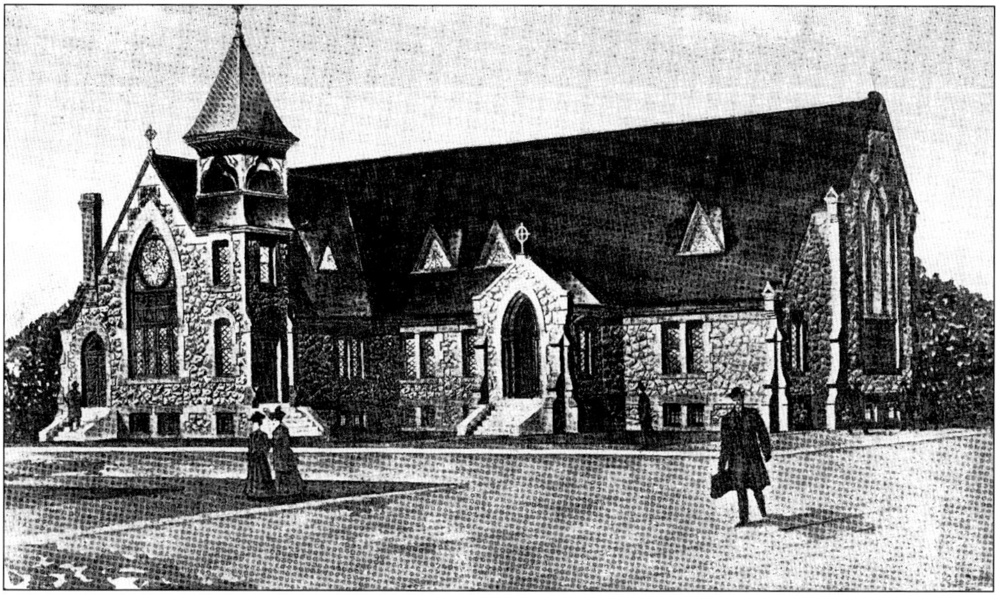

The original chapel of the Church of the Incarnation was built on Estes Street in 1886. The addition, which extends to Broad Street, was added in 1909. Many of Lynn's wealthiest citizens were Episcopalians, and the Incarnation, which was only the second church of that denomination in Lynn, served both permanent and summer residents of the Diamond District.

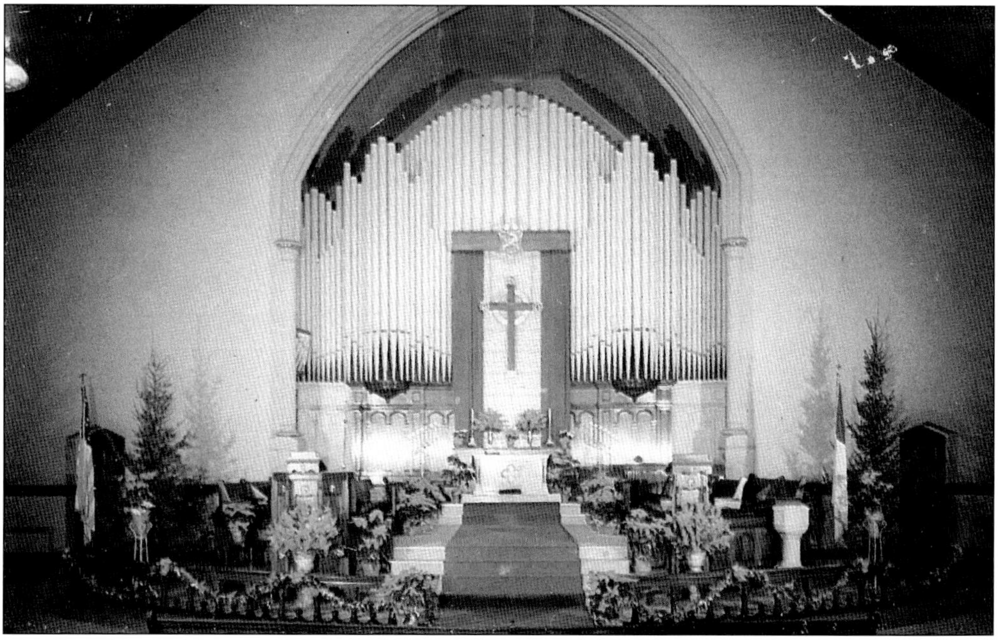

The first Methodist church in Massachusetts was established by Jesse Lee in Lynn in 1791. This is a 1960s view of the interior of the congregation's third home, which stood at City Hall Square from 1878 until it was destroyed by fire in 1972.

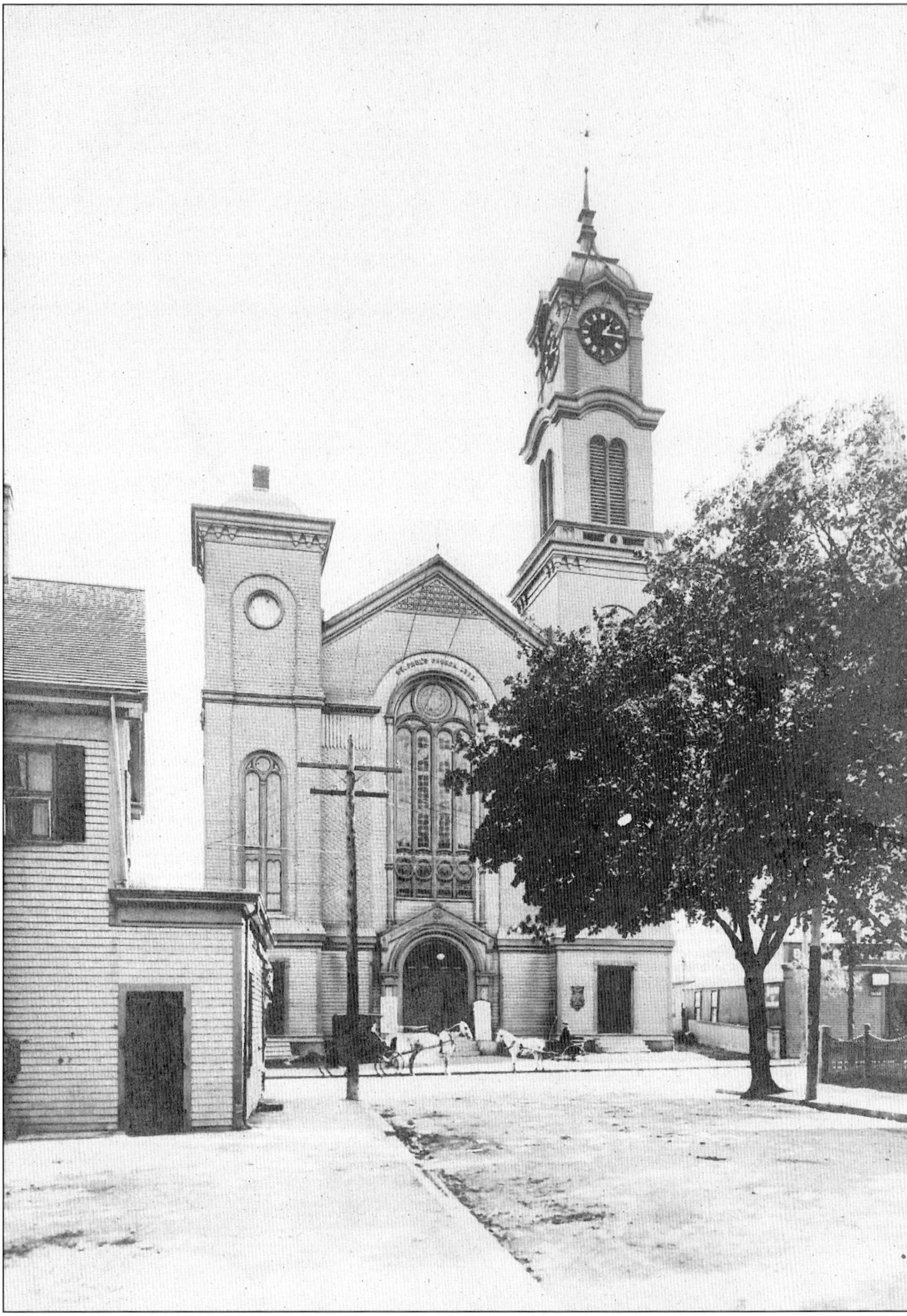

Founded in 1811, St. Paul's was the second Methodist church established in Lynn. The Union Street edifice shown here *c.* 1905 was built in 1864 to replace the original church, which had burned in 1859. The new church was itself destroyed by a 1968 blaze. That same year, St. Paul's and the First Methodist Church joined to form Christ Church United Methodist.

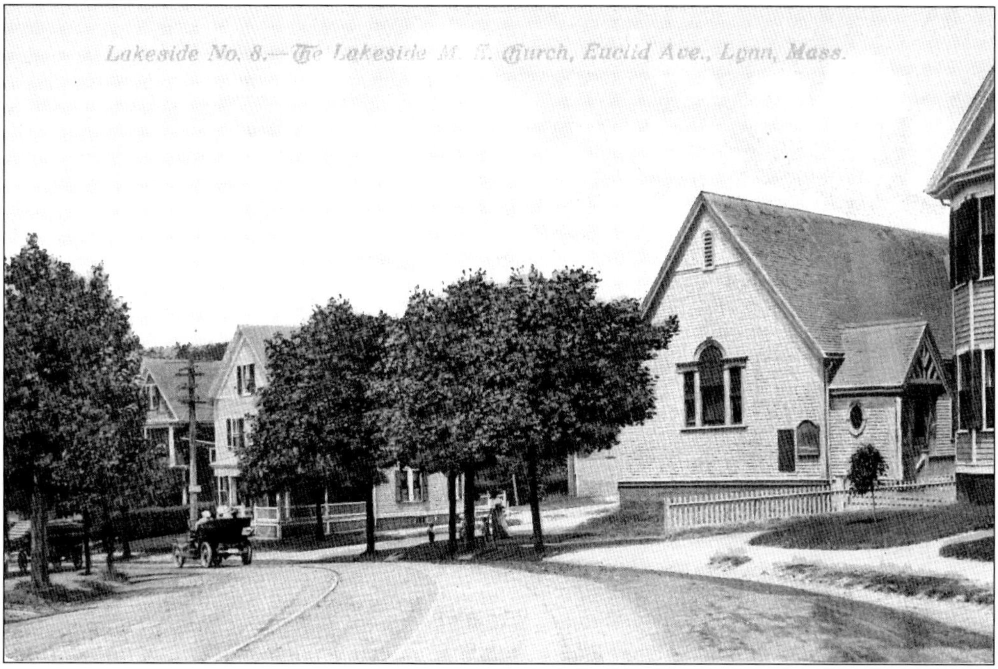

The Lakeside Methodist Episcopal Church on Euclid Avenue, seen here *c.* 1910, was organized in 1893 to serve the needs of that growing part of the city.

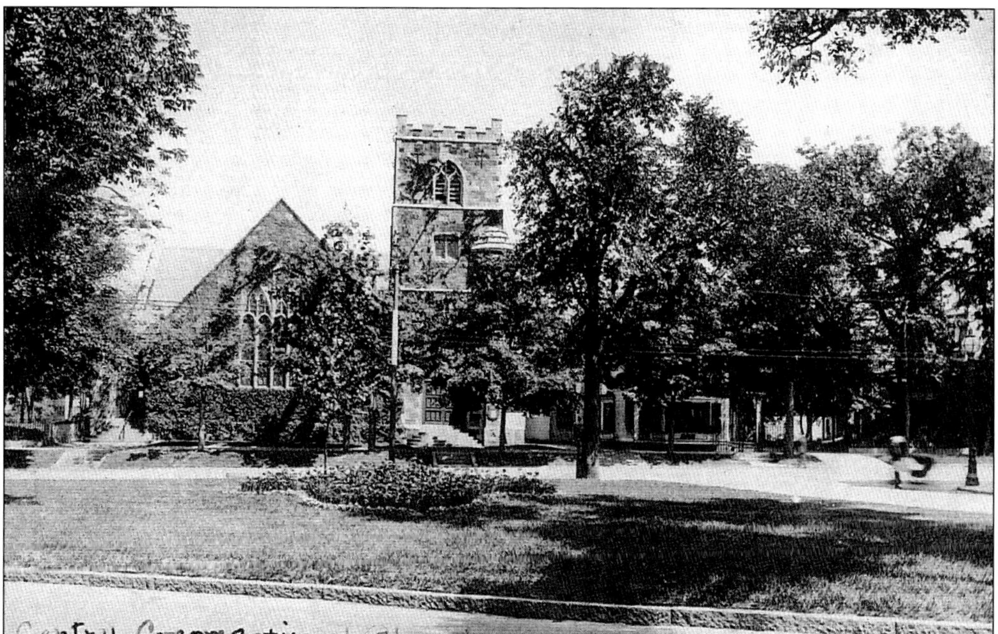

After twice losing their home to fire, the Central Congregational Church built the edifice on Broad Street that it still occupies. The society was founded in 1850 to serve the central district.

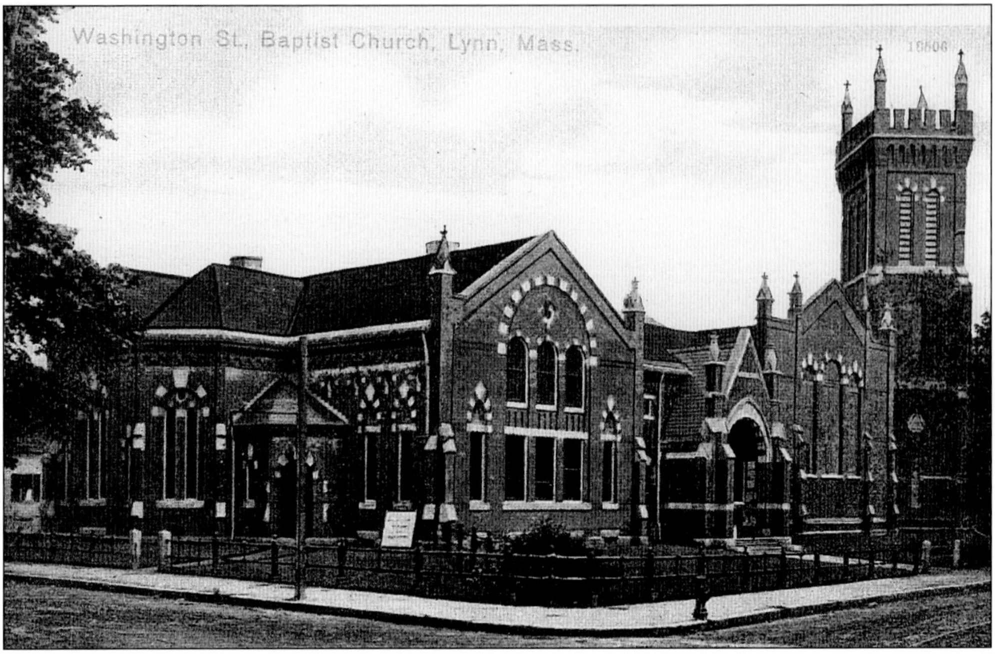

The Baptist faith was represented in Lynn as early as 1651 but its first practitioners were fined for what the established church considered their "erroneous" opinions. By the time of this photograph in 1910, there were six Baptist churches flourishing. Like so many other societies, the Washington Street Baptist Church had lost an earlier home to fire.

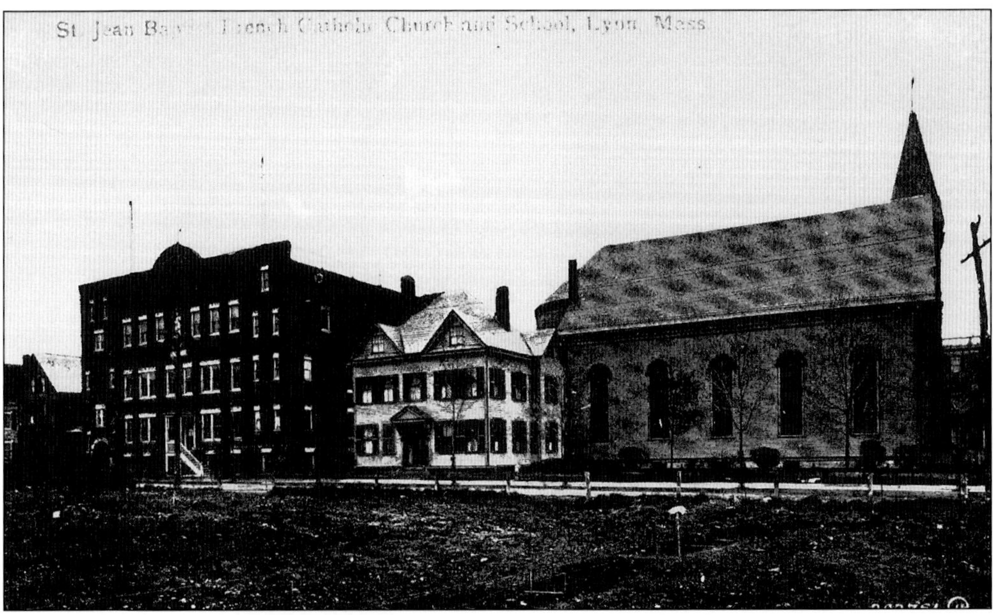

The St. Jean-Baptiste Church was founded in 1886 to accommodate the large influx of French-Canadian immigrants. The original church on Franklin Street was in use for over one hundred years until the parish closed in 1996.

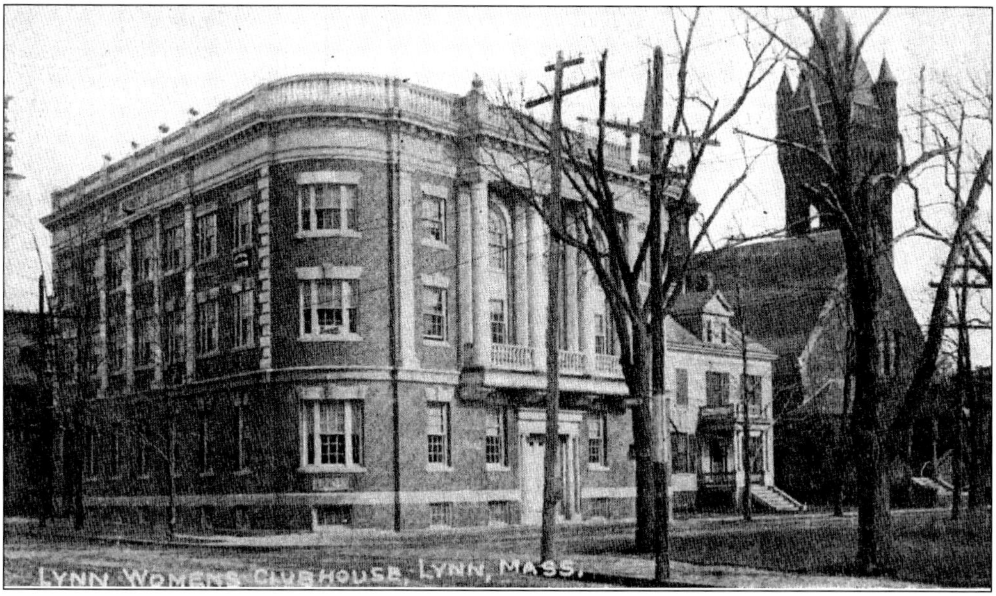

The Lynn Women's Clubhouse Corporation was founded in 1904 to establish a common headquarters for Lynn's numerous and active women's clubs. The design was by New York architect Josephine Chapman and is still in use today as Girls, Inc. The rather unpleasantly named White Plague Exposition referred to on the card was in fact a citywide fund-raiser for tuberculosis research.

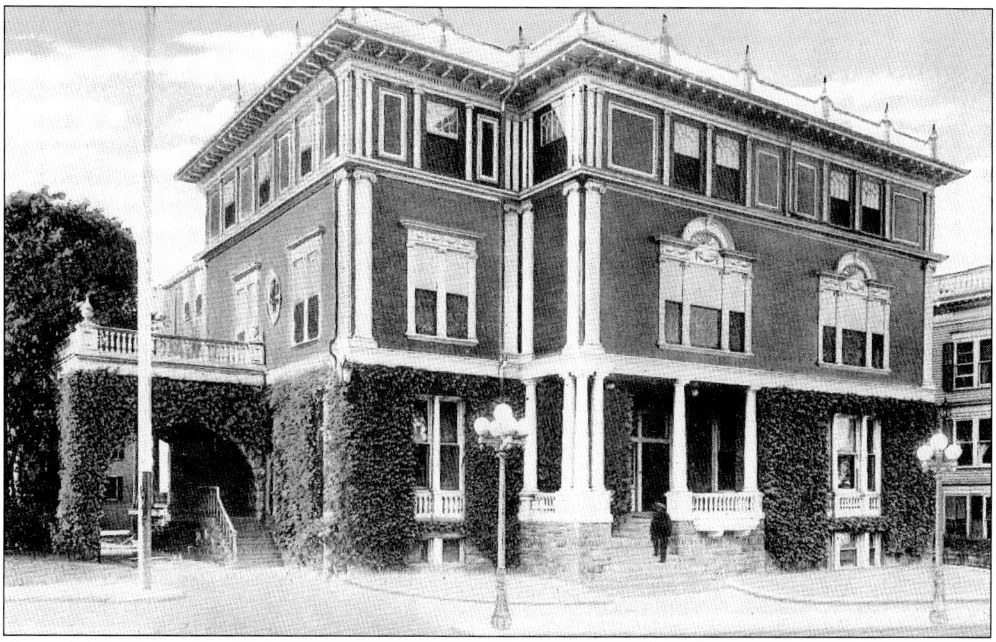

One of the premier private men's clubs of the state, the Oxford Club was a fixture at Washington Square for 80 years. The club's membership, which was drawn chiefly from among Lynn's wealthiest citizens, peaked in the 1920s, just about the time of the stock market crash.

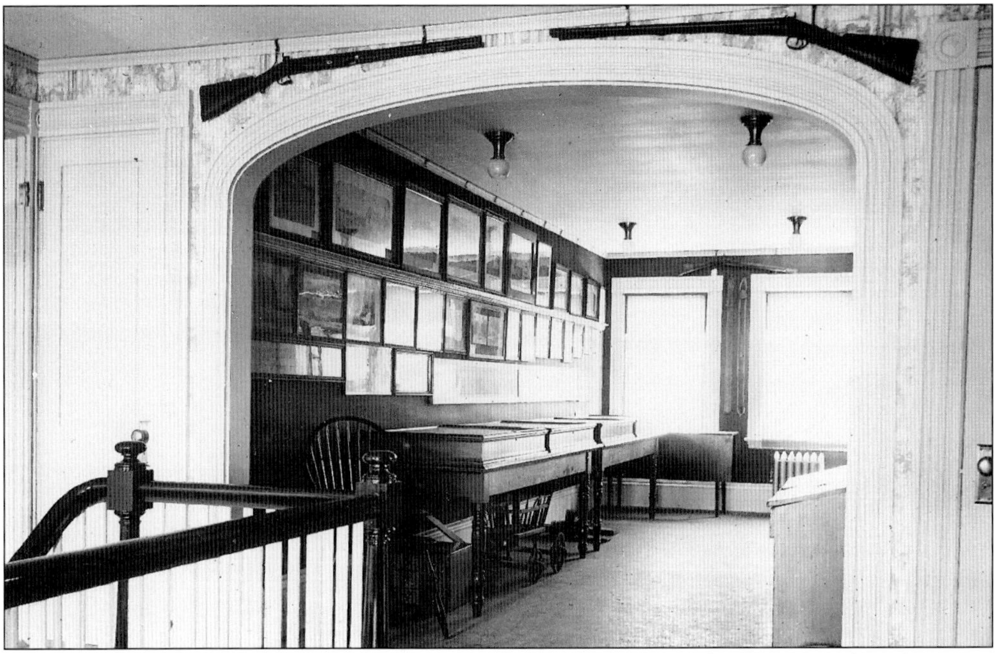

After having rented rooms at various locations, the Lynn Historical Society purchased its own headquarters in 1913. The second floor of the Hyde-Mills house at 125 Green Street has been converted to exhibit space in this 1915 view.

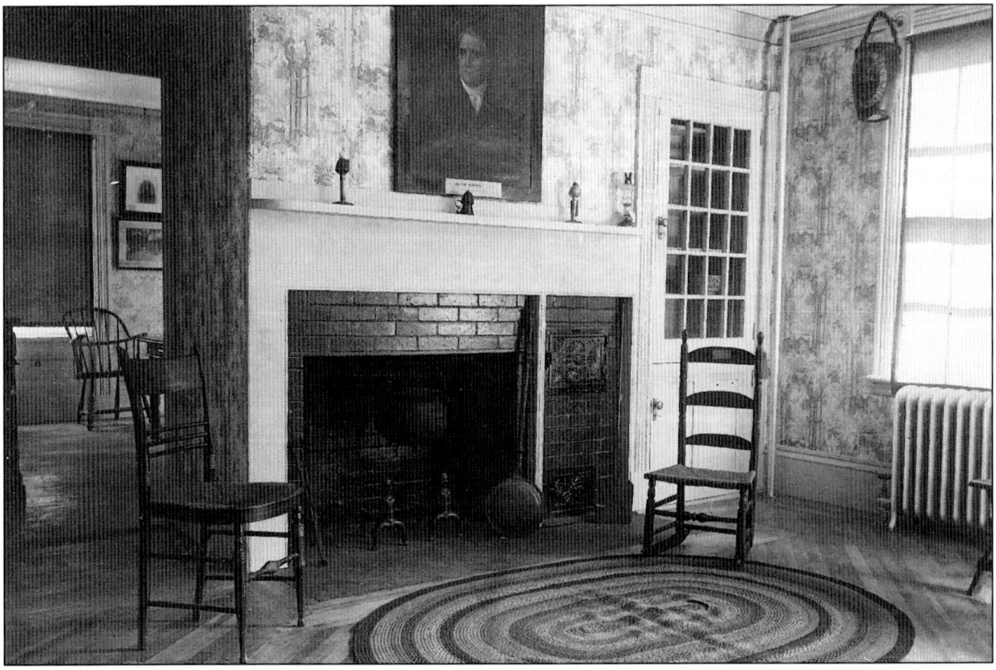

This cozy, hearthside arrangement is very characteristic of what the public expected to see displayed at a local historical society. This room is now the society's meeting hall.

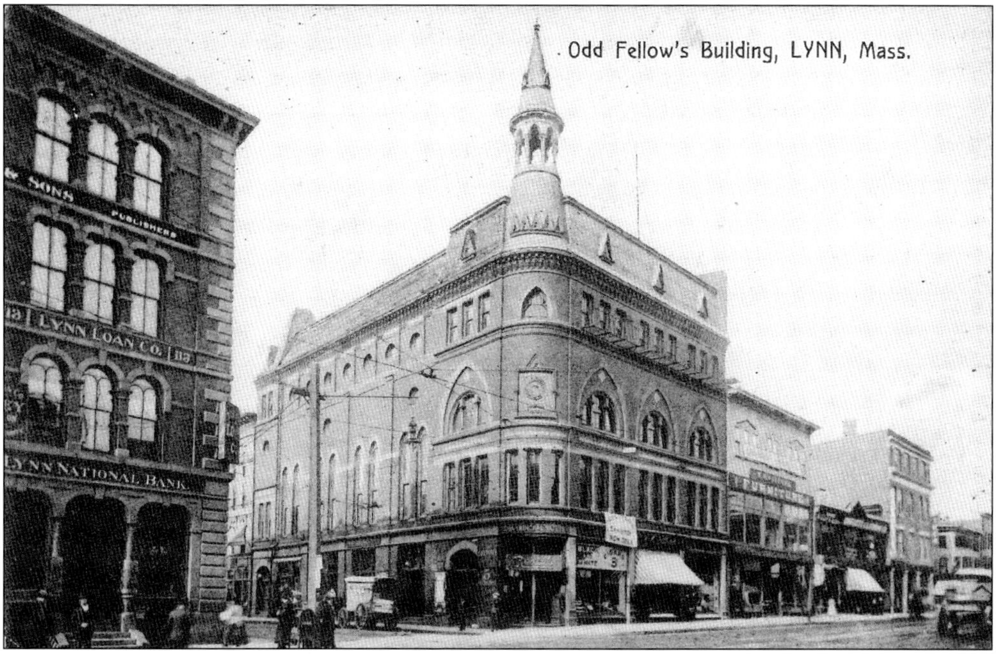

One of several elaborate homes constructed by the various lodges of the benevolent society, the Odd Fellows building stood at the corner of Market and Summer Streets from 1871 to 1964. This view is from 1909. (Conway collection.)

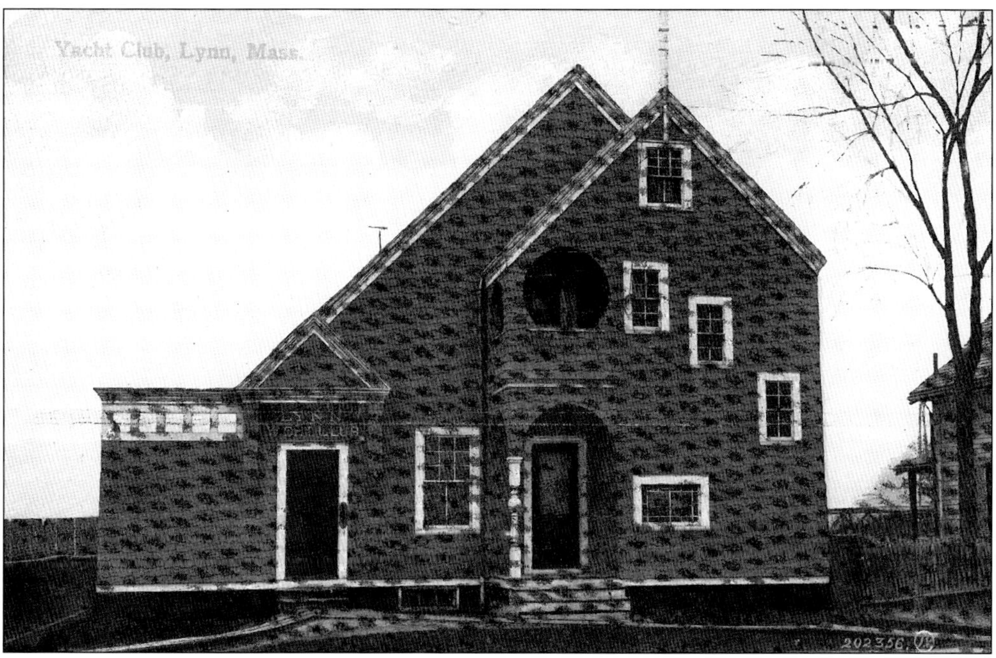

The Lynn Yacht Club has been active since 1870. This early clubhouse on Washington Street, shown here in 1915, was demolished when the Lynnway was built.

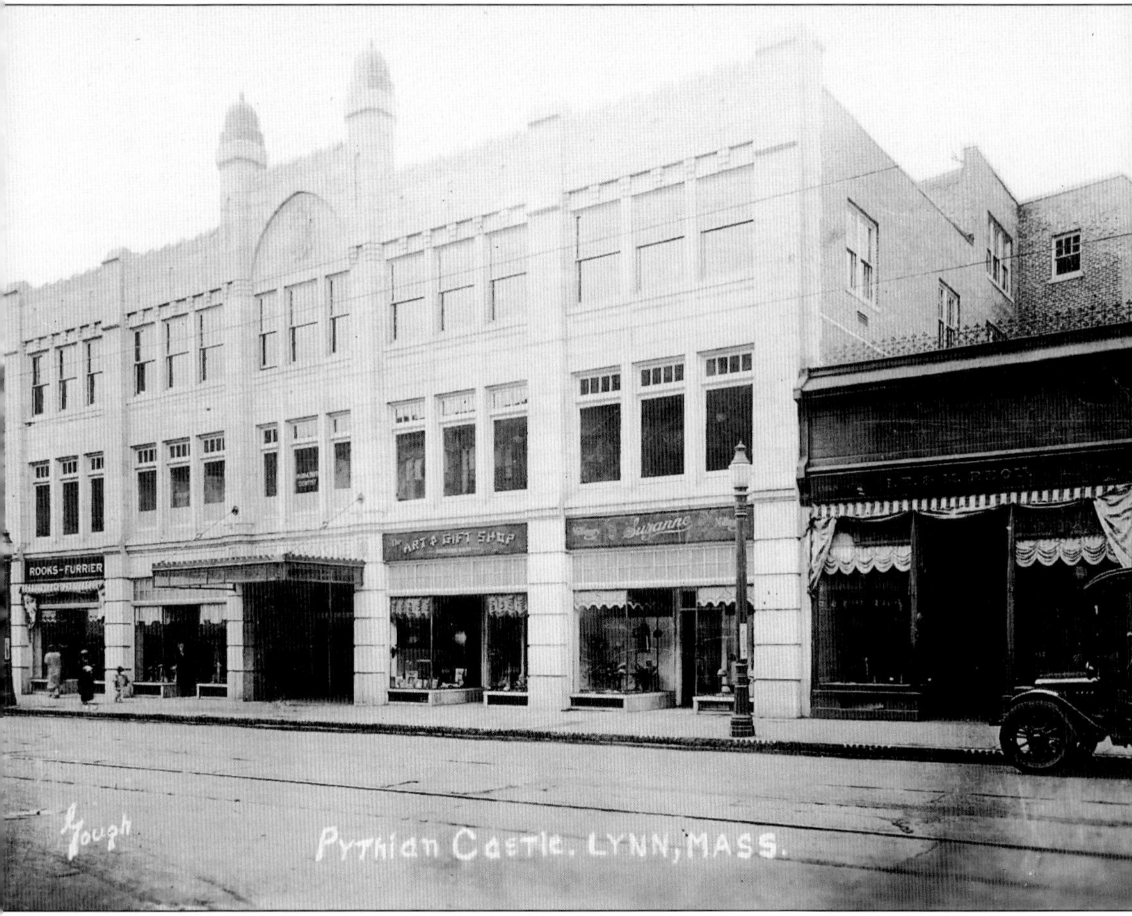

The Knights of Pythias was formed in the wake of the Civil War to "revive the spirit of fraternity in the hearts of the men of America." By 1926, when the Pythian Castle was built on Market Street, Lynn had 11 lodges, including two designated as "colored."

Seven

THE BUSINESS OF LYNN

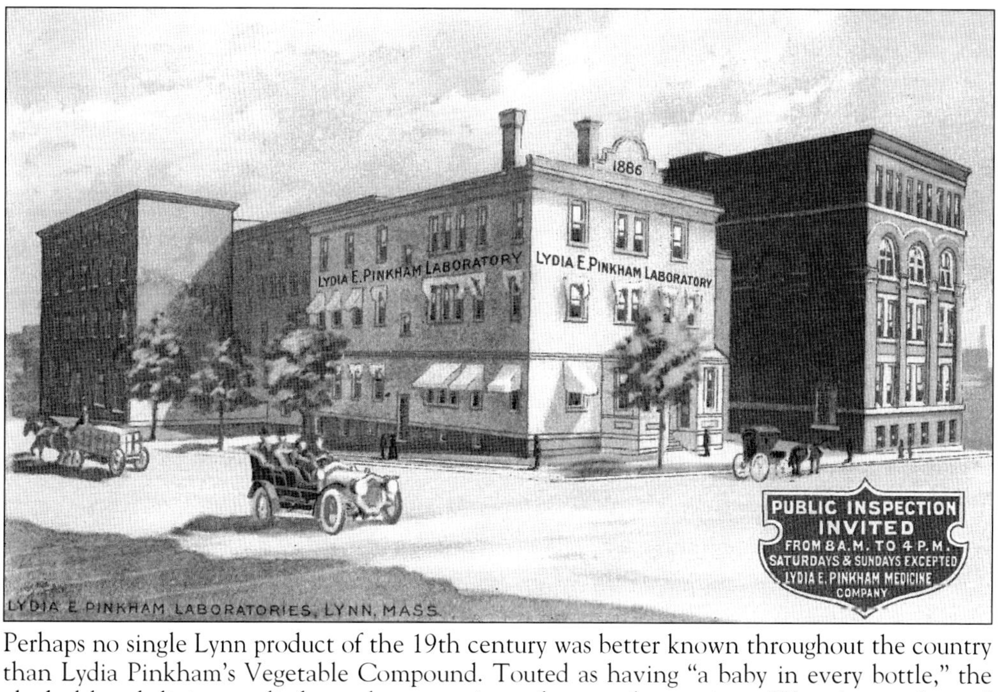

Perhaps no single Lynn product of the 19th century was better known throughout the country than Lydia Pinkham's Vegetable Compound. Touted as having "a baby in every bottle," the alcohol-laced elixir was relied upon by generations of women for a variety of "female complaints." The Pinkham building is still standing on Western Avenue, although the company moved out of Lynn in 1972. (Conway collection.)

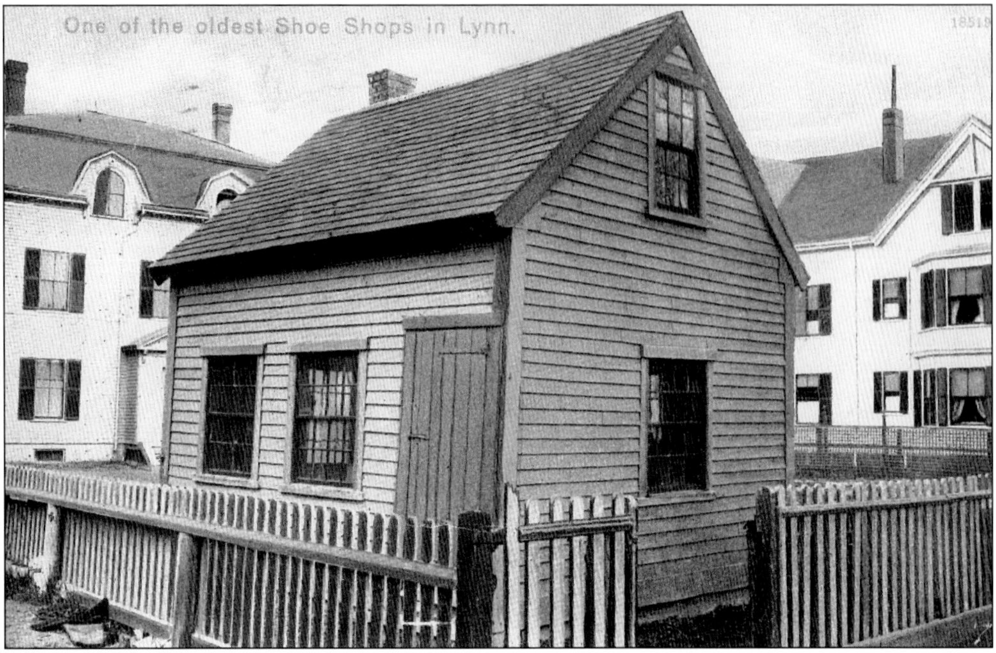

Ten-footer shops such as this one once dotted Lynn's landscape in the days when shoes were made by hand and most Lynn farmers spent at least part of the year engaged in the trade. The shop shown here, which once stood on Mall Street but is now at the Peabody- Essex Museum in Salem, belonged to Joseph Lye. Lye left behind an extraordinarily detailed series of diaries that offer great insight into the activities of an early-19th-century shoemaker.

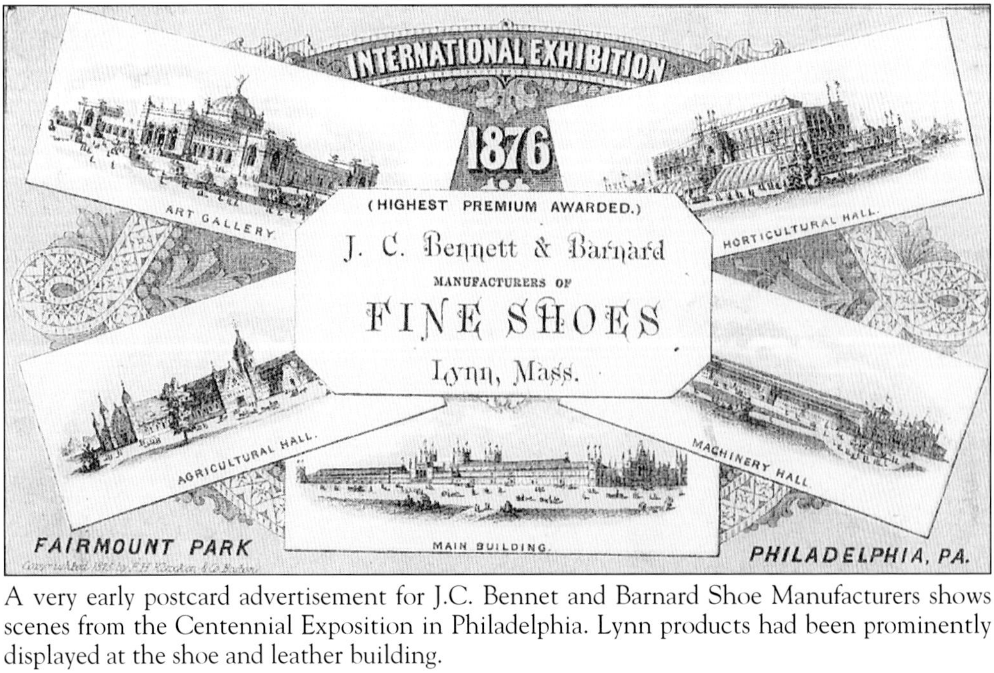

A very early postcard advertisement for J.C. Bennet and Barnard Shoe Manufacturers shows scenes from the Centennial Exposition in Philadelphia. Lynn products had been prominently displayed at the shoe and leather building.

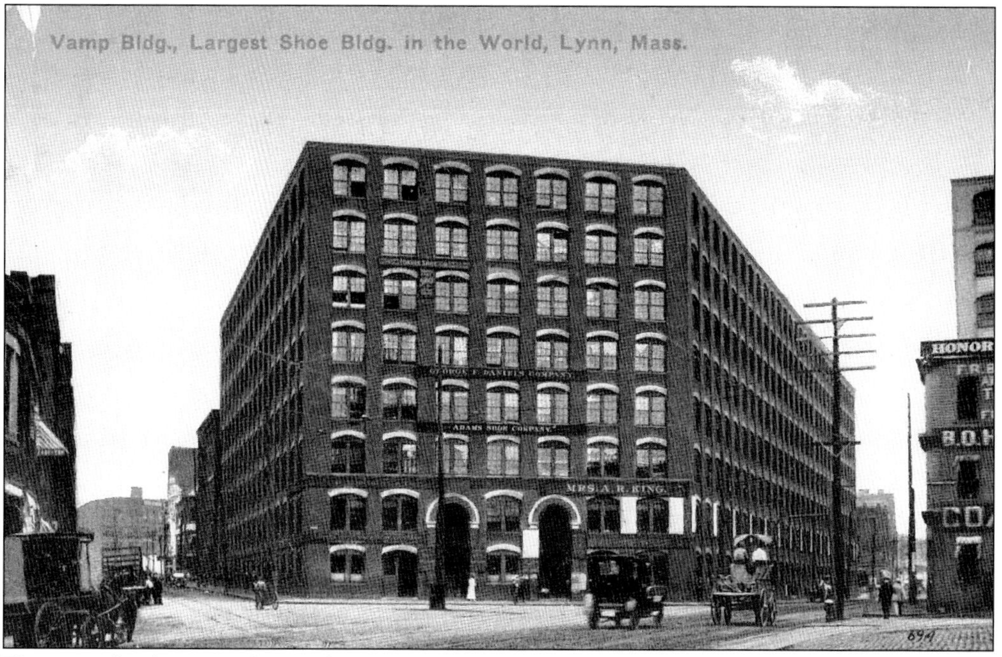

The growth of Lynn's shoe industry over the 19th century is reflected in the Vamp building. Constructed in 1903 and enlarged in 1907 to relieve Lynn's chronic shortage of factory space, it was the largest factory in the world devoted solely to shoe manufacturing.

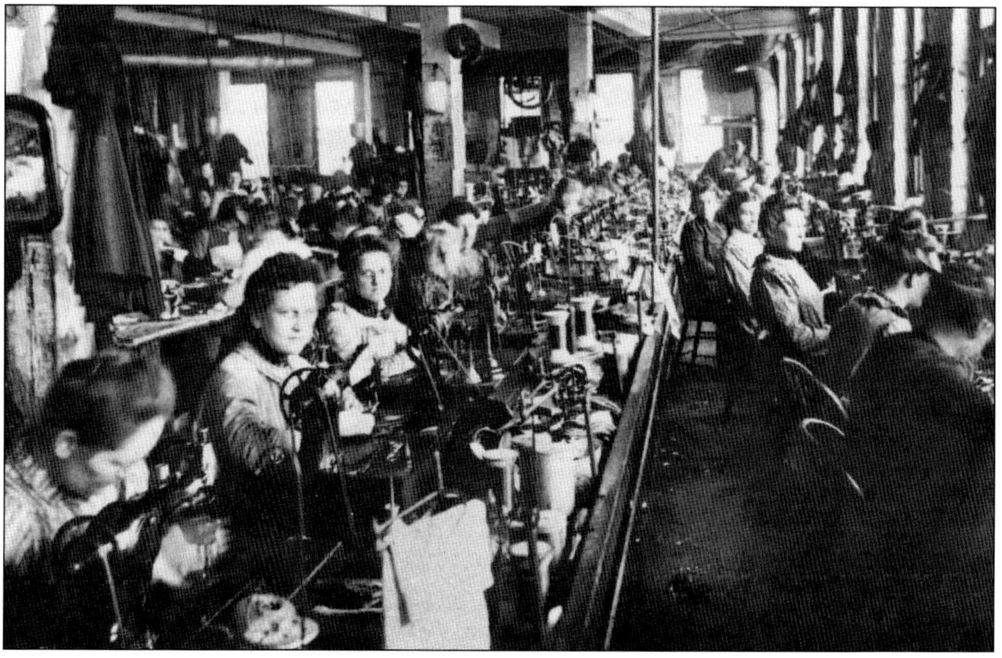

The stitching room at the Brophy Shoe Company illustrates the crowded working conditions as well as the fact that tasks in the shoe factory were generally divided by gender. This 1890 view has been reproduced on a modern postcard.

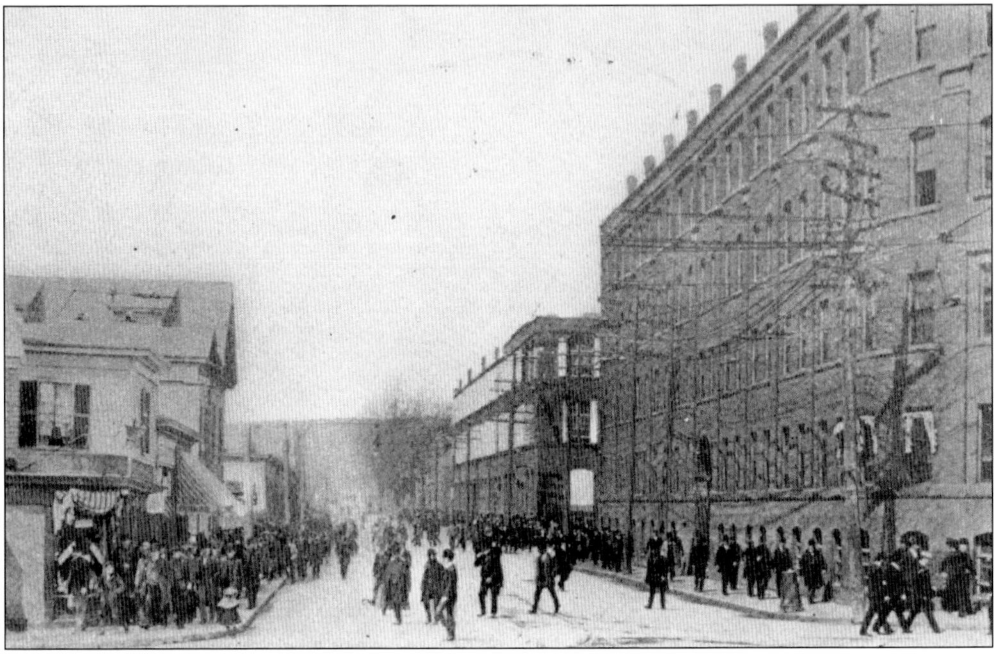

Lynn's Thomson-Houston Electric Company merged with Thomas Edison's American Electric in 1892 to form the General Electric Company (GE). Thomson-Houston had occupied a large complex on Federal Street, which continued to be used by the new company. About the bustling scene shown here, the sender of this 1905 card proudly asked, "Can you do as well in Elmira?"

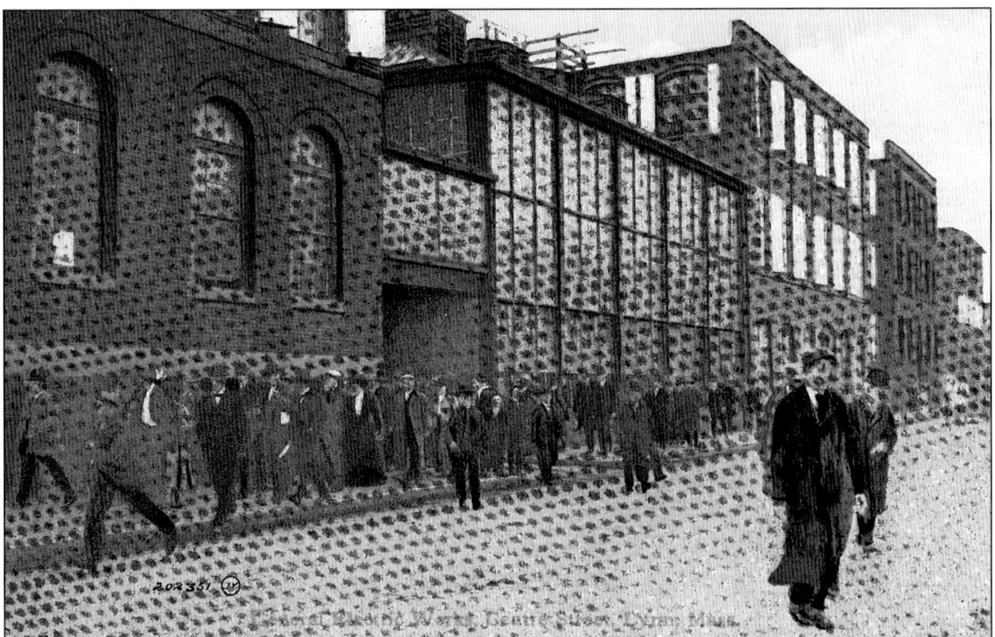

The Centre Street entrances to GE's West Lynn Works are shown *c.* 1905 at the blowing of the noon whistle.

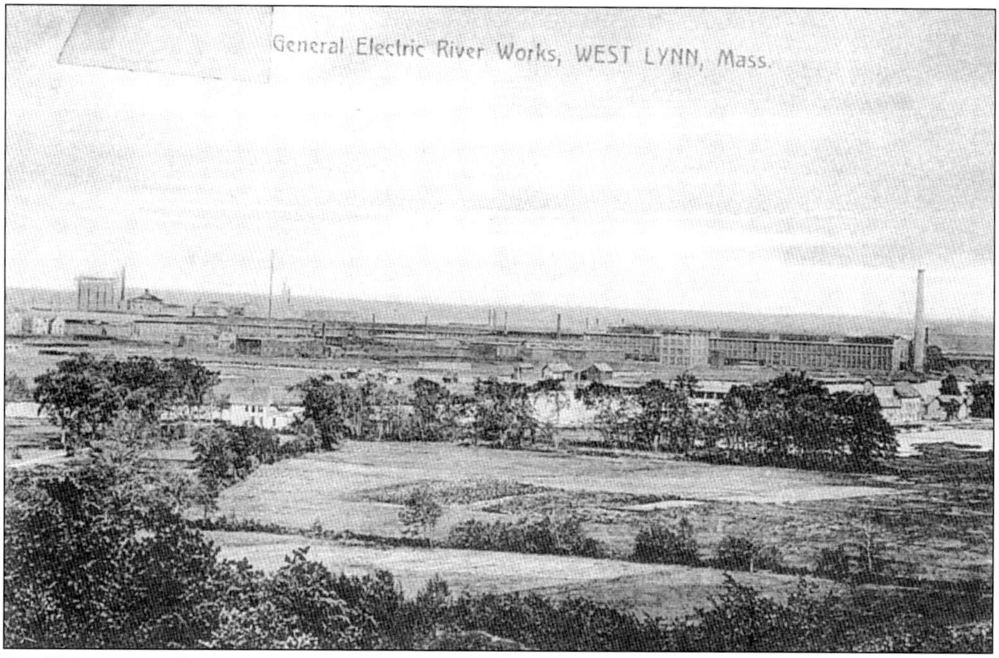

As GE continued to grow, its operation expanded with the construction of the sprawling river works alongside the Saugus River in 1893. Although the shoe industry would reign supreme through the 1920s, GE became an increasingly important part of Lynn's economy as the century progressed.

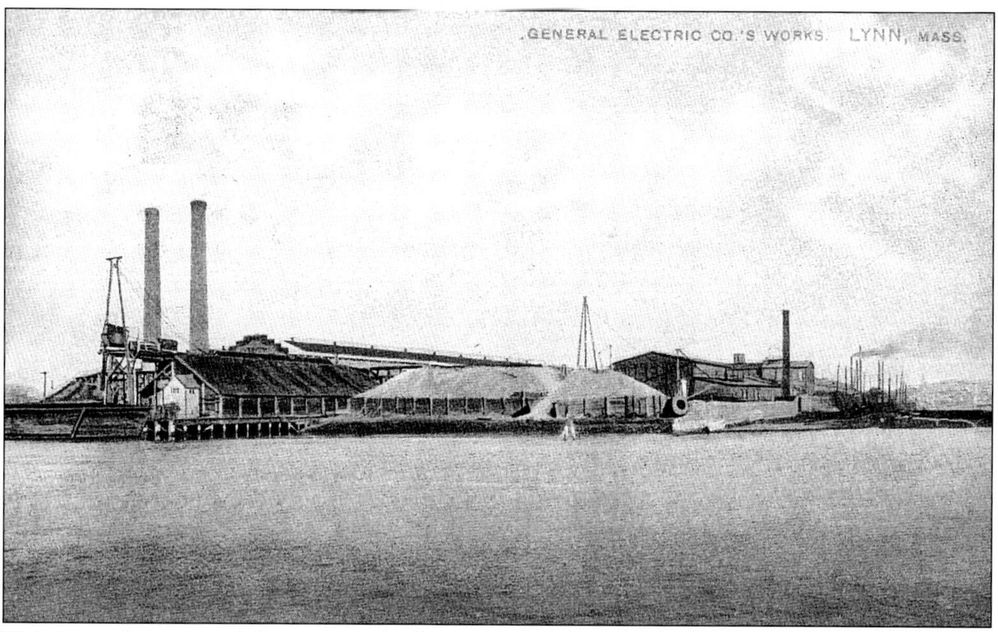

This is another view of the river works from across the river, taken *c.* 1910.

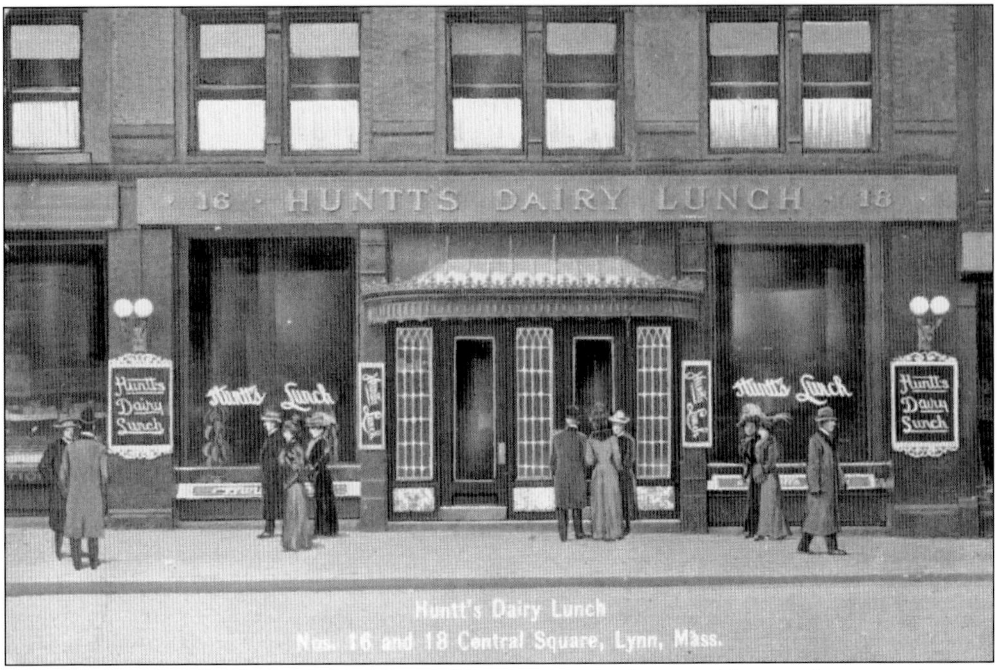

Huntt's Dairy Lunch was a popular Central Square fixture for over 60 years that specialized in modestly priced fare. (Conway collection.)

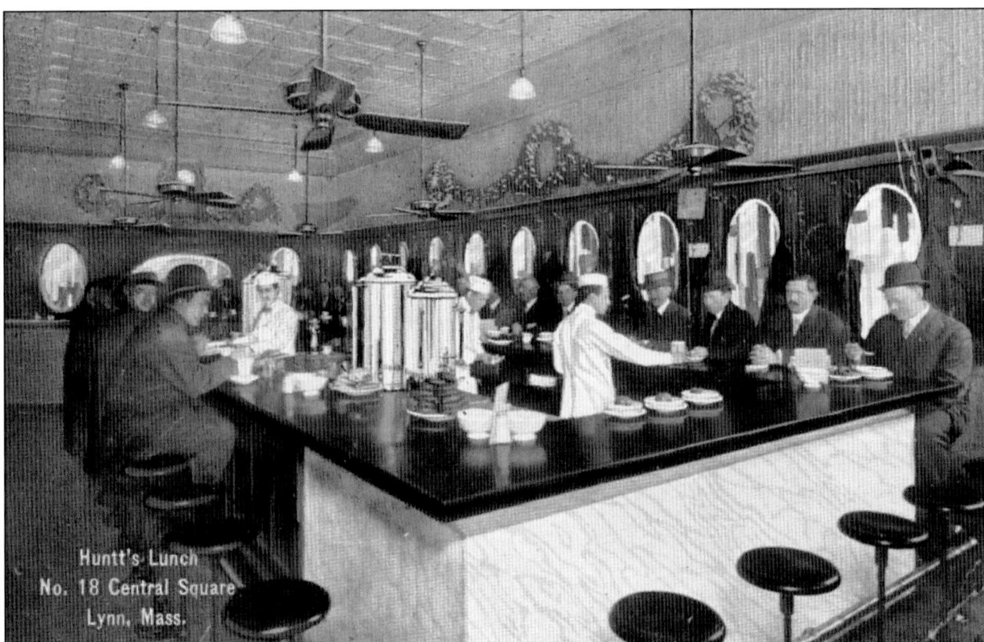

The interior of Huntt's Central Square lunchroom was decorated for the Christmas holidays c. 1905. Huntt's also had restaurants at Market Square and Willow, Andrew, Broad, and Washington Streets by the 1920s. (Conway collection.)

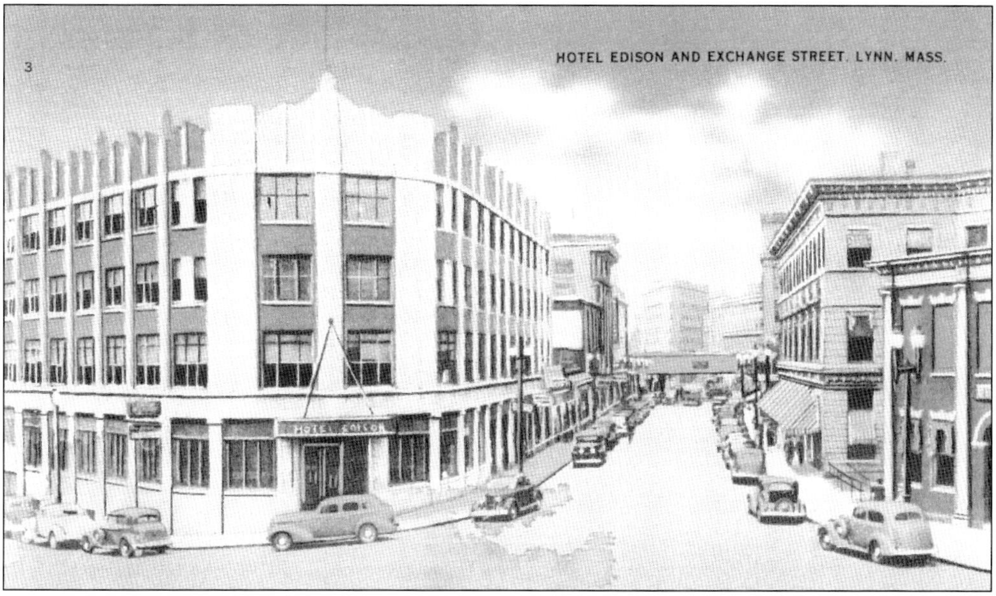

The Hotel Seymour, built in 1907, was the first hotel at the corner of Broad and Exchange Streets. Later it changed its name to Hotel Lennox and burned in a spectacular fire in 1931. The present Hotel Edison, shown here in the 1940s, was built at the same site in 1932. (Conway collection.)

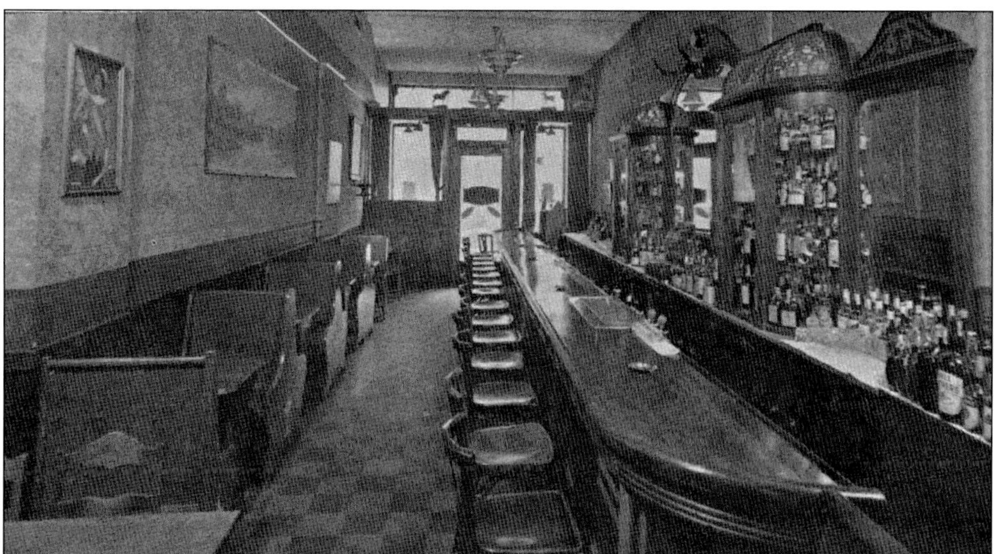

The Edison's handsome oak bar is the centerpiece of the men's grill and taproom in this photograph from the early 1950s.

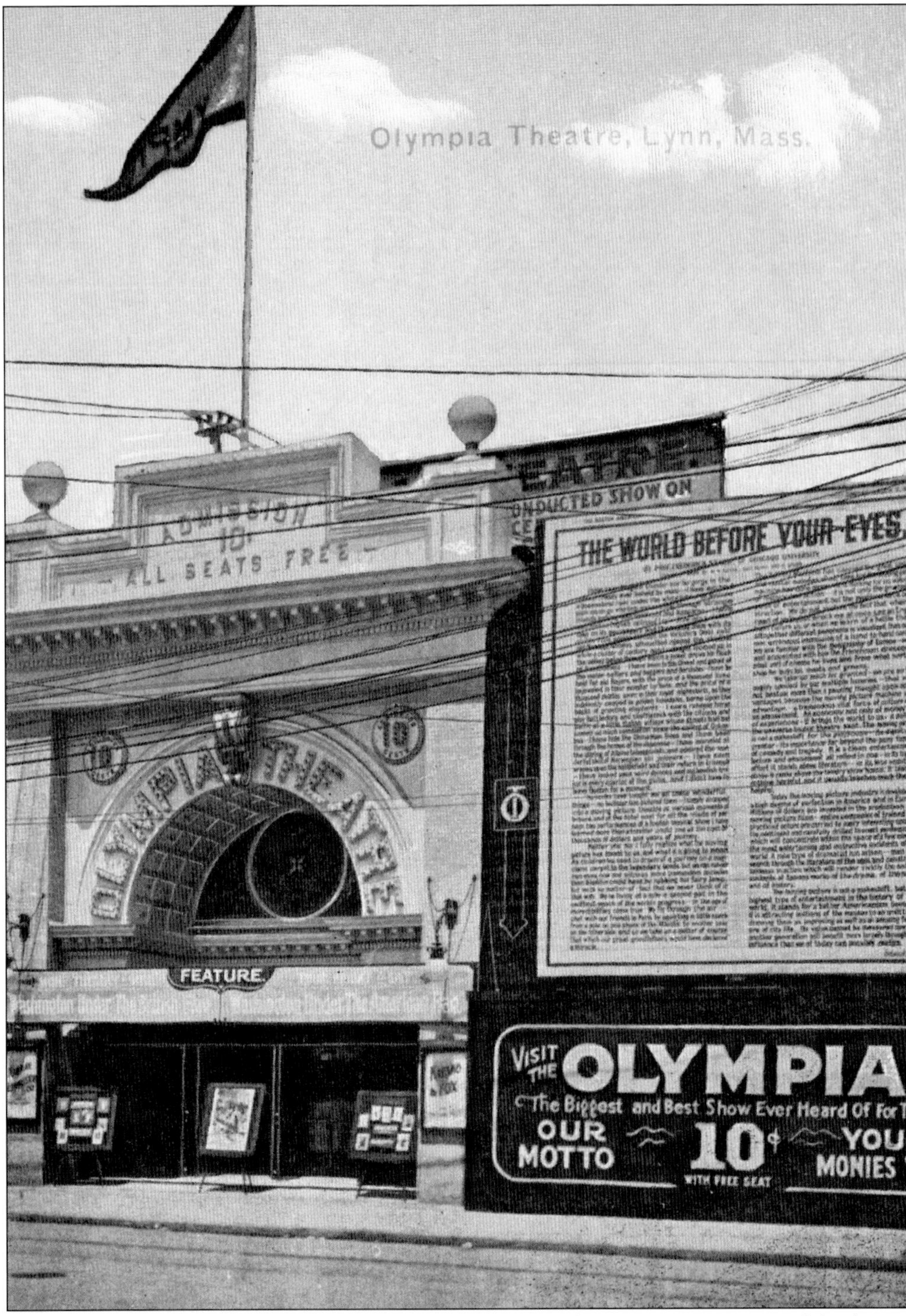

When the Olympia Theatre on Washington Street opened in 1908, it was one of the largest motion picture houses in New England, with a seating capacity that would eventually reach 3,200. Some theaters charged both admission and seating fees, but the Olympia proudly advertised, "Admission ten cents, all seats free." This picture was taken *c.* 1912.

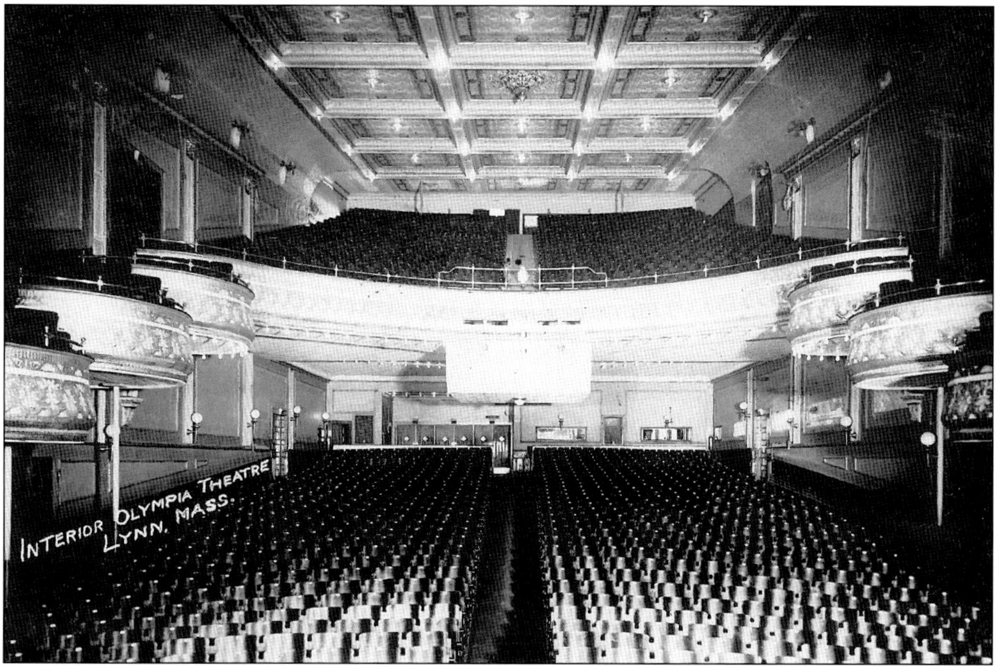

The interior of the Olympia Theatre appears here before being expanded in 1915. The Olympia was a popular stop on the vaudeville circuit and featured slightly more highbrow entertainment in its Sunday afternoon concerts. The theater was demolished in 1953. This card was published by Moering and Groesach of Lynn. (Conway collection.)

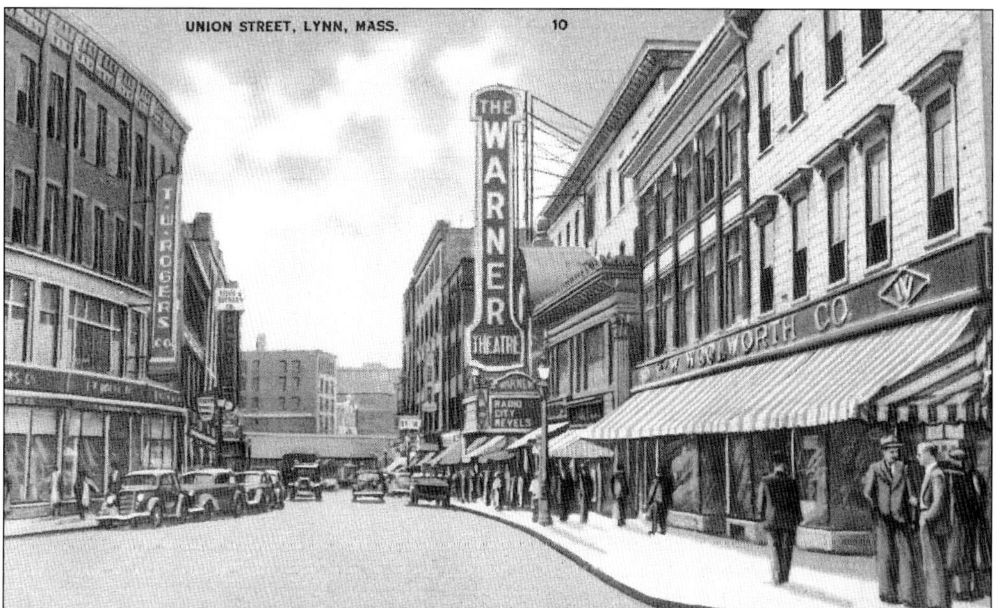

The Strand Theatre on Union Street was remodeled and opened as the Warner in 1930. The electric sign in front was the largest of its kind in New England at the time. (Conway collection.)

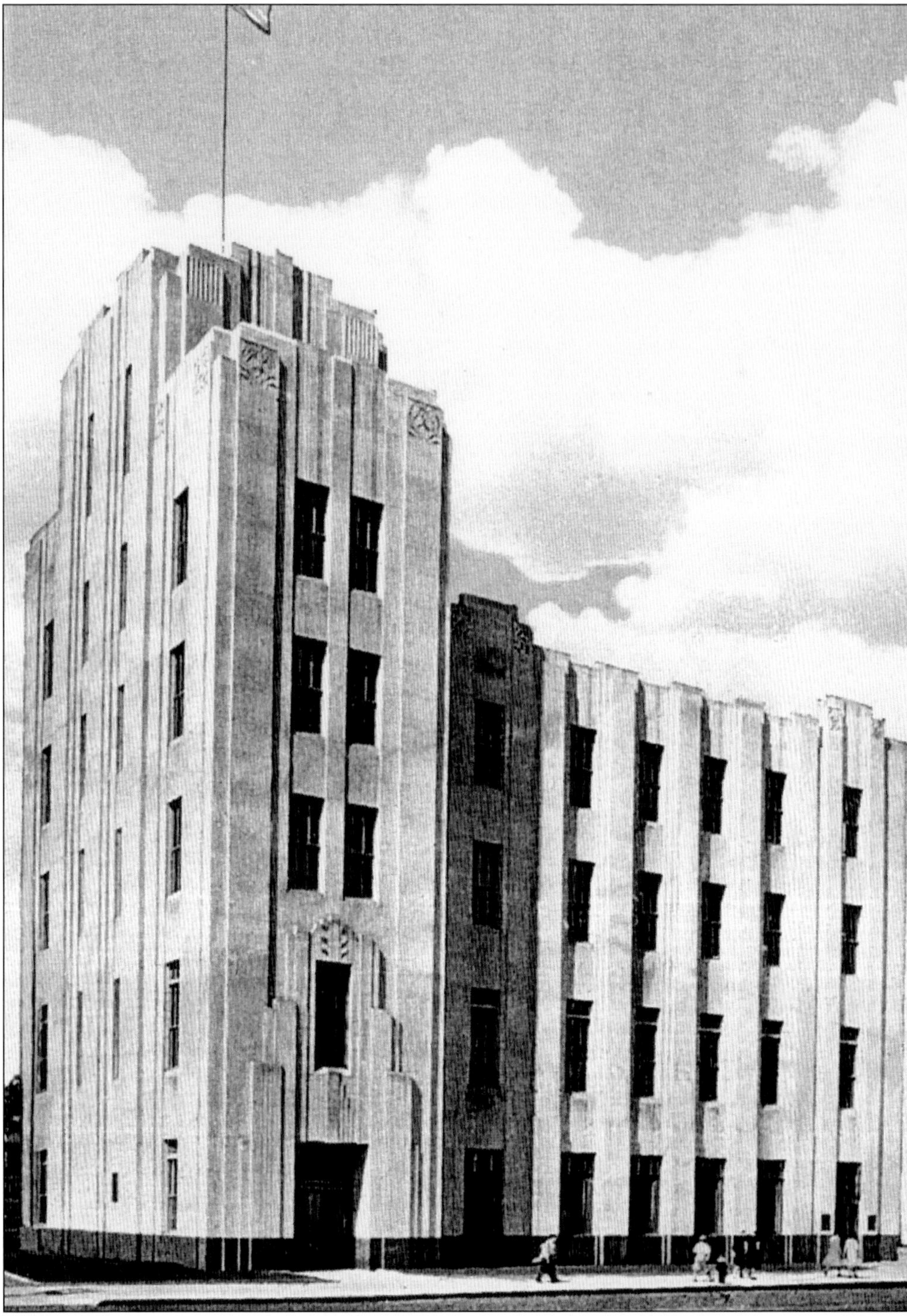

The first telephone in Lynn was installed between the Breed and Sprague Coal Company's office at Central Square and its wharf on Broad Street in 1876. New England Telephone built its Art Deco headquarters, one of Lynn's few skyscrapers, at City Hall Square in 1932 and still occupies the site.

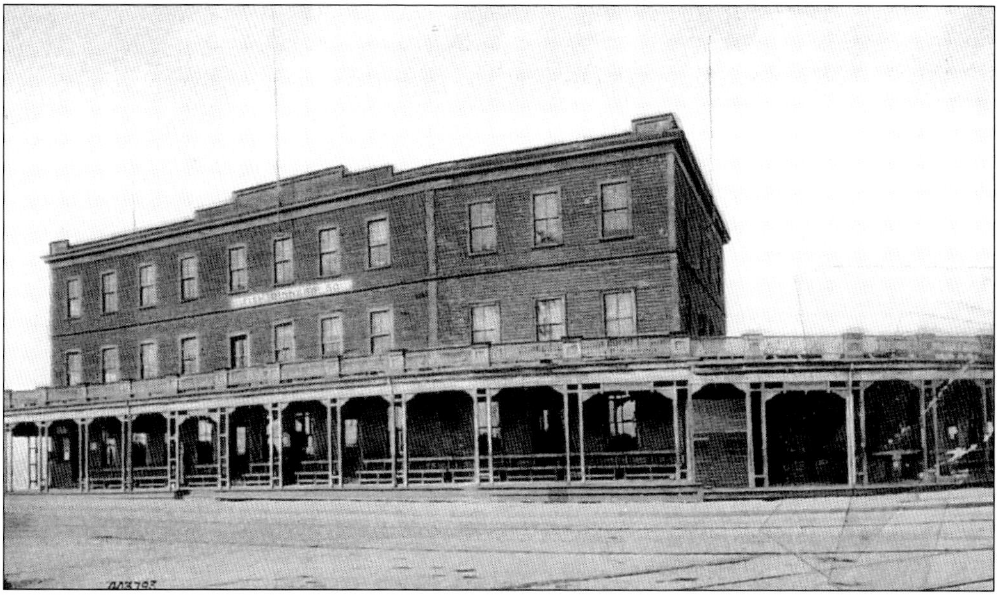

Tibbett's Hotel was a popular restaurant also, well-known for its seafood dinners. It stood at the foot of Washington Street, just before the Nahant town line, from 1889 until it fell to fire in 1922.

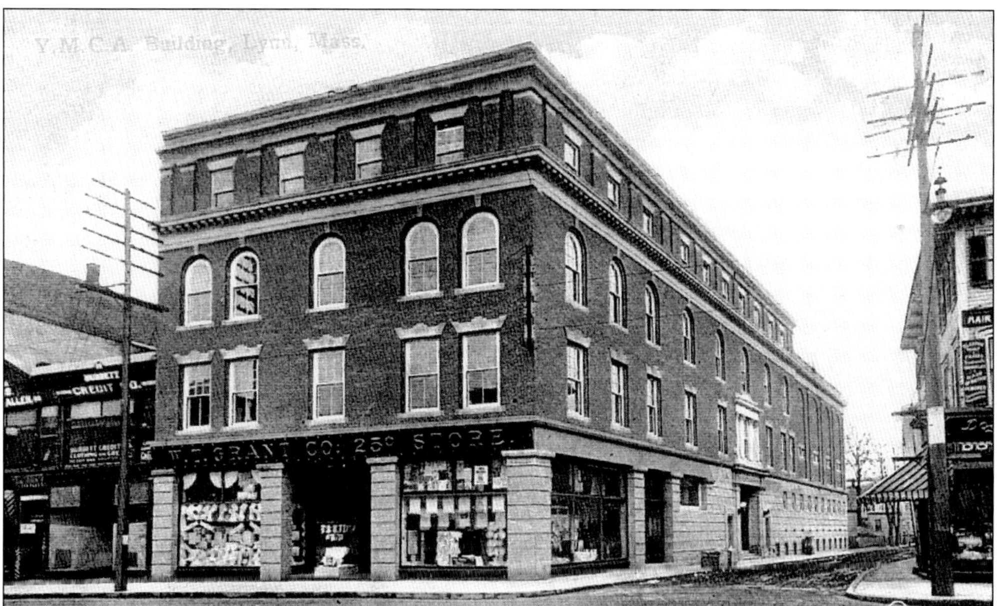

The 25¢-store of W.T. Grant opened in 1906 in rented space in the YMCA building on Market Street. Grant's would eventually grow into a major retail chain, with its stores a mainstay of downtowns nationwide until its demise in 1976.

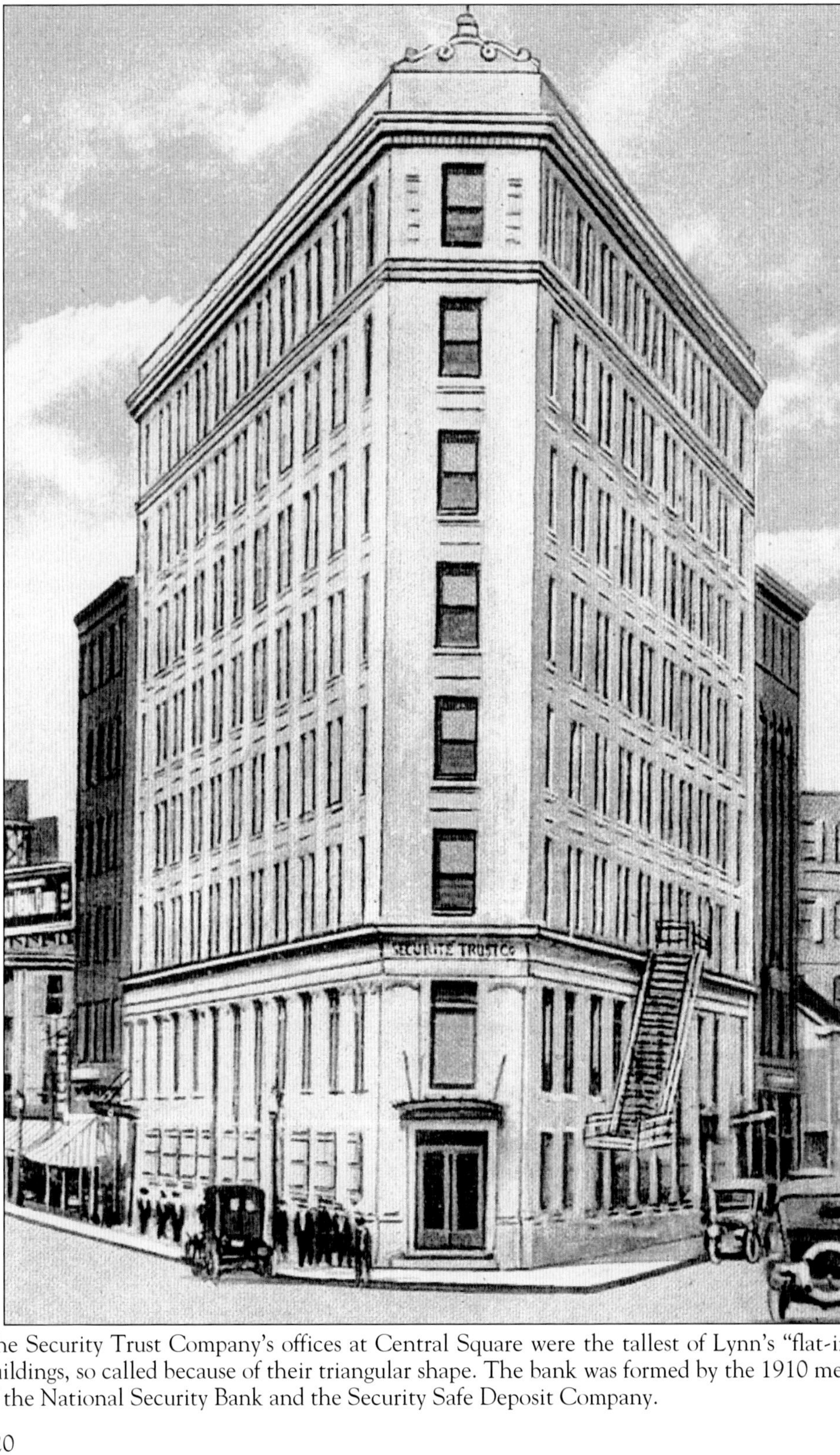

The Security Trust Company's offices at Central Square were the tallest of Lynn's "flat-iron" buildings, so called because of their triangular shape. The bank was formed by the 1910 merger of the National Security Bank and the Security Safe Deposit Company.

Eight

Souvenirs and Novelties

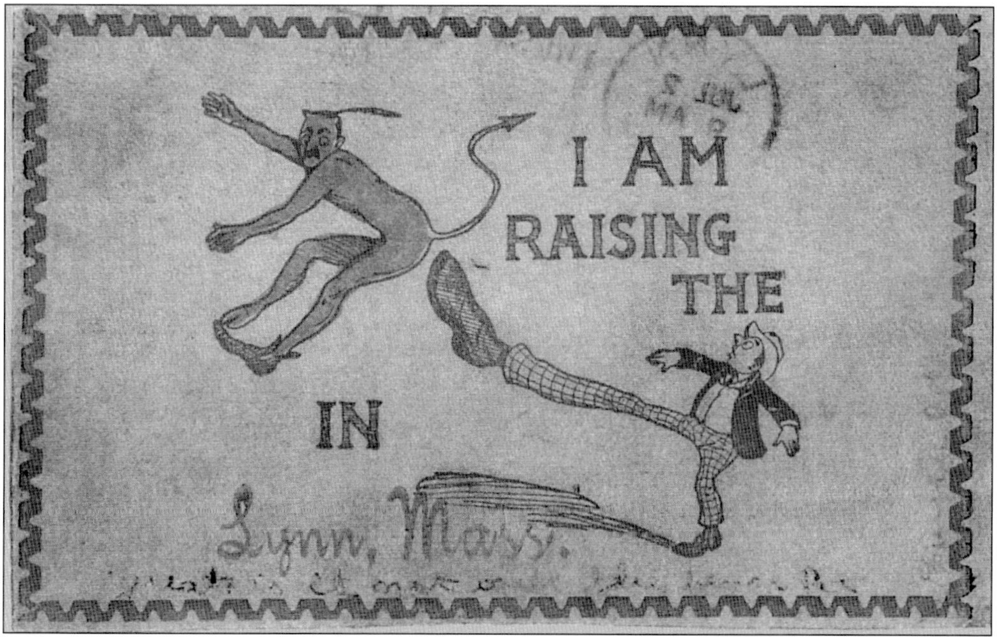

Manufacturers used a variety of materials to produce eye-catching novelties. This leather card was probably mass-produced, with "Lynn, Mass." simply stamped on. (Conway collection.)

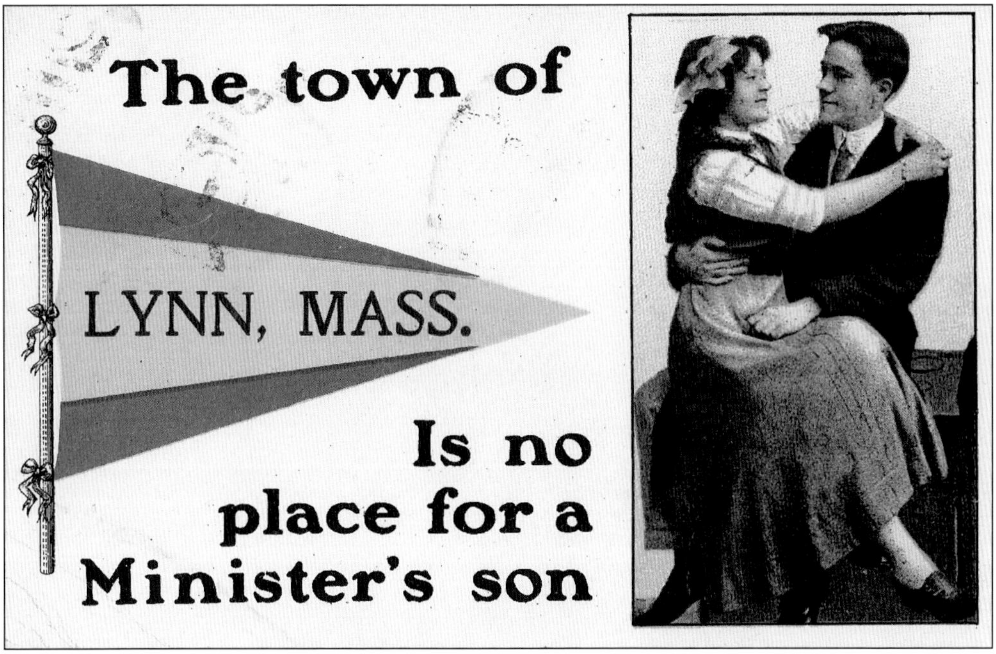

Slightly risqué themes made cards like this popular souvenirs c. 1910. The different typescript of the word "Lynn" indicates that this card, too, was sold in other markets.

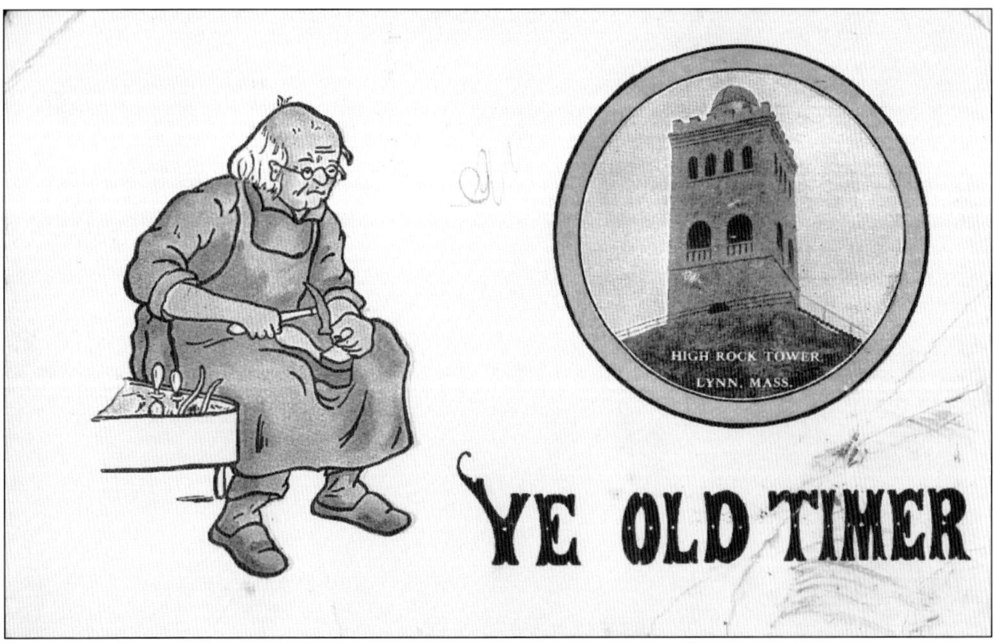

This nostalgic 1912 representation of an early shoemaker includes the ubiquitous High Rock Tower.

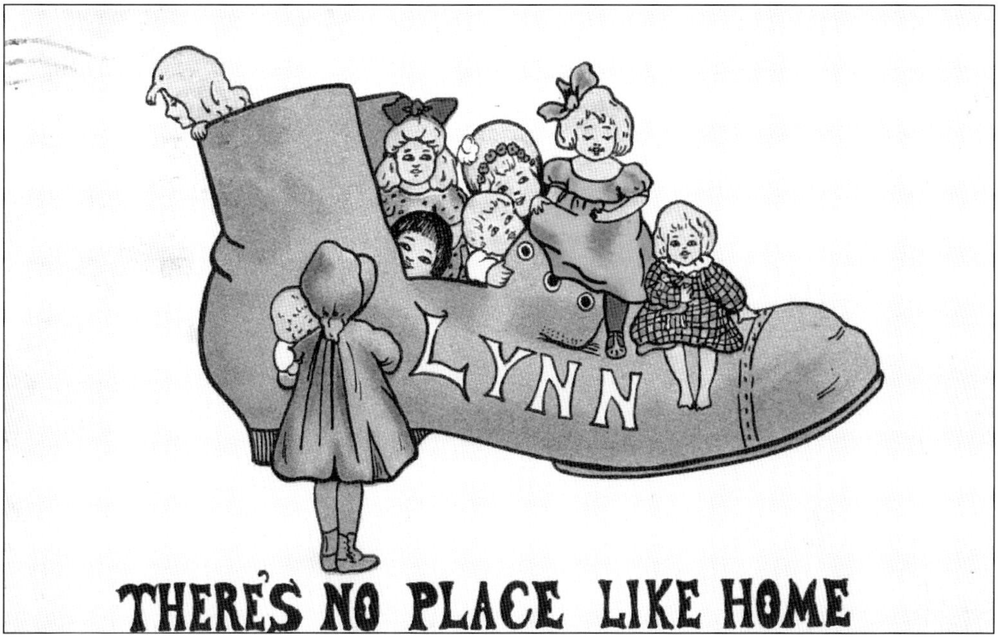

Shoes were an irresistible theme in any depiction of Lynn, particularly in the early 20th century as the industry reached its peak. This 1917 card is reminiscent of the style of some of the popular children's book illustrators of the time.

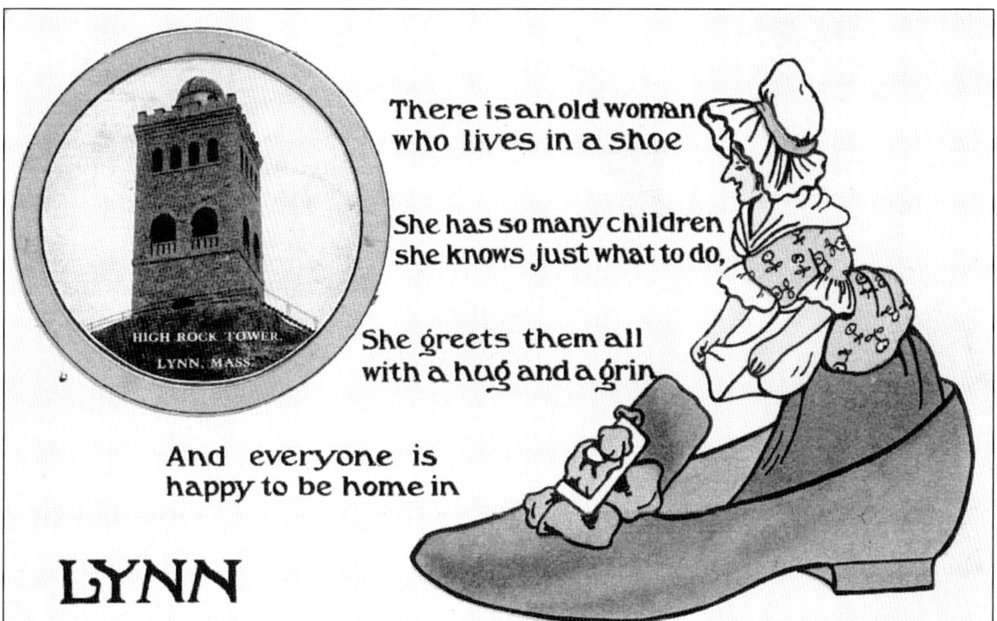

One of the same series as the one above, this card reworks a well-known Mother Goose rhyme with Lynn in mind. (Conway collection.)

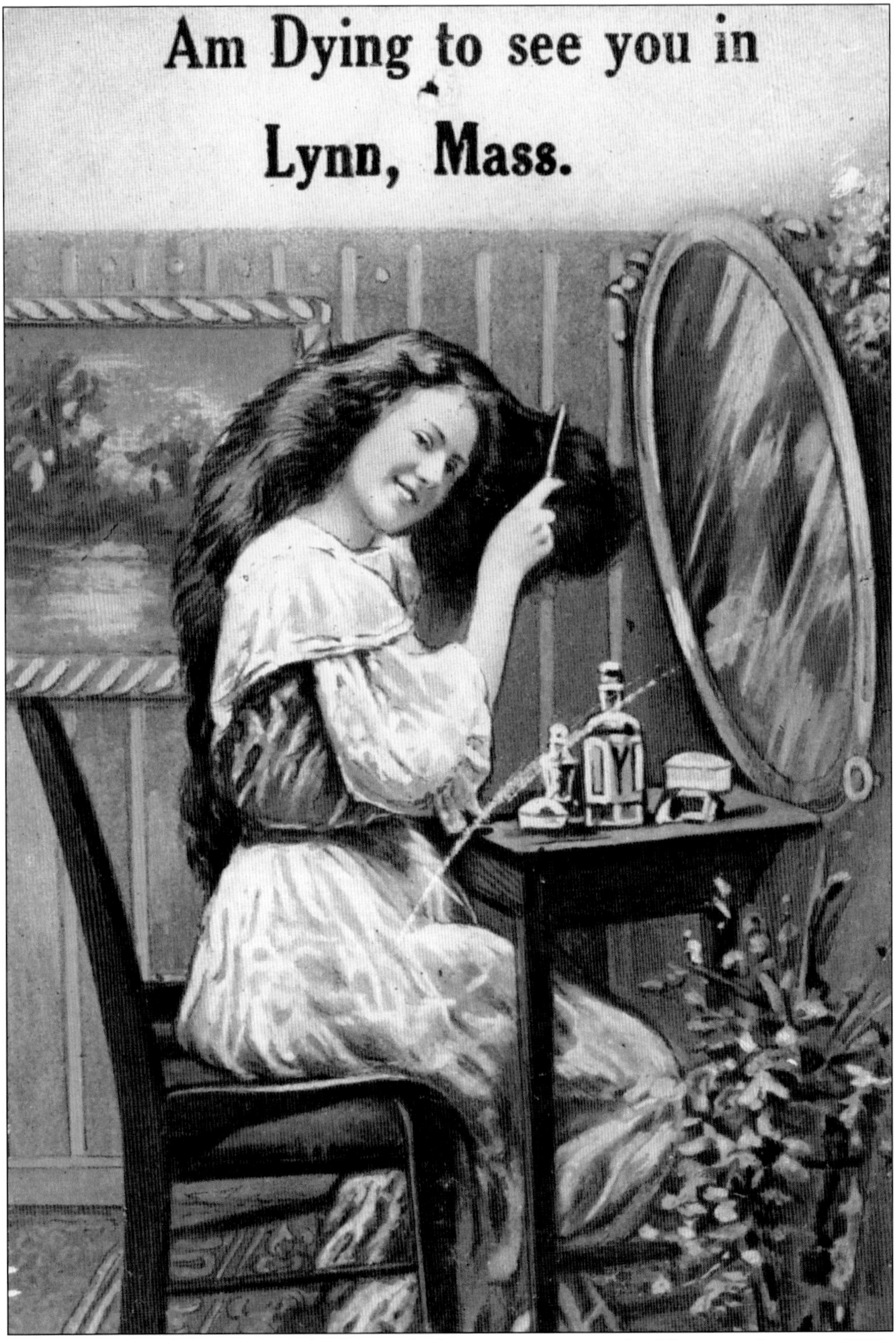

A pretty girl and a pun were both standards on souvenir cards. This one dates to 1911. (Conway collection.)

Nine

Bird's-eye Views

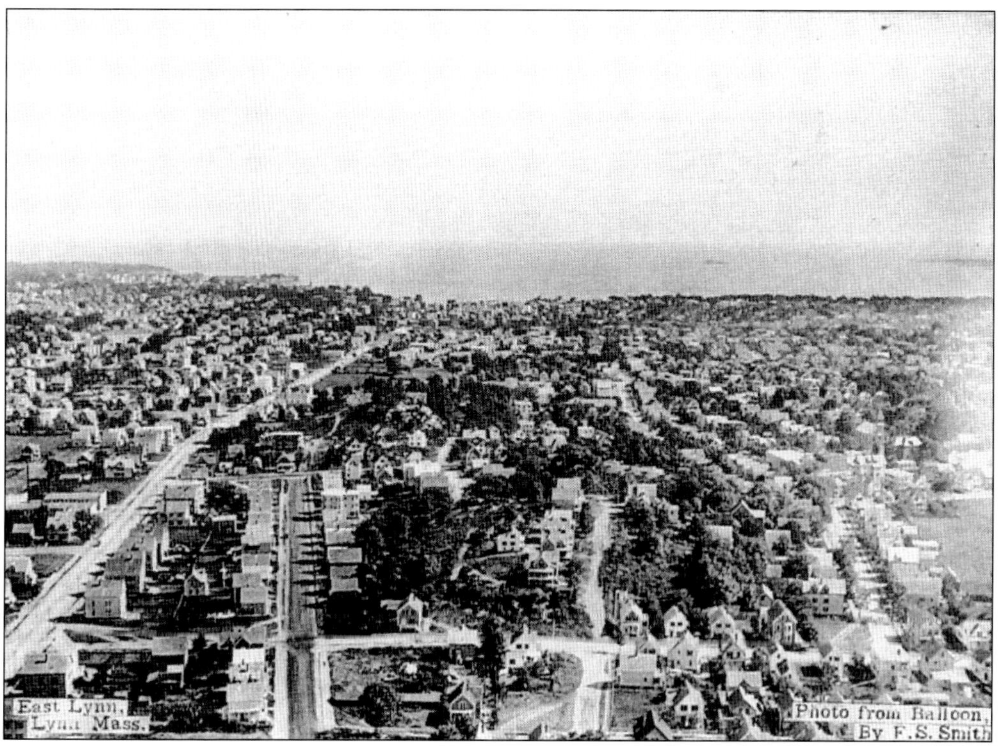

The first successful photograph from a balloon was taken in 1860. This *c.* 1885 view is of East Lynn, looking toward the water with Eastern Avenue on the left.

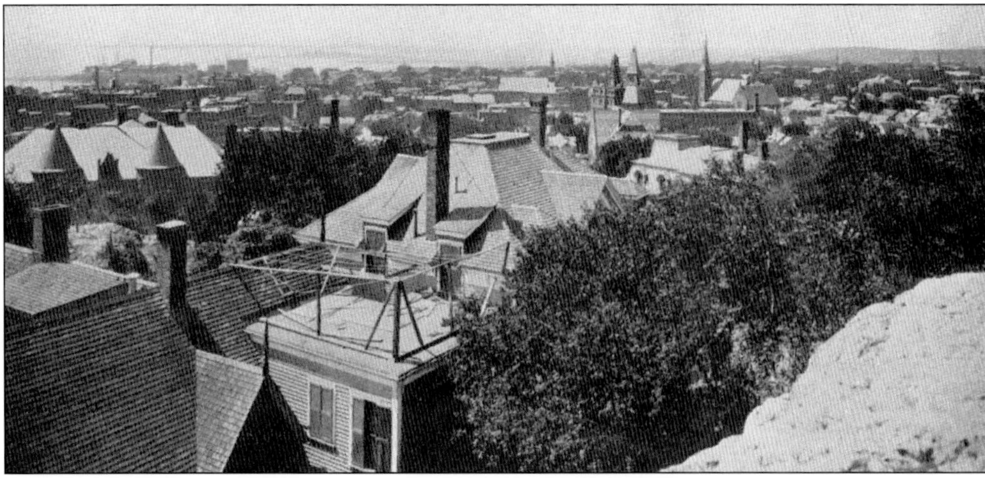

High Rock Tower afforded an ideal position for sweeping views of the entire city. Near the center of this 1880 photograph are the towers of the old city hall and the Washington Street Baptist and First Methodist Churches. The old English High is on the left.

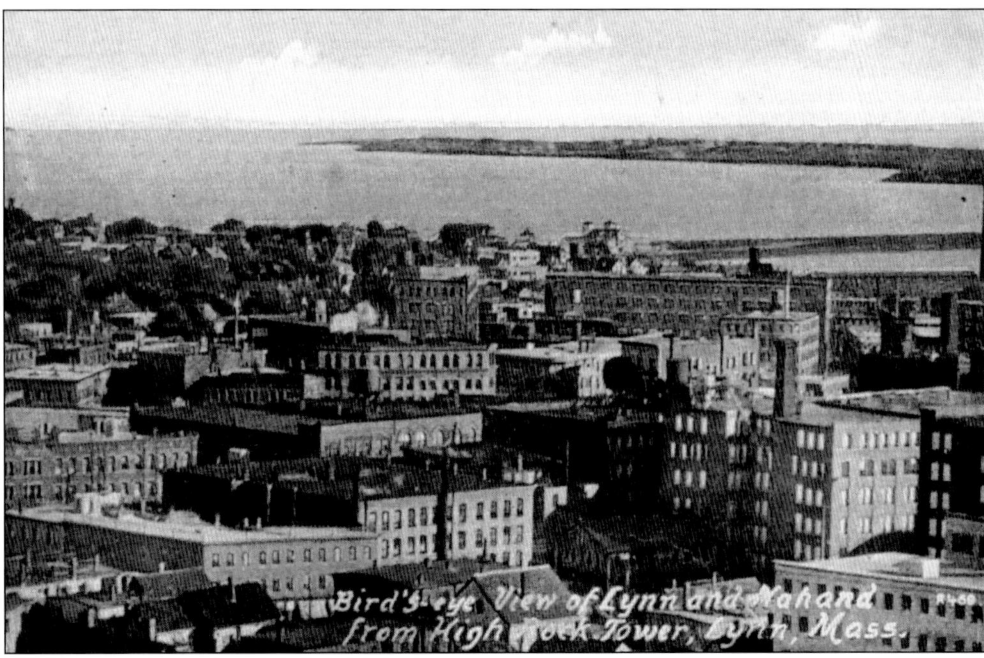

This 1905 view from High Rock looks into the heart of industrial Lynn with Nahant in the background.

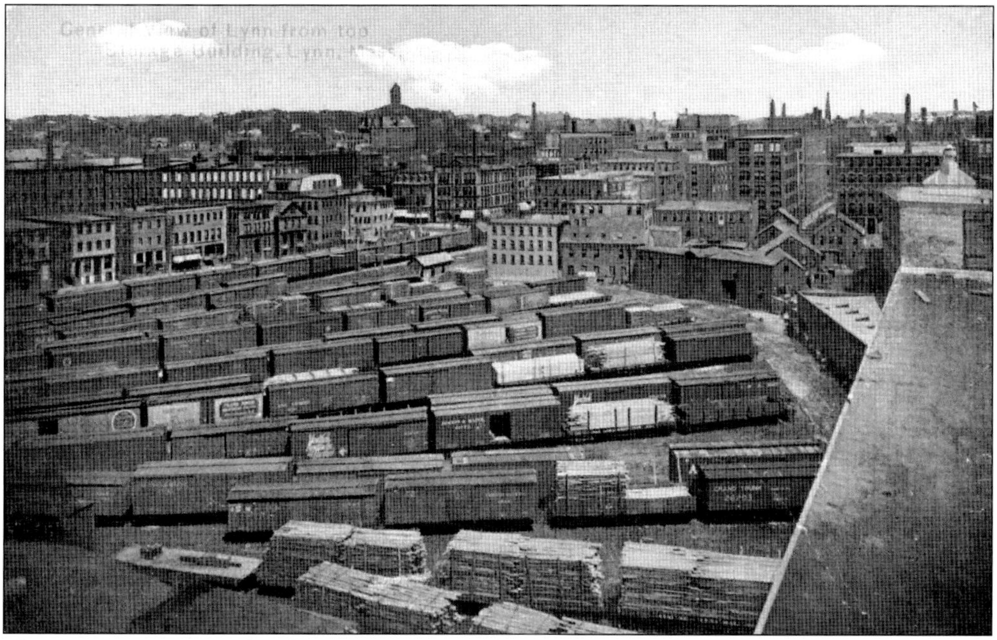

The Boston & Maine freight yard is seen from the roof of the Lynn Storage Warehouse on Pleasant Street *c.* 1910. High Rock Tower can be seen in the far distance.

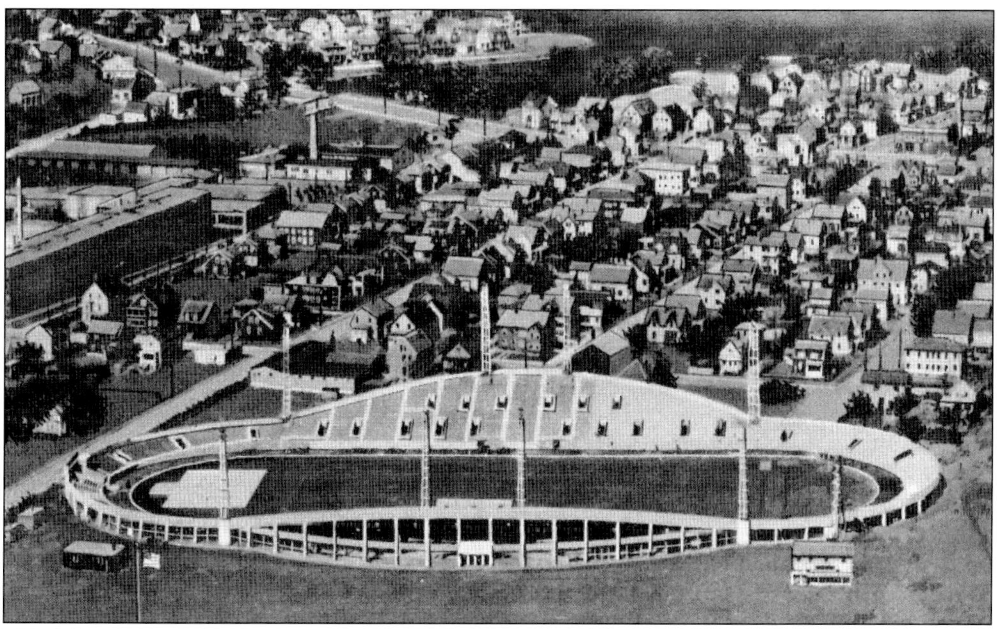

The Manning Bowl was a WPA project begun in 1936. This aerial view shows the stadium shortly after its completion, before the 1940 addition of Fraser Field.

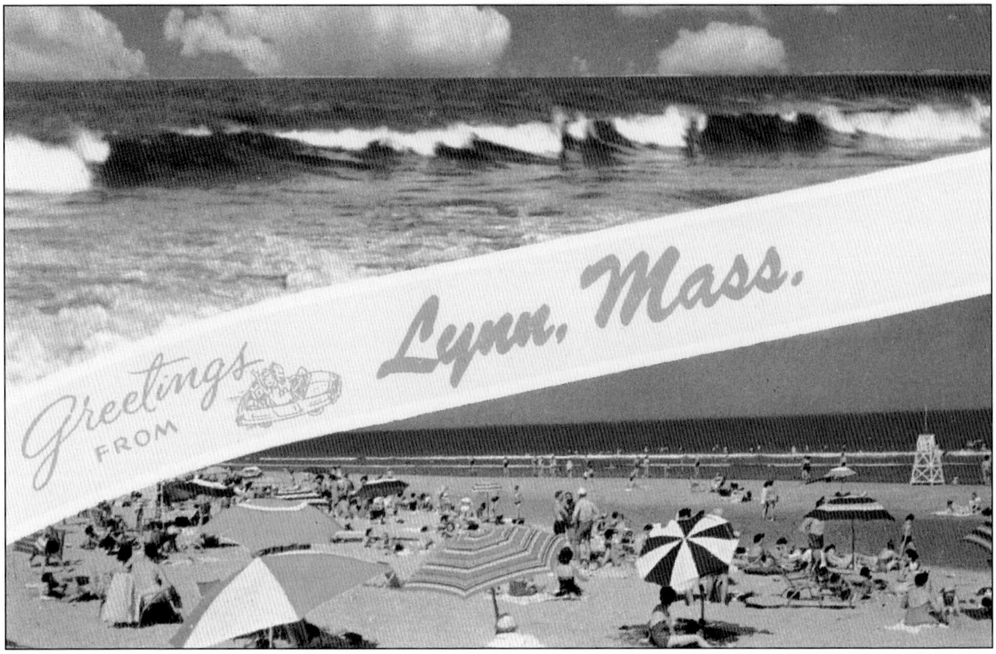

Greetings from Lynn, MA, in 1960.

Other Publications by the Lynn Historical Society

Cushing, Elizabeth Hope. *The Lynn Album: A Pictorial History*, 1990.

Cushing, Elizabeth Hope, ed. *No Race of Imitators: Lynn and Her People, An Anthology*, 1992.

Grover, Kathryn. *Lynn Album II: A Pictorial History*, 1996.

Howlett, D. Roger. The *Lynn Beach Painters: Art Along the North Shore (1880–1920)*, 1998.

Newhall, Benjamin Franklin. *Sketches of Saugus*, 1997.

Sammarco, Anthony. *J. Sanger Atwill and His Craftsmen: The Art of Furniture Making*, 1995.

Turino, Kenneth C., ed. *Civil War Diary of Lt. J.E. Hodgkins, August 1862 to July 1865*, 1994.